RETURN
OF THE
KING

The Restoration of

CHARLES II

CHARLES FITZROY

SUTTON PUBLISHING

To my parents
with love

First published in 2007 by
Sutton Publishing Limited · Phoenix Mill
Thrupp · Stroud · Gloucestershire · GL5 2BU

British Library Cataloguing in Publication Data
A catalogue record for this book is available from the British Library.

Hardback ISBN 978-0-7509-4635-3
Paperback ISBN 978-0-7509-4636-0

Typeset in Garamond.
Typesetting and origination by
Sutton Publishing Limited.
Printed and bound in England.

CONTENTS

INTRODUCTION

At 3 p.m. on the afternoon of 3 September 1658 Oliver Cromwell, Lord Protector of the three kingdoms of England, Scotland and Ireland, breathed his last. As if the elements themselves were celebrating his passing, 'the greatest storm of wind that had ever been known which overthrew trees, houses, and made great wrecks at sea' blew itself out. With military precision, the Lord Protector died on the anniversary of two of his most famous victories, at Dunbar in 1650 and Worcester in 1651.

Before we consider the events that were consequent on his deathbed, Cromwell's career must be swiftly rewritten; it is one of the most extraordinary in British history. In an age of unprecedented political and religious ferment, this provincial gentleman of modest means rose to become the sole ruler of Great Britain and led the nation to victory in wars with Holland and Spain. Despite widespread opposition, no effective challenge was mounted during his lifetime, and, unlike so many opponents who crossed his path, he died peacefully in his bed.

There was little foretaste of the momentous role that Cromwell was to play during his early career. He first entered the public stage on his election as Member of Parliament for Huntingdon in 1628, where he immediately joined the ranks of the opposition to Charles I. Two years later he suffered a serious loss of social status following the bankruptcy of his wealthy uncle. During the 1630s, the period of Charles I's personal rule without parliament, Cromwell worked as a humble farmer in the Fens. As a devout Puritan, and a fervent champion of the right to follow his own religious beliefs, Cromwell strongly disapproved of Archbishop Laud's High Church Anglicanism and his persecution of religious

1

dissenters, and was tempted to emigrate to New England. But he remained and was elected to the Long Parliament in 1640.

Cromwell made his reputation during the First Civil War. On its outbreak in 1642 he raised a troop of cavalry, and became an influential member of the war party, determined to enter into negotiations only after defeating Charles I in the field. Following his victory at Marston Moor in 1644, he was instrumental in setting up the New Model Army, a formidable force of professional soldiers with an immensely strong *esprit de corps*. At its first major engagement, the battle of Naseby in June 1645, with Cromwell acting as second in command to Sir Thomas Fairfax, the Royalists were decisively defeated.

During the aftermath of the First Civil War, the Army, with Cromwell as its leading spokesman, became increasingly political as the soldiers demanded a greater say in running the Government, and the right to express their religious views. Although sympathetic to his men's grievances, Cromwell did not accept the more radical social demands of the Levellers, advocates of manhood suffrage, equality before the law, and the abolition of the monarchy, and suppressed a mutiny by their leaders. But he adopted a more radical position after a secret agreement between Charles I and the moderate Presbyterian Scots led to the Second Civil War in 1648. Following the Royalist defeat at Preston, Cromwell, like so many of his soldiers, incensed at all this bloodshed, and by the King's renewed negotiations with the English parliament behind the Army's back, determined to hold Charles directly accountable for his actions and to bring him publicly to trial. To give a veneer of parliamentary legitimacy to this unprecedented act, an act of 'cruel necessity', Col Pride purged the majority of those members, mostly Presbyterian, who were against rule by the Army and were likely to object strongly to the soldiers' decision to put the King on trial. The remaining members, known as the Rump, were prepared to carry out this unprecedented, unconstitutional act.

Following Charles I's execution on 30 January 1649, the Commonwealth set about creating a new order, voting for the abolition of the monarchy and the House of Lords, and the disestablishment of the Church of England. Meanwhile, Cromwell, who succeeded Fairfax as commander-in-chief of the Army in 1650, led the New Model Army to victory over the Irish and the Scots enemies of the Commonwealth. Cromwell's final win as a commander in the field, at the battle of Worcester on 3 September 1651, was so overwhelming that it seemed that the Royalists would never be able to mount another military challenge. Cromwell was equally successful in Europe, where he gained success in a naval war against the Dutch in 1652–4. A deeply religious man, Cromwell came to see this endless succession of victories as a sign of God's providence.

Political success, however, proved much more elusive. During the 1650s Cromwell struggled to construct a settlement that would replace the regime that he had played such a prominent role in destroying. The Army, on whom his power depended, became increasingly disillusioned with the Rump Parliament. Although initially a radical body, it became progressively apparent that the Rump's primary aim was ensuring its own survival, and Cromwell dismissed it in a fit of rage in April 1653, uttering the memorable words: 'In the name of God, go.'

Cromwell now embarked on a series of political experiments. The Barebones Parliament (named after a religious fanatic named Praisegod Barbon) of July–December 1653, an attempt to establish a government of the godly, ended in failure, and Cromwell was appointed Lord Protector. His power, based on the Instrument of Government, a written constitution, was shared with a council. Ominously, however, although the constitution made provisions for liberty of conscience, those officers who disagreed with the Instrument were cashiered and imprisoned without trial. When the First Protectorate Parliament was elected in September 1654, soldiers refused entry to Westminster to all those who opposed the constitution. But, far from being cowed, the members who took their seats refused to ratify Cromwell's new powers, and were dismissed in January 1655. The Royalists were encouraged by the division among their enemies to plan a rising, but Col John Penruddock, the only Cavalier to raise a sizeable force, was soon defeated. Although many Royalists had agreed to rise in revolt, in the event the majority, including the major landowners, stayed at home.

Cromwell, however, was now determined to crush his Royalist foes forever. He instituted the rule of the Major-Generals in August, a naked display of military force. The enforcement of a strict moral code, exclusion of the traditional ruling class and arbitrary imprisonment of their enemies without trial were particularly unpopular. Those who refused to conform were to be punished. The Decimation Tax was harshly enforced, making many Cavaliers, in the words of Lt Gen Ludlow, 'desperate and irreconcilable'. To give some semblance of legality to his military government, a Second Protectorate Parliament was summoned in September 1656, but, once again, up to 100 elected members were excluded on orders of the Council. Sir Edward Hyde, chief adviser to Charles II, and later Earl of Clarendon, summed up the bitterness of the majority of the population: 'We are now without any right or title to anything we enjoy, and are at your mercy to dispose of us as you please; which is the lowest condition of traitors.' There was widespread relief when the rule of the Major-Generals came to an end in January 1657, followed by the prorogation of the Second Protectorate Parliament in July.

Despite these setbacks, Cromwell continued to enjoy undisputed control of Britain, more powerful than his Stuart predecessors James I or Charles I. In acknowledgement of this, a new constitution, entitled the Humble Petition and Advice, gave Cromwell semi-regal status. A number of Cromwell's protégés now proposed that he accept the title of King. The Protector, though sorely tempted, was, as so often, wracked with indecision when confronted with a vital political decision.

If he accepted, he would be in a much stronger position to cement his rule by thus taking on the mystique of monarchy. Most Royalists were certain to remain hostile, but they had proved no match for the New

Model Army, and their military capability would not be increased by Cromwell's taking the crown. On the other hand, he had agonised over ordering the King's execution in 1649, which had been followed swiftly by the abolition of the monarchy. If he now ascended the throne, he would face the charge of hypocrisy. Furthermore, he knew that many of his soldiers were hostile, their fears orchestrated by three leading generals, his brother-in-law John Desborough, his son-in-law Charles Fleetwood, and the able and charismatic John Lambert, all of whom were to play a decisive role in the months to come.

After much hesitation, Cromwell decided against such a bold move. The prorogued parliament met again in January 1658 but was no more successful at imposing a settlement than its predecessors, and was dismissed within a month. A series of family tragedies affected the Protector deeply, and when the 'tertian ague', probably a form of malaria, struck him down in the summer, it soon proved fatal. At his death in September it was still uncertain who would claim his inheritance, though his son Richard had been proclaimed heir apparent.

Cromwell aroused and still arouses deep divisions between his admirers and his detractors. To his enemies he was a 'brave, bad man', to his admirers he was, in the words of the nineteenth-century prime minister Lord Rosebery, product of an era that identified with Cromwell's moral certainty, 'a practical mystic, the most formidable and terrible of all combinations, uniting an aspiration derived from the celestial and supernatural with the energy of a mighty man of action; a great captain off the field seeming, like a thunderbolt, the agent of greater forces than himself; no hypocrite, but a defender of the faith; the raiser and maintainer of the Empire of England'. There is a dichotomy at the heart of Cromwell's career. The staunch champion of English liberty and firm believer in the importance of parliament, he was only able to impose his deeply held beliefs by relying on force. Much as he desired legitimate government through parliament, it was ultimately the Army that represented power.

When Cromwell died, it was still unclear what the future would hold. The months to come were to show that his son Richard was unequipped to follow in his father's footsteps, while many of his father's lieutenants were willing to place their own personal ambition above any loyalty to the regime as they made their bids for supreme power. But, like a gigantic poker game, as the stakes gradually rose, player after player fell out until there was only one left at the table.

1

CROMWELL'S HEIR, HIS GENERALS
AND HIS PROTÉGÉS

Although Oliver's complete dominance of the political stage meant that there was an enormous vacuum to fill, he hoped that the loyalty of all those who had served him would be transferred to his eldest son and heir. To counter Richard's political inexperience and his minimal knowledge of the Army, or the Army of him, his father had promoted him in the last year of his life. He was appointed chancellor of Oxford University, a member of the Council of State and of the other house (a substitute for the House of Lords), and given command of Col Goffe's regiment in the Army.

Richard was a very different character from his father. All observers were united in admiring his affable nature, his gentlemanly behaviour and his good breeding. William Hooke, writing to John Winthrop, founder of the colony of Massachusetts, noted: 'His son seemeth to be of another frame, more soft and tender . . . yet he is of a sweete countenance, vivacious, and candid.' But his self-effacement proved a severe handicap. An anonymous Royalist gave a less charitable verdict: 'The Vulture died, and out of his ashes arose a Titmouse.'

The key question was whether the new Protector could control the Army, the basis of his father's power. The generals of the New Model Army constituted arguably the most able and ambitious group to have emerged from the Civil Wars. Cromwell had promoted them on the basis of merit, and they owed him their personal loyalty, but as the Royalist threat diminished in the early 1650s, divisions began to appear, and several of the most senior generals had fallen out with their commander-in-chief.

The most brilliant of Cromwell's generals was John Lambert. He was
a member of the Yorkshire gentry, who had won rapid promotion
during the Civil Wars. His military success rivalled that of Cromwell
himself. A general at the age of 26, he had played a leading part in
defeating the Royalists at Preston, Dunbar and Worcester. Lambert was
as decisive in politics as he was on the field of battle, and proved himself
an able administrator. His Instrument of Government, published in
1653, advocated rule by a small Council of State backed by parliament,
elected every three years, and formed the basis of the Protectorate
instituted in December of that year.

Lambert was an ambitious man. Now that he had helped to create the
Protectorate, he hoped that he would be designated as Oliver's successor.
On the way to the ceremony installing the Protector at the Court of
Chancery in 1653, Lambert drove in Cromwell's coach, and then for
several years basked in his favour. He was instrumental in persuading
the Protector to institute the rule of the Major-Generals in 1655.

The two men fell out in 1657 over the idea that Cromwell should
accept the crown, which deeply offended Lambert's republican
sentiments. After hesitating over taking the oath of loyalty to the
Protector, he resigned his commissions and retired from active life.
For the year preceding Cromwell's death, Lambert enjoyed a quiet
life at Wimbledon House, his splendid residence formerly owned
by Queen Henrietta Maria, which he now adorned with magnificent works of art and laid out spacious grounds around it. Lucy
Hutchinson, wife of the regicide Col Hutchinson, who had fallen out
with Cromwell and Lambert over their championship of military
over civil government, described how the general 'fell to dress his
flowers in his garden, and work at the needle with his wife and maids,
while he was watching an opportunity to serve again his ambition'.
Although out of office, Lambert continued to command widespread
support among the soldiers, but his perceived ambition made men
suspicious of his motives.

The most radical of all the generals was Thomas Harrison, an ardent champion of the Fifth Monarchy Men, who believed that it was their duty to overthrow the established order and bring in the reign of Christ on earth, as expounded in the prophecies of the book of Daniel. They expected imminently the second coming of Christ and the setting-up – in succession to the Assyrian, Persian, Greek and Roman empires – of his Kingdom on Earth. Harrison rivalled Lambert in his daring on the field of battle and had been a signatory of Charles I's death warrant. A strong advocate and instigator of the Barebones Parliament of 1653, filled with members of extreme religious sects, he had quarrelled with Cromwell on its dismissal, had been cashiered and had subsequently been twice imprisoned.

The most senior military figure, and a man of great bravery and moral integrity, was Thomas, Lord Fairfax (appointed 3rd Baron on the death of his father in 1648), first commander of the New Model Army. Fairfax had fought for parliament in the First and Second Civil Wars, but had always viewed the Army as a means of ridding Charles I of his worst advisers and bringing him back to the negotiating table. He had strongly disapproved of Pride's Purge, and of Cromwell's subsequent decision to put Charles I on trial. When his name was read out at the trial, his masked wife called out boldly from the gallery that he had more wit than to be present. And when the charge was read out on behalf of 'the people of England', she cried: 'It's a lie, not half nor a quarter of the people.' In objection to the invasion of Scotland in July 1650, Fairfax had resigned his commission and had retired to his native Yorkshire. Nevertheless, he retained widespread respect, and it was likely, should he re-enter public life, that he would exert great influence.

Lambert's retirement in 1657 had led to the promotion of a number of Cromwell's extended family. Richard had been proclaimed heir apparent. His younger brother Henry had been ruling Ireland with a firm and judicious hand, at first as commander-in-chief and, since 1657, as Lord Deputy. Henry was a firm believer in the supremacy of the civil over the military, and, despite opposition from the Protestant settlers, wanted to broaden the basis of government so that it would include opponents of his father, both Royalists and former Parliamentarians, who had been excluded from the political process. Charles Fleetwood and John Desborough, two senior generals, both of whom had married into Cromwell's family, were devoutly religious, and members of the Independent sects that had formed such an important part of the New Model Army. Desborough possessed the stronger character, but it was Fleetwood, following the retirement of Lambert, whom Cromwell had chosen as his right-hand man. Thomas Belasyse, Viscount Fauconberg, a former Royalist, had married another of the Protector's daughters, and had been assigned diplomatic missions by his father-in-law. Maj Gen Whalley, Richard's cousin, provided a further family ally within the New Model Army.

The Protector's relatives had become used to their favoured status and began to see themselves as a surrogate royal family. A Capt Titus, writing to Sir Edward Hyde in February 1656, described the arrogance of one of Cromwell's daughters, Mrs Claypole: 'There was lately a wedding . . . whither all the grandees and their wives were invited, but most of the major-generals and their wives came not. The feast wanting much of its grace by the absence of those ladies, it was asked by one where they were? Mrs Claypole answered, "I'll warrant you washing their dishes at home as they used to do." This hath been extremely ill taken, and now the women do all they can with their husbands, to hinder Mrs Claypole from being a Princess, and her Highness.'

As well as his extended family, Cromwell was also heavily reliant on men whom he had promoted and who owed him personal loyalty. George Monck, a gruff, stocky Devonian, had been a professional soldier all his adult life. He had learnt his trade in Holland in the 1630s during the Thirty Years War, alongside Lambert, Fleetwood and Fairfax, before serving under the Royalist Marquis of Ormonde in Ireland during the First Civil War. Ormonde sent Monck back to England under arrest in 1643 for refusing to take an oath of loyalty to the King, and he was interviewed by Charles I at Oxford, before being sent to join the Cavalier forces under John, Lord Byron besieging Nantwich in Cheshire. At the battle on 29 January 1644, the Royalists were defeated by Fairfax and Sir George Booth, both to prove key figures in the run-up to the Restoration. Monck was captured and imprisoned for two years in the Tower of London, where he wrote a military textbook.

Despite the King's attempt to retain his loyalty (he even sent the prisoner £100 in gold coins), Monck transferred his allegiance to parliament in 1646 and agreed to serve again in Ireland, since this involved fighting predominantly Catholic rebels. The war in Ireland, where the Catholics had been in revolt since 1641, was regarded as very different from that on the mainland (Ormonde himself had appealed for help to parliament as the best source of Protestant assistance in defending Dublin), and Sir Edward Hyde, no admirer of Monck, wrote: 'when he [Monck] left the Tower he did so as a patriot and not as a partisan'. He served the parliamentary regime loyally in Ireland in 1647–9, and was thus absent during Charles I's trial.

Although criticised by parliament for coming to terms with Owen Roe O'Neill, the leader of the Catholic rebels in Ulster, Monck's tactical ability had caught the attention of Cromwell, who summoned him to join his invasion of Scotland in 1650. Monck repaid his faith by leading the English infantry at the hard-fought battle of Dunbar, and was left behind in command when Cromwell marched south in the summer of 1651. He then completed the defeat of the Royalists in the northern kingdom. In 1652, on the outbreak of the Anglo-Dutch war, Monck was appointed one of three generals-at-sea, alongside Robert Blake, and fought with conspicuous success. In 1654 he returned to Scotland as commander-in-chief, and subdued the Highlands in a brilliant campaign, using well-supplied and highly mobile patrols of mounted infantry. Monck showed himself equally able as an administrator, ensuring the peace of the Highlands by the leniency with which he treated the defeated Royalists. As a contemporary witness recorded: 'The English gave tolerable terms to them all, and by this wisdom has gotten them all quiet.'

11

During the 1650s, as Cromwell struggled to provide a lasting political settlement, and with an ever-increasing number of enemies, his most loyal basis of support continued to be the Army. Even their staunch opponent Sir Edward Hyde admitted that, during the Civil Wars, the New Model soldiers had comprised 'an army whose order and discipline, whose sobriety and manners, whose courage and success, made it famous and terrible over the world'. Its commanders were to play a key role in the events of the following months.

Alongside the generals, there were a number of men who had risen to prominence as Cromwell's protégés. These can be loosely termed his courtiers, several of them with a military background. Their leaders were Edward Montagu, Lord Broghill, Viscount Fauconberg, John Thurloe and Oliver's son Henry. Now that Cromwell was dead, they had no wish to see one of the generals become a military dictator. Consequently, they were united in their desire to bring the Army under control of the civil authorities. All were strong supporters of Richard.

These Cromwellians were men of varied talents. Montagu had fought with the New Model Army in the First Civil War, before being elected MP for Huntingdonshire, Cromwell's home county. In 1653 he had been chosen by Cromwell to be a member of the Council of State, before serving with distinction under Blake in the Navy. After Blake's death, he became senior admiral of the fleet. At Oliver's second installation as Protector in 1657, it had been Montagu who had filled the role as chief companion previously held by Lambert. Roger Boyle, Lord Broghill, an Anglo-Irish grandee, had fought for the Royalists before Cromwell persuaded him to change sides by offering him a senior command in the Irish campaign of 1650. Thereafter, he served the Protector faithfully in Ireland and Scotland and was a principal proponent of Oliver accepting the crown.

Oliver's son Henry had succeeded Fleetwood as Lord Deputy in Ireland. For the first time in many years, it appeared that this troublesome country was at peace. Although Henry was a prickly character, prone to take offence, he had made progress over the tricky question of finding a compromise between the demands of the Protestant settlers and the Catholic inhabitants. Oliver's son-in-law Fauconberg, who had married his daughter Mary, had also joined the regime, heading a successful diplomatic mission to Louis XIV. As a reward, he had been awarded Lambert's regiment, a highly sensitive post considering the popularity of the ex-general.

The most able administrator of this group of Cromwellians was John Thurloe, Secretary to the Council and, from 1657, Secretary of State. More importantly, Thurloe was head of the highly effective secret service. Despite his many enemies, the information Thurloe received from his spies and informers meant that Cromwell had almost as much knowledge of any Royalist plot and intrigue as Hyde or Charles II himself, and projected risings and revolts were soon put down. Thurloe's information on European affairs was equally extensive. As the Royalist Col Birch was later to put it: 'Cromwell carried the secrets of all the princes of Europe at his girdle.'

Cromwell's ministers abroad were among his most able followers. George Downing, at the Hague, had been heavily involved in negotiations during the First Dutch War of 1652–4. Downing was also trying his best to protect English shipping interests in the Baltic, which the Dutch regarded as their own preserve. Sir William Lockhart, Governor of Dunkirk, and victor of the battle of the Dunes, when an Anglo-French force had defeated the Spanish, aided by their Royalist allies, was also keeping a careful watch on the exiled Court in Brussels. A subtle diplomat, Lockhart had formed a close relationship with Mazarin, the ruler of France, whose alliance with Cromwell had formed the cornerstone of English foreign policy since 1654.

Without a strong personality to control them, there was little to hold Cromwell's followers together. They had been united by a desire to fight for 'the Good Old Cause', a defence of the political and religious freedom of Englishmen against the tyranny of Charles I, but each man interpreted this idea differently. For some, such as Lambert, the Army was the decisive force in defending this freedom; for others, such as Broghill and

Thurloe, parliament reigned supreme in the body politic. Harrison and his fellow religious extremists, highly influential in the Army, wanted an elect group of the godly to determine the future. For Richard Cromwell, these shifting and complex interrelationships were to assume increasing importance in the succeeding months.

The careers of these men illustrate the complexity of Commonwealth politics and the difficulty in using generic terms such as Royalists and Parliamentarians. Monck, Broghill and Fauconberg had all started the First Civil War as Royalists before changing sides. These men had close relations who were Royalists. Lambert had fought fiercely throughout the Civil Wars for the Parliamentary cause, but he was related to John, Lord Belasyse, a Cavalier and himself a cousin of Fauconberg. Belasyse was a founding member of the Sealed Knot, a Royalist secret society led by a number of younger sons of the great landed families, based in East Anglia, which coordinated operations against the Commonwealth. Although he was opposed to his kinsman's activities on behalf of Charles II, Lambert was prepared to secure his release from imprisonment in the Tower. Monck, commander of the Commonwealth armies in Scotland, had a cousin, Sir John Grenville, who was a leading Royalist in the south-west of England. Lockhart had the distinction of being knighted by both Charles I and Cromwell. A Scottish Presbyterian, he had fought for parliament, then the King, in the first two Civil Wars, before switching allegiance to Cromwell in 1652.

2

PRESBYTERIANS, REPUBLICANS, ROYALISTS AND FOREIGN POWERS

The new Protector was only too aware of the need to rally his father's supporters when he surveyed the enemies ranged against him. Some of his most dangerous opponents were Parliamentarians who had fallen out with Cromwell. The more moderate of these were the predominantly Presbyterian members of the Long Parliament who had been purged by Col Pride in 1648 owing to their objections to the trial of Charles I. These men, known as the secluded members, totalling 276 MPs, were to be out of office for a decade, but then were to play a crucial role in the run-up to the Restoration. As Presbyterians, they supported a restrained and disciplined Church governed by elders, and strongly objected to the High Church Anglicanism of Charles I and Laud, with their love of pomp and ritual. But the Presbyterians contrasted with the more radical Independent sects who dominated the Army and were opposed to any form of organised Church. Some Presbyterians had become Royalists, including William Prynne, a polemicist of genius, who had once been a formidable critic of Charles I, and had suffered the indignity of having both his ears clipped in the pillory, but was then a vociferous opponent of the Commonwealth during the 1650s. Many of these former Parliamentarians were prepared to support the restoration of the monarchy, but only on the basis of the Newport Treaty they had negotiated with Charles I in 1648, in the aftermath of the Second Civil War. By this the King had agreed to drastic limitations to his powers and to support a Presbyterian Church.

The forcible dissolution of parliament in April 1653 had turned leading members of the Rump, such as the headstrong Sir Arthur

Hesilrige, a major opponent of Charles I, into the Protector's implacable foes. The more subtle and intelligent Sir Henry Vane had once been a close friend of Cromwell, with whom he shared a belief in religious tolerance, and a desire to reform Englishmen so that they would be 'holy as well as free'. He had, however, been outraged by the Protector's dismissal of parliament in 1653. Another Rumper and regicide, the radical Edmund Ludlow, felt that Cromwell had betrayed his republican heritage, 'sacrificing it to the idol of his ambition'. Thomas Scot, a fellow regicide, was even fiercer in his denunciation of the authority granted to the Protector, regarding him as little better than a military dictator and no champion of liberty. The Republicans, as these men were called, failed to see the irony that they had been the beneficiaries of Army violence in Pride's Purge in 1648. They were, however, anxious to regain office and determined to prevent the new Protector assuming his father's mantle.

Other opponents of the Government were less resolute in their republicanism but had strongly disapproved of Cromwell's arbitrary dismissal of the parliament in 1653. One of the brightest of this group was Anthony Ashley Cooper, who had changed from a Royalist to a Parliamentarian during the First Civil War. Later to become Earl of Shaftesbury and a member of the Cabal before leading the opposition to Charles II during the Exclusion Crisis of 1679–81, his political abilities had already been recognised, as well as his slippery nature. The King had failed to persuade him to revert to his former allegiance. Cromwell had been little more successful in securing Ashley Cooper's loyalty, and had prevented him from attending the Second Protectorate Parliament in 1656, exclaiming: 'No-one was so difficult to manage as the little man with three names.'

One of Cromwell's hopes in the last year of his life had been to bring peers who had supported the Parliamentary cause in the Civil Wars into the Government. The Second Protectorate Parliament, which reassembled in January 1658, had two houses, the House of Commons and the Other House, as it was known, resembling the House of Lords abolished in the aftermath of Charles I's execution. But former Parliamentarian peers such as the Earls of Manchester and Warwick, and Viscount Saye and Sele, all held back, uncertain of how their acceptance of this institution might affect their constitutional position in any future House of Lords. With the Protector visibly ageing, they feared for the future.

The most numerous opponents of Cromwell were of course the Royalists. Since the later 1640s their leaders had been living in impoverished exile, latterly in the Spanish Netherlands. The two central figures were the young King Charles II and Sir Edward Hyde, his chief minister since 1644 and appointed Lord Chancellor in 1658. The close relationship between master and servant formed the bedrock on which the Restoration was to be based.

By 1658 Charles II, now aged 28, had spent almost half his life in exile. As a boy he had attended several battles in the First Civil War, before going into exile in 1646. Three years later he had inherited the crown on hearing the tragic news of his father's execution. The young King had formed an uneasy alliance with the Scottish Covenanters, extreme Presbyterians who had fought with parliament during the First Civil War before falling out with the English parliament over the execution of Charles I. In 1650 he had set off for Scotland determined to regain his throne. But the Covenanters were religious fanatics who subjected Charles, brought up as an Anglican, to months of humiliation in order to test the depth of his conversion to their cause. He played no part in the defeat of the Scots by Cromwell at Dunbar and was forced publicly to confess the sins of his parents, regarded as idolators, particularly his Catholic mother, Henrietta Maria, before being crowned King at Scone on New Year's Day 1651. When he was finally able to lead an army into England that summer, he suffered a disastrous defeat at Worcester, and then spent a traumatic six weeks on the run, hunted like an animal, before reaching France.

The events of 1650–1 had taught Charles II a number of vital lessons. He must establish himself, as Hyde wished, as a symbol of the traditional order, a rallying point for all those disaffected with the regime. Rather than dwelling on his disastrous alliance with the Scottish Covenanters and his defeat at Worcester, Royalists celebrated his near-miraculous escape from his enemies. Charles himself realised that he must never again alienate his predominantly Anglican followers by indulging in a political marriage of convenience with his erstwhile Presbyterian opponents.

After his escape to France, Charles II had resumed a life of inactivity and penury on the Continent, forced to observe events from the sidelines. In 1654, following a treaty between France and the Commonwealth, the King had left France for Cologne, before moving to the Spanish Netherlands in 1656 after the Commonwealth's declaration of war on Spain. Although Charles had signed a treaty with the Spanish guaranteeing the Royalists a pension, Spain was bankrupted by forty years of continuous warfare and the money was rarely paid. Consequently, morale was very low among the hungry and penniless Cavaliers, whose prospects of a return from exile seemed to grow ever more distant after years of defeat and failed attempts to overthrow Cromwell and the English Commonwealth. The Royalists vented their frustrations in drinking, quarrelling and duelling. Although Charles was tempted on several occasions to cross the Channel to join his followers on the mainland, the King was restrained by the widespread indifference and hostility he had witnessed first-hand in the aftermath of the Worcester campaign.

Physically Charles cut a tall, imposing figure. While he was at the French Court a decade earlier, Madame de Motteville had noted approvingly: 'He was well-made, his dark complexion suited his fine black eyes: his mouth was large and ugly, but he had a fine figure.' Another female admirer had been much taken with his hair, 'of a shining black, not frizzled, but so naturally curling into great rings, a comely ornament'. Now it was streaked with grey and his features had coarsened but his courteous manner charmed all who came into contact with him.

The charming exterior was, however, deceptive. Charles's character had been moulded by his experiences in exile. Years of failure and disappointment had merely stiffened his resolve. He remained single-minded in his determination to regain his throne. Throughout the long years that succeeded Worcester, the King never failed to maintain a cheerful exterior, paying careful attention to his senior advisers, and encouraging his intriguing, fractious supporters. James Butler, Marquis of Ormonde, an Anglo-Irish grandee and resolute champion of the Royalist cause in Ireland throughout the Civil Wars, was one of many to note his natural intelligence, and how he possessed 'more judgement and understanding, by many degrees than many who pretend to it'.

The Marquis noted the toll that the years of enforced inactivity had taken, when Charles was obliged to 'sit still and dream out his life' instead of going into action 'with his sword in his hand'. He was compelled to listen to the unrealistic schemes for his restoration advanced by his followers, and spent countless hours sorting out the bitter personal feuds that beset the exiled Court. Little wonder that he should have preferred the company of the younger, high-spirited Cavaliers who gave him some escape from his arduous responsibilities. Ormonde lamented his sovereign's 'immoderate delight in empty, effeminate and vulgar conversation', and Hyde was sharply critical that the King 'did not enough delight in his business'.

Others had noted the young King's love of pleasure and his determination to enjoy the moment and seize any chance of happiness when it occurred. As Madame de Motteville commented, he 'bore the ills of poverty with reckless nonchalance, snatching at whatever pleasures came his way'. Charles's boon companions were his contemporaries Henry Bennet, later Earl of Arlington, Secretary of State and member of the Cabal, Will Crofts, and the Irishmen Daniel O'Neill and Lord Taafe. Charles's correspondence with Bennet throughout the 1650s makes frequent reference to dancing and parties, and the King's desire to purchase the most fashionable articles of clothing. These easy-going, cynical men shared their sovereign's love of pleasure and his love of beautiful women, and were to set the tone for the relaxed morals of the Restoration Court.

During the years of exile, Charles enjoyed a number of mistresses, and sired several illegitimate children. His first serious affair was with Lucy Walter, by whom he had a son James, future Duke of Monmouth, in 1649, and rumours abounded that they had been secretly married. But no evidence has ever come to light, and it seems very unlikely that the King would have jeopardised his chances of a restoration by making such an unfavourable match. His affair with Lucy ended in scandal, when her lifestyle became so dissolute that the King ordered the forcible removal of his son, who was brought up by Charles's mother Henrietta Maria in Paris.

The King's love of pleasure, however, was always secondary to his determination to regain his throne. In order to do this, he relied heavily on the advice of Sir Edward Hyde. This high-minded, clever and gregarious lawyer had proved a resolute champion of the Royalist cause. There was something of the schoolmaster about Hyde. He had taken it upon himself to instruct Charles II (as he became in 1649) in the art of kingship. He also saw it as his mission to teach Englishmen the error of their ways in condoning the execution of their lawful sovereign and then supporting the illegal regime that had replaced the monarchy. In order to maintain the Royalist cause, and to undermine the Commonwealth, Hyde carried on a vast correspondence with his agents on mainland Britain, who were constantly testing the loyalty of servants of the regime. His success can be measured not only in converts to Royalism, but also in the sense of insecurity bred in an unpopular regime founded on force.

The Chancellor's policy was one of passive resistance to the Common-wealth. The King represented tradition and order. The temporary rulers were impostors, the basis of their government was illegal, relying on nothing more than military might, and Cromwell had committed the unforgivable crime of regicide. Throughout the 1650s Hyde strove to his utmost to prevent Cromwell from imposing a new order. He fervently believed that the English would eventually welcome back the King they had driven into exile and was convinced that his enemies eventually would fall out. 'If I did not assuredly believe', he wrote to Secretary of State

Sir Edward Nicholas, 'that they will at last determine the confusion and be each other's executioners, I should be very melancholic; for I have really more hope from that than from all the armies and fleets you and your enterprising friends will be able to draw together.'

It was inconceivable that a nation so steeped in tradition should not wish to restore the long-established pillars of the monarchy, the English constitution and the Anglican Church. Despite the years of penniless exile, when the restoration seemed an ever-more-distant prospect, Hyde kept faith that England would revert 'to its old good manners, its old good humour, and its old good nature – good nature, a virtue so peculiar that it can be translated into no other language, and hardly practised by any other people'. Each failed attempt by Cromwell to effect a settlement showed the impossibility of replacing these essential components of English life. It was the English themselves who held the key, for 'it must be the resurrection of the English courage and loyalty must recover England to the king'. To back this policy of passive resistance, Hyde supported the setting-up of the Sealed Knot, the Royalist secret society which was to coordinate operations against the Commonwealth.

Hyde's closest ally during the long years of exile was the Marquis of Ormonde. The Chancellor greatly admired the Irish nobleman's unimpeachable loyalty, which involved the sacrifice of his entire fortune in the Royalist cause and his steadfast belief in the Anglican faith, although most of his family were Catholics. Ormonde was, however, a bon viveur, a lover of women and a man of action, temperamentally closer to the King, and it was he who accompanied Charles whenever there seemed a chance of crossing over to England. The Marquis was also used on delicate missions, such as the removal of Charles's youngest brother Henry from France in 1654, when his mother Henrietta Maria was attempting to convert him to Catholicism. More recently, he had been on a secret mission to London to try to rally Royalist support.

The Chancellor was aware that many Royalists in England were demoralised after witnessing numerous abortive plots and risings. Some remained sitting on the fence and had 'warily distributed their family to both sides'. Many more, rather than risk losing everything, followed the advice of Col Gervase Holles, a Cavalier who had fought in the Civil Wars: 'If we keep our swords in their sheaths, they will soon cut their own throats.' The majority of Charles I's supporters in the First Civil War had been staunch Anglicans. Even in defeat they remained committed to Royalism, but punitive fines, sequestration and sums sent abroad to help the exiled King had sapped their willingness to fight for the cause. The bishops remaining in England had either been arrested or had become taciturn, refusing all Hyde's entreaties that they consecrate new bishops to vacant sees. It was left to more active junior members of the clergy, such as John Barwick, later dean of St Paul's, and Gilbert Sheldon, the future Archbishop of Canterbury, to lead a clandestine resistance. Roman Catholics, who had fought enthusiastically for the King, had been equally persecuted.

There were younger and more energetic Royalists who longed to mount a challenge. The Action Party, encouraged by Prince Rupert, first cousin of the King and a leading general and admiral during the Civil Wars, despised what they perceived to be the vacillating and ineffective policies of the Sealed Knot. They were not prepared to wait indefinitely for the fall of the regime. Their leaders wanted to attract the support of anyone disaffected with the Commonwealth. Many of these were Presbyterians turned Royalist who had originally fought for parliament and had gained estates from dispossessed Royalists. They were, therefore, keen on a conditional restoration, enabling them to retain their possessions, and the imposition of Presbyterianism as the state religion, something Charles I had agreed to during secret negotiations preceding the Second Civil War in 1648. Furthermore, they never forgot that Charles II had taken the Covenant in the summer of 1650, and that he had been crowned a Covenanter King in Scotland on New Year's Day 1651.

Charles favoured a more active opposition to the regime than Hyde. There were two reasons for this: one was to keep the Royalist flame alight; the other was to keep the Government feeling insecure. During his escape after the battle of Worcester, Charles had witnessed great indifference and often hatred of his cause. While hiding at Trent Manor in Somerset, he had even seen the villagers celebrating his putative death. Although the chances of a successful rising seemed remote, he feared that the cause would wither and die without visible evidence of Royalist resistance. The longer the Cromwell family remained in power and the House of Stuart in exile, the more distant appeared the prospect of a restoration. He therefore encouraged his followers on the mainland to be prepared to fight for the cause.

Although the Royalists suffered greatly – subjected to punitive fines, denied any office in government and prevented from practising the Anglican religion – the Government remained fearful of them. Edward Phillips, a nephew of John Milton and dedicated opponent of the House of Stuart, admitted their success: 'It was nothing else, but the restless and invincible spirit of the Royal Party, that by keeping the Usurpers in a perpetual distraction, and Alarm, hindered them from proceeding to a final Establishment of their Power.' And there was always the possibility that they might prevail. Penruddock's rising in the south-west in 1655 had been a failure, undermined by Thurloe's superior intelligence service, the hesitation of the Sealed Knot, the lack of unity between the traditional Anglican Royalists and the more recent Presbyterian converts, and the reluctance of the great magnates, such as the Marquis of Hertford, to participate, for fear of losing their estates. Nevertheless, Cromwell was shocked by his inability to crush the Royalist movement. He determined on more serious measures, and the rule of the Major-Generals was set up to crush Royalism once and for all. In Cromwell's words, his soldiers were to instruct their countrymen 'not what they want but what is good for them'. But even John Lambert, Cromwell's leading lieutenant and a strong supporter of the rule of the Major-Generals, one of whom he was, was uneasy at the antagonism it aroused. Beneath the surface, he worried at the Cavaliers' implacable hatred of the regime: 'They are as careful to breed up their children in the memory of the quarrel as can be. They are, haply, now merry over their Christmas pies, drinking the King of Scots' health, or your confusion.' And fear of the Royalists, as Thurloe admitted to Hyde after the Restoration, was the determining factor in Cromwell's foreign policy.

The reaction of European powers to the news of Cromwell's death and the appointment of Richard as the new Protector showed the impact of Oliver's personality throughout Europe. Once foreign ambassadors in London had reported that all was calm, rulers made haste to acknowledge Richard. This demonstrates not only the respect with which the Protector was held for his victories on land and sea, but also his striking success in isolating Charles II. Although the King was related by blood to most of the rulers in Europe, who expressed shock and outrage at the execution of Charles I in 1649, they had been only too happy to acknowledge the Commonwealth and had distanced themselves from the Royalist cause.

In 1654 Cromwell had made an alliance with the brilliant, wily Cardinal Mazarin, who was ruling France during the minority of Louis XIV. He was reputed to be the lover and possibly the husband of Louis's mother, Anne of Austria, and even possibly the father of Louis XIV. As part of the alliance, Cromwell persuaded the Cardinal to expel the English King, although he was Louis's first cousin. Now that Cromwell was dead, the Cardinal, conscious of the close links between the Stuart family and their Bourbon cousins, hastened to visit Charles II's mother, Henrietta Maria, who was living in Paris. The Cardinal offered his congratulations on the death of the 'old monster'. At the same time he was careful not to offend the Protectorate, and directed the French Court to go into mourning for Oliver's death.

The Dutch had always found Cromwell particularly enigmatic. The vast majority shared his passionate espousal of republican and Protestant values, but resented his encouragement of the two nations' fierce trading rivalry, which had led to naval war in 1652–4. Nevertheless, the Government, led by the republican Jan de Witt, was determined not to admit the exiled Stuart Court, since it feared the popularity of the House of Orange, with Charles II's sister Mary, mother of the young Prince William, at its head. Even when the Commonwealth was at war with Holland, the States General still refused to form an alliance with Charles. The Dutch, however, hated Cromwell for the destruction the Anglo-Dutch war caused, and celebrated the news of his demise by dancing through the streets of Amsterdam, chanting: 'The Devil is dead.'

The Spanish had, in theory, supported the Stuart cause since the English Commonwealth declared war on Spain in 1655. In practice, however, they had treated Charles as an embarrassment from the moment he arrived uninvited in the Spanish Netherlands in 1656. He was hastily sent to provincial Bruges, away from the capital in Brussels, where he and his fellow exiles were living in desperate poverty. Royalist troops under Charles's brother James, Duke of York had fought alongside their Spanish allies at the battle of the Dunes in 1658, but they had been defeated by Turenne's Frenchmen and a contingent from the New Model Army. Spain, after a generation of warfare, was bankrupt and longing for peace. There was little chance that it would provide troops or transport for a Royalist invasion. Even so, the exiled Cavaliers based in Brussels remained a threat the Protectorate could not ignore. In addition, Flemish privateers operating with impunity out of Ostend were preying with devastating effect on English shipping in the North Sea.

But the real problem of the war with Spain was the ever-rising cost of keeping an army in the field and a navy at sea. At the time of Cromwell's death, the Army was costing some £1,100,000 p.a. while the Navy was almost as expensive, costing £900,000. In addition, the cost of running the civil government was £300,000. Despite draconian taxation and years of punitive fines on Royalists, income stood at no more than £1,900,000, leaving a shortfall of £400,000. With each passing year, the debt to the military rose, increasing discontent and the threat of mutiny. The only realistic means of reducing the debt was to disband part of the armed forces but, in order to do this, the Government needed to make peace with Spain, and it needed to believe that the Royalist threat had receded permanently.

3

TROUBLE IN THE ARMY

Although Oliver had only made his wishes known just before his death, and there had been no public announcement, Richard's succession was immediately ratified by the Privy Council, dominated by Thurloe. To enlist the support of the Army, the Council immediately sent the proclamation of his eldest son as Lord Protector to the influential Council of Officers based in London, who offered unconditional support. Declarations of loyalty poured in from all parts of the kingdom, and from the important figures of Monck, commander-in-chief in Scotland, and Montagu, commander of the Navy.

In the immediate aftermath of Cromwell's death, his many enemies felt a surge of optimism. The Leveller William Howard wrote: 'All men's hearts (almost quite dead before) are of a sudden wonderfully revived to an expectation of some great change.' The Royalists were similarly euphoric. In spite of the fact that Richard had now inherited 'all his father's greatness and all his glory,' as Sir Edward Hyde noted, 'I cannot believe all will submit to the government of this young coxcomb.' But this optimism soon subsided. Although Cromwell's troops were pelted with carrots and turnip-tops by students in Oxford, Thurloe, keeping a close eye on any potential troublemakers, noted the general passivity: 'There is not a dog that wags his tongue, so great a calm we are in.' A plea by Sir Edward Nicholas, the Royalist Secretary of State since 1641, for all 'lovers of the honoure and peace of the 3 kingdoms . . . to take up arms immediately and end the usurpation' was never issued. 'So the King's condition never appeared so hopeless, so desperate,' Hyde declared mournfully shortly afterwards; he was 'no more apprehended or talked of than if he were in the Indies'.

Richard Baxter, originally a parliamentary chaplain and one of the leading Presbyterian divines, a natural conservative and an opponent of all forms of arbitrary rule, summed up the feelings of the majority of the population: 'Many sober Men that called his Father [Oliver Cromwell] no better than a Trayterous Hypocrite, did begin to think they owed him [Richard] Subjective. They knew that the King was by birth their rightful Sovereign . . . But they were astonished at the marvellous providence of God, which had been against that Family [the Stuarts] all along, and they thought that there was no rational probability of his [Charles II's] Restoration.'

Richard was an unknown quantity. This worked to both his advantage and disadvantage. He did not excite the same passions as his father did, and stood a fair chance of reconciling his father's many enemies. The numerous proclamations and declarations of loyalty from all over Britain that greeted his succession indicated the populace's desire for a peaceful transfer of power. Many of these tributes compared Richard with great religious leaders of the past, and hailed him as a new Joshua or Elisha. The citizens of Sudbury waxed lyrical in the expectation that Richard's government 'may still be a morning without clouds, till righteousness may fully dwell in the midst of us'. An ecumenical document, published by the clergy of the Independent sects, led by John Owen, a great favourite of Oliver Cromwell, attempting to make common ground with their Presbyterian rivals, was a further indication of the desire for reconciliation. There were other reassuring signs. Scotland and Ireland, so often the scenes of trouble, remained passive.

However, if the new Protector was to profit from this desire for peace he needed to belie his reputation as a charming, self-effacing nonentity, and provide leadership. Richard's brother Henry analysed the problem in a letter to Thurloe written on 8 September, within days of his father's death: 'Where is that person of wisdom, courage, conduct, and (which is equivalent to all) reputation at home and abroad, which we see necessary to preserve our peace?' His best chance was to take advantage of the widespread support he enjoyed in the immediate aftermath of his father's death. But there were a number of powerful factions eager to test Richard's ability to rule.

The New Model Army posed the greatest immediate threat. The officers and men declared their allegiance but were acutely conscious that the new Protector, unlike his father, had never fought in their ranks. With a Government debt of £2,500,000 and an annual deficit of £400,000, Richard's most pressing concern was to raise money to maintain some 40,000 men in arms throughout Britain, a crushing financial burden. He had two choices: to raise taxes, certain to alienate the civilian population, or to disband some of the soldiers, with the risk that the dissatisfied troops might mutiny. Oliver had an intimate knowledge of the New Model Army, in which he had served since its creation, and had formed a close bond with his men, but even he had been unable to make a substantial reduction in their numbers. Richard, in contrast, was an outsider, a stranger to the soldiers.

The generals were acutely aware of their men's propensity for violence if they were not paid. The difficulty of paying the troops had led to the award of debentures, a certificate of deferred payment secured 'upon the public faith'. Parliament assigned the sale of land belonging to the crown, the Church and Royalist delinquents to redeem the debentures, but this was a very slow and complicated process. Impoverished soldiers were prepared to offer their debentures for sale, although this was prohibited by the Government, and there was widespread resentment among the poorer soldiers when they saw their officers enriching themselves at their expense. Lambert was regarded as particularly unscrupulous in this way. Col Lilburne offered the general the magnificent palace of Nonsuch, built by Henry VIII, stating that his men would take 12 shillings in the pound for their debentures.

Desborough, one of the most aggressive of the senior commanders, anxious to placate his men and showing little concern for the civilian population, suggested that people should be forced to pay taxes, an example of the Army's insolent aggressiveness that had earned it such widespread hatred and distrust. There was a mutinous outbreak in Dunkirk shortly after Richard's accession, easily suppressed but an ominous sign for the future, especially as the governor, Sir William Lockhart, suspected that 'there is something else at the bottom of it, and I hope to find it out'. Unsurprisingly, the ordinary civilian felt embittered that his taxes should be used to pay for the maintenance of such a hated institution.

These problems were enough to try the most experienced leader. In addition to the prestige of his name, there were two ways in which the new Protector could dominate the Army: through the Privy Council and through parliament. But it was unclear whether either of these bodies was capable of controlling the military. On the very day of his father's death, the Privy Council thought it necessary to gain the support of the leading officers. This was easily obtained, the officers queuing up to show their loyalty. But there were soon signs of discontent. On 7 September Thurloe wrote to Henry Cromwell in Ireland: 'I must need acquaint your Excellency that there are some secret murmurings in the army, as if his Highness [Richard] were not general of the army, as his father was . . . I am not able to say what this will come to, but I think the conceit of any such thing is dangerous.' Fauconberg reiterated the warning a week later: 'a cabal there is of persons and great ones held very closely, resolved, it's said, to rule themselves or set all on fire'.

The Army, meanwhile, was relying on the same tactics that it had used when it became heavily involved in politics in 1647–8 and in 1653. Fired with religious zeal, the soldiers had originally gathered for prayer and fasting and these meetings, where all were encouraged to air their views, had often led to demands for constitutional change, usually in the form of a petition submitted to parliament. On both the previous occasions, when parliament had failed to heed its wishes, the Army had dismissed it. The soldiers were very conscious that they had been recruited on the basis of ability and determination, regardless of their social status, with their officers chosen on merit. The majority of the men were members of Independent sects, inspired by a fervent belief in their cause. They included Fifth Monarchy Men, who believed in the imminent second coming of Jesus, and the rapidly growing sect of Quakers, regarded as still more dangerous, with their refusal to accept any religious hierarchy and their belief in social egalitarianism. Debates were held between the generals and their colonels and other officers before military action.

Initially, the soldiers were inspired by a united vision of liberty, but, gradually, this cohesion had broken down and there was no longer the close bond that had united the Army a decade earlier. Their increasing unpopularity, aggravated by the rule of the Major-Generals, led to the civilian population regarding them as little better than expensive mercenaries intent on self-preservation. As the high-minded republican Member of Parliament Algernon Sidney remarked sadly, soldiering had 'become a trade', not a calling. More than ever, they wanted to be paid for it, and were prepared to mutiny if their demands were not met.

Nevertheless, the Army still wielded enormous influence and Richard ignored the soldiers' wishes at his peril. In the autumn of 1658 the men began holding meetings on Fridays, ostensibly to pray together, the officers gathering at Fleetwood's residence at Wallingford House, the more radical elements at the house of the rough and aggressive Desborough. Many of the men present at these meetings were genuinely religious, but others used the occasion to discuss politics. As Thurloe noted, 'under the notion of godliness' they were 'indeed serving lusts of their own'. Fleetwood, a man of weak-minded vanity and pious affectation, was the vehicle for the soldiers' protests. Oliver Cromwell had summed up his son-in-law Fleetwood when he tried to dissuade him from the dissolution of parliament two years previously: 'You are a milksop, by the living God, I will dissolve the House.' Henry Cromwell, who succeeded the ineffective Fleetwood as Lord Deputy of Ireland, added: 'I believe the milk, wherein Fleetwood was sopped, had much water in it.' Ironically, Henry was probably one of the few men who could have controlled Fleetwood, but Richard considered his position in Ireland too important for him to be brought back to London.

Despite, or perhaps because of, the weaknesses in his character, Fleetwood was popular with his soldiers, and Oliver had made him his right-hand man during the last months of his life, responsible for ensuring the loyalty of the Army. Without Cromwell to control him, his natural propensity for intrigue resurfaced. He had one advantage that became increasingly apparent. As a born procrastinator, unwilling to take tough decisions, the longer the period of instability lasted, the stronger his position became at the expense of the new Protector's. Fauconberg was suspicious of Fleetwood, and had written to Henry Cromwell as early as 29 August, even before Oliver's death, that he was one of two officers not summoned to a meeting called by Fleetwood of leading officers, 'by which you may guess something'. Henry was equally suspicious of his brother-in-law's intentions and wrote scathingly of his 'lust and ambition. . . . I thought those whom my father had raised up from nothing would not so soon have forgot him, and endeavour to destroy his family, before he is in his grave.'

Richard was aware of the need to control the Army and issued orders for an oath of loyalty to him to be taken by all the troops in September. This was done, but, on the 21st, Fleetwood presented an address asserting the Army's right to full participation in government alongside the Protector and the Privy Council, which was to be composed of sober and godly men. Fauconberg, highly aware of the threat of the military, commented on the petition: 'They are demanding things which no magistrate in the world can grant without divesting himself of all but the shadow,' adding 'in the end I fear it will prove a serpent.' Rumours abounded that Fleetwood was to be appointed 'Generalissimo of the forces'. Fauconberg reported to Henry Cromwell on 28 September that some officers had already approached Richard 'to give away his power of disposing all command in the army to Fleetwood but this is a great secret yet'. The fact that the senior officers in the Army continued to meet regularly for prayer and fasting gave them ample opportunities to indulge in political debate.

Unrest increased in early October as senior officers sought to influence political events. Following a meeting of 300 officers at St James's on 8 October, Fleetwood presented a petition, declaring in ringing tones the soldiers' loyalty to Oliver's memory, but advocating that he replace the Protector as commander-in-chief, and urging that no officer be dismissed without a court martial, i.e. the Army would regulate itself. Richard knew that he must impose his authority. On 18 October he stressed that he was 'resolved to live and die' for the Good Old Cause, to the troops a powerful if nebulous appeal to a nostalgic ideal of freedom for which they had originally taken up arms against the tyranny of Charles I. Richard, however, insisted that he would retain control of the militia and, more importantly, would remain commander-in-chief, with Fleetwood promoted to be his lieutenant-general. For the moment it appeared that his firm action had defused the crisis. Towards the end of October, however, the weekly meetings of officers on Fridays recommenced at St James's, the main object of complaint being their inability to influence the Protector's choice of officers, so that 'good men were put out and worse put in'.

If Richard wanted an example of how to cope with the problems in the English Army, he need look no further than the example set by three of his key supporters: his brother Henry in Ireland, Montagu at the Navy and Monck in Scotland. Each man advocated a similar policy: firm discipline, a refusal to let his officers indulge in politics, with the threat of cashiering those who did, and an attempt, whenever possible, to ensure regular payment of wages.

The three men offered Richard their best advice. Henry, who had already cashiered some of his own officers in Ireland and was highly suspicious of the officers in the English Army, suggested that his brother order the dispersal of troops outside the capital, where they would be less inclined to involve themselves in politics. Montagu, soon to leave London to take up his command at sea, spoke eloquently in parliament of the danger of the soldiers' petitions, a way for them to become involved in politics. He attempted to unite support behind Richard by issuing a declaration by the Navy on 12 October to defend the Protector 'against Charles Stuart and his adherents'.

Soon after his succession, Richard sent to Monck for advice. His messenger, the general's brother-in-law Thomas Clarges, returned to London with Monck's stern warning of the urgent need to tackle the power of the military. Monck urged Richard to take immediate action and remodel the English Army, using this as a pretext to dismiss 'insolent spirits' and other potential opponents. On religious matters he advocated a moderate form of Presbyterianism. He disagreed with Oliver's policy of toleration, which had been so damaging, for 'we have almost no religion amongst us, which is crumbled into dust by seperations and devisions, and we are become the scorn of our enemies, and the greif of our friends'. It was time to take a firm hand and 'put a stop to that progresse of blasphemes and profanes, that I feare is too frequent in many places by the great extent of toleration'. Monck himself had already purged his army of known Quakers and Anabaptists, and had forbidden his men from holding meetings 'to interpose in public affairs'. He had also been ruthless in cashiering officers he suspected of disloyalty, in particular religious extremists, and was able to report to Thurloe: 'The army was never quieter nor in better condition since I commanded here.' Monck further advised Richard to rely on Thurloe, Broghill and Oliver St John, another Cromwellian loyalist who championed the civil authority over the military. Unfortunately, Richard was not confident enough to take Monck's advice.

The exiled Royalists noted the divisions among their opponents and made a careful evaluation of the key figures. It was the astute John, Lord Colepeper, a senior member of Charles's Council, who saw the solution. Immediately after Cromwell's death he wrote prophetically:

The person my eye is chiefly upon as able to restore the King, and not absolutely averse to it, neither in his principles nor in his affections . . . is Monck, who commands, absolutely at his devotion, a better army, as I am informed, than there is in England, and in the king's quarrel can bring with him the strength of Scotland. . . . I need not give you his character; you know he is a sullen man that values him[self] enough, and much believes that his knowledge and reputation in arms fits him for the title of Highness and the office of Protector better than Mr Richard Cromwell's skill in horse-racing and husbandry doth. You know, besides, that the only ties that hath hitherto kept him from grumbling have been the vanity of constancy to his profession, and his affection to Cromwell's person. . . . Nothing of either can now stick with him. The way to deal with him is, by some fit person to show him plainly, and to give him all imaginable security for it, that he shall better find all his ends, those of honour, power, profit, safety, with the King than in any way he can take. . . . When he is engaged past a retreat he will want you as much as you will want him, and you may mould him into what form you please.

Charles decided that Sir John Grenville, son of the Cavalier general Sir Bevil Grenville, victor of the battle of Lansdowne Hill, and a cousin of Monck's, was the man most suited to the task of contacting the general. This was not the first time that the King had communicated with Monck. Three years earlier he had written to him from Cologne, but without eliciting a response. The general had in fact immediately forwarded to Cromwell a copy of the letter (while carefully retaining the original), but the Protector was not wholly reassured. He wrote to Monck shortly afterwards: 'There be some that tell me that there is a certain cunning fellow in Scotland, called George Monk, who is said to lie in wait there to introduce Charles Stuart; I pray you use your diligence to apprehend him, and send him up to me.' Cromwell was on his guard.

After his death, it had been noted, when Richard was declared Protector to muted response in Edinburgh, that the soldiers' reaction was: 'Why not old George? He would be fitter a protector than Dick Cromwell.' But Monck was to prove impeccably loyal to the Protectorate during the winter months. The Royalists, however, were prepared to wait, and one of their agents, Dr Barwick, had won over Col Clobery, one of Monck's most trusted officers, whom he described as 'honest, silent, wary'.

The Royalists were also busy in England. Charles continued to encourage the activities of John Mordaunt, the most active of all his followers in England despite the Parliamentarian sympathies of his father, 1st Earl of Peterborough. Mordaunt's capture, following an abortive rising in Sussex, led to his imprisonment in the Tower. At his trial in Westminster Hall, he escaped the death sentence by just one vote. Free again after his acquittal, he accepted his new appointment as King's Plenipotentiary, with the authority to widen Royalist support, offering pardons and rewards to former rebels. Mordaunt, following Hyde's dictum, was against relying solely on French or Spanish military help, 'when more nobly we may do it ourselves', but traditional Cavaliers, including members of the Sealed Knot, saw him as rash, vain and overbearing. The divisions among the Royalists were exacerbated by the number of spies and double agents who had infiltrated their ranks. Sir Richard Willis, one of the leaders of the Sealed Knot, was reporting the group's every move to Thurloe.

Fortunately for the Royalists, there were even more serious divisions in the ranks of the Government. In the Privy Council, Montagu was one of the few senior military figures on whom the Protector could rely. Fleetwood and Desborough, the two senior generals (Lambert was still in retirement), blocked the appointments of his brother Henry, Fauconberg and Broghill. Instead, they advised the new Protector he should promote sober and godly men, and that Maj Gen Berry and Col Thomas Cooper were more suitable candidates. Richard's supporters in the English Army, Maj Gens Goffe and Whalley, and Col Ingoldsby, were junior in rank to

Fleetwood and Desborough. They were unable to prevent the latter from passing a resolution that Richard was not to cashier officers without a court martial. There was a dangerous implication that the Army would be accountable only to itself, and claim the right, as it had done so often during the past decade, to interfere in civil affairs. The Protector's position was not helped by a serious illness contracted by his secretary, Thurloe, on whom he relied heavily for advice, which laid him low for most of September and October.

One of the major successes of Oliver's Protectorate had been in raising England's reputation on the Continent. His alliance with France had led to military and naval triumphs against Spain. Richard, however, was far less successful. He hoped to capitalise on his father's alliance with Mazarin, and had tried to approach France for a loan of £50,000. But the Cardinal deftly put aside Richard's request, offering him some Barbary horses instead.

Richard was equally ineffective in the Baltic, where Sweden was at war with Denmark, both countries aiming to control the Sound whose shores formed the entrance to that sea. The two nations were looking for allies, and eagerly sought the help of the English Government. Cromwell had advocated an alliance with Charles X of Sweden, a warrior king after his own heart, to counter the influence of the Dutch, who were extremely protective of their trade in grain and naval supplies coming through the Sound, and favoured the Danes. At the time of Cromwell's death, Sweden and Denmark were still at war, despite England's and the Netherlands' desire for peace so that they could benefit from peaceful trade in the Baltic. Despite warnings from Downing, the English resident in Holland, that the Dutch were about to enter the fray, Richard and his Privy Council were unprepared when a Dutch fleet sailed north, defeated the Swedes and relieved Copenhagen, which they had been besieging. Belatedly, Vice Adm Goodson was authorised to sail to the Baltic, but this was not the season to mount an expedition and he was driven back by heavy gales.

With little success abroad, and growing problems with the Army, Richard needed to bolster confidence in the regime. One way of doing this was to stage a magnificent funeral for his father. No trouble was spared to ensure that the occasion would match the splendour of a royal event, and the ceremony was based on the funeral of James I. The public had already been admitted to Somerset House for the previous month, where the wax effigy of the Protector, clad in purple velvet, holding an orb and sceptre, lay upon a bed of state. On 23 November the effigy, now wearing a crown and placed upright, was taken from Somerset House to Westminster Abbey in a splendid procession, attended by the ambassadors and envoys of the foreign powers. The effect was, however, rather ruined by the late departure of the procession. By the time it reached the Abbey it was dark, and the dearth of candles and of heating meant that the service was conducted in near darkness and in freezing cold.

Few were impressed by this display of pomp. Republicans such as Ludlow were scandalised at the regal honours bestowed on Cromwell. Others, such as the poet Abraham Cowley, lamented the 'vain-glory; briefly a great show, and yet after all this, but an ill sight'. More importantly, the soldiers begrudged a reputed sum of £60,000, which could have been used to pay their wages, being spent on the ceremony. Although a vast crowd of mourners accompanied the procession, there was little sorrow. The Royalist John Evelyn wrote: 'It was the joyfullest funeral I ever saw; for there were none cried but dogs, which the soldiers hooted away with a barbarous noise, drinking and taking tobacco in the streets as they went.' Thurloe was happy when the event was over. 'Much endeavour', he recorded, 'there hath been to blowe the coal among the soldiers, to have begotten some disturbance this day, but all is ended in peace.'

The funeral, however, could not disguise increasing signs of discontent among leaders of the regime, as Monsieur de Bordeaux, the French ambassador, reported back to Mazarin on 18 November: 'It is remarked that some ministers of the Council, who were once very zealous for the Protector, are now deserting him, for fear that they may fall with him.'

The funeral brought to the surface the simmering resentments between the factions surrounding the new Protector, who used arrangements for the ceremony as a means of testing their strength. Desborough, a fervent anti-monarchist, and strongly against Oliver being given a funeral befitting a reigning monarch, wanted all Royalists to be ordered out of London on the day as a security measure. Montagu, on the other hand, who had urged Oliver to accept the crown, dismissed Desborough's concerns, retorting that 'there was no fear of any disturbance except his [Desborough's] procurement'. There was already bad blood between the two men due to Montagu's appointment as colonel of a regiment of horse and a member of the General Council of the Army, although he had not fought in the New Model Army since 1645. Consequently, he had not participated in the Army's political activity of the past twelve years and was therefore regarded as little better than a spy by Fleetwood and Desborough. In early December tempers boiled over, with the two generals accusing Montagu, Fauconberg and Ingoldsby of conspiring against their lives. When Richard appeared to take Montagu's side, Desborough, with studied arrogance, marched out of the Council meeting.

Despite the superficial splendour of the funeral, the months of continuing intrigue and unrest had undermined Richard's belief in his abilities to rally support for the Protectorate. He had not shown the authority necessary to enforce the obedience of the Army. The Privy Council was divided. His best hope lay in summoning parliament as a counterbalance to the military, but his father had not set a good precedent. Oliver had refrained from holding free elections, knowing full well that a majority of the voters would never support his candidates. And even with a very restricted electorate, he had been unable to find a parliament to do his bidding. Could his son be more successful? Or would Henry Cromwell's pessimistic verdict prove correct, that 'the calling of a Parliament signifies nothing until the army be sufficiently modelled'. On 3 December the decision was taken to issue writs.

4

THE FALL OF THE PROTECTORATE

Richard hoped that the new parliament would reinforce his own mandate to rule and raise taxes to pay off the Army. Thurloe advised that the number of members should be enlarged so that they would represent as broad a range of views as possible, with the usual exception of known Royalists and Catholics. This led to the election of many inexperienced men, leaving the way for open for the new parliament to be taken over by Richard's opponents. Moreover, Thurloe and his aides failed to prevent Hesilrige, Vane and their Republican allies from gaining election. These men, with their great experience of parliamentary affairs, but excluded from office since the Rump's dismissal in 1653, had never forgiven Oliver Cromwell. Lambert, another potentially dangerous opponent, was one of the few soldiers who were elected, reflecting the general unpopularity of the military.

The Protector opened parliament in regal fashion on 27 January 1659, impressing the members with his speech, delivered 'with such a grace and presence, and with such oratory and steadinesse, without the least interruption and so pertinently to the present occasion, as it was beyond all expectation'. But, as with his father's funeral two months earlier, the superficial splendour of the ceremony masked the lack of a political programme. He hoped that he would be immediately approved as Protector. There were, however, a recalcitrant but highly influential Republican minority, headed by the Rump leaders, who were determined to take the initiative and challenge the constitutional basis of Richard's right to assume power. They opposed successfully the Bill of Recognition (recognising Richard's rank as Lord Protector), effectively a vote of no confidence in the regime. Hesilrige, in particular, used all his famed eloquence in objecting to Richard's title as lawful chief magistrate, which implied that events since the expulsion of the Rump in 1653 were legitimate. 'If this pass,' the old warrior declared in ringing tones, 'we shall next vote canvas breeches and wooden shoes for the free people of England.'

Seizing the initiative, Richard's opponents proceeded to undermine the authority of the Government by indulging in endless insignificant arguments over the inclusion of Scottish and Irish members and why the counties were overrepresented, as opposed to the boroughs. There was more dissension over the composition of the Upper Chamber. It was generally agreed that it was better for parliament to have two Houses, but no accord was reached as to the composition of a replacement for the old House of Lords. Many members of the Commons objected to the number of Cromwellians elected to the Upper House. They were condemned by Richard's opponents as his placemen or soldiers with no interest in constitutional affairs, 'not fit to give laws in Parliament'. Moreover, their exclusion from the House of Commons greatly reduced their confidence. It is little wonder, with this fatal lack of leadership, that the Speaker, the lawyer Chaloner Chute, should have stated despairingly: 'We are indeed in a wood, a wilderness, a labyrinth.'

One way of opposing the Government was to concentrate on the illegality of the past actions of the Protectorate. When Maj Gen Robert Overton, once a senior commander in the New Model Army and a prominent Leveller, who had been imprisoned for the past three years without charge in Jersey, was brought to London, he was given a hero's welcome. On 16 March 1659 a crowd of 1,500 greeted him at Brentford and he was escorted in triumph by 500 horsemen to Westminster, where his coach was crowned with laurel wreaths. When the Government attempted to present the case against him in the Commons, it was decisively rejected and Overton was released, to the delight of the crowd assembled outside.

The indignation expressed at Overton's arbitrary arrest was indicative of the growing hatred of the military. Despite the heated debates in parliament, nothing was done to address the question of the Army's pay, now some forty weeks in arrears. Not only were members dismissive of the military, but they were reluctant to court unpopularity by increasing taxation. No attempt was made to augment the monthly assessment, the main way of raising money. 'It is a bad time to set up with a debt of two million a half [the overall national debt],' Vane wrote. 'A rat has got among the merchants. They break [go bankrupt] every day, ten at a time.' This was scarcely likely to placate the common soldiers who were clamouring for action from their leaders. The radical Col Okey expressed their bitterness in parliament: 'I see it will be a crime to be an army man. Is the expense of our blood nothing?' One member gave a succinct answer: 'The little fingers of major-generals have I found heavier than the loins of the greatest tyrant kings that went before.'

This attack on the Government's legality did not, however, mean a swing back to the Royalist cause. A petition was presented on behalf of seventy Cavaliers from Salisbury, who had been sent to Barbados in 1654, where they were sold as slaves and set to work in the sugar mills. But, despite a heart-rending account of their suffering, 'attached as horses and beasts for the debts of their masters, being whipped at the whipping-posts (as rogues) for their masters' pleasure, and sleeping in styes worse than hogs in England', the petition was ignored. One of the few to speak up for the Cavaliers was a former stalwart Parliamentarian, Sir George Booth, soon to lead a revolt against the Government.

Charles had encouraged secret Royalists to try for parliament. Not all had been willing to take the oath of loyalty to the Protectorate, but Hyde instructed such candidates to hinder the work of Government by opposing it on constitutional rather than Royalist grounds. The more disagreement there was in parliament, the more people would look back with longing to the rule of a peaceful monarchy that had preceded these troubled times. Hyde, like the Republicans, had seen the value of the attack on the legality of the regime, 'a sharp prosecution of those criminals whom he [the Protector] must protect'. At the end of February

41

he urged his agent Alan Brodrick, the witty, intelligent and dissolute
secretary of the Sealed Knot, to contact 'all friends who are in Parliament
to pursue all occasions for making war with Holland'. The Chancellor
knew full well the expense of warfare, and the unpopularity of raising the
taxes needed to pay for the ships that would have to be sent to sea.

Charles and Hyde were also pursuing plans for a national rising.
Mordaunt, who had been made a viscount by the King at the beginning
of March, was charged with the task of coordinating all Royalist activity
in England, with the grandiose title of Plenipotentiary of the Great Trust
or Commission. Privately, Mordaunt assured Hyde of his Anglican beliefs,
and that 'Nothing can secure the Crown that destroys the Mitre.' But his
new Trust included Lord Willoughby of Parham, Sir William Waller,
Sir Edward Massey and Sir George Booth, all prominent Presbyterians
who had fought for parliament in the First Civil War. He also hoped to
attract the support of Maj Gen Richard Browne, a strong Cromwellian in
the early 1650s, who was reputed to be wavering in his allegiance.

But the Royalists in England were disunited. On a personal level,
Brodrick's feud with Mordaunt, and the bitter recriminations it
provoked, was to hinder plans for a rising. Furthermore, as has been said,
the support of the leading Presbyterians was conditional. They wanted
the King to guarantee the supremacy of their religion, something Hyde
was determined not to concede. But he was clever enough to see that he
could appear to give in on this key issue if he insisted that it must be
subject to later parliamentary approval, calculating that the King's
restoration would lead to the election of an ultra-Royalist parliament.

The disunity among the Royalists, and their record of failure,
persuaded some Cavaliers to desert the cause. The Duke of Buckingham,
childhood friend of the King, and his companion on his Scottish
expedition, had come back to England the previous year, seeking the hand
of the daughter of Lord Fairfax, a great Yorkshire heiress. Cromwell had
been suspicious of this spectacular switch of allegiance and imprisoned
Buckingham in the Tower. But the fabled Villiers charm worked its

customary magic. Following Cromwell's death, the handsome Duke was released and claimed his heiress, carefully distancing himself from the King. On 11 March Hyde heard that he was going before parliament 'to profess himself an open enemy of the Stuarts'. For Charles this act of treachery by his closest friend, with whom he had been brought up after the assassination of his father, must have been particularly bitter.

Other former Royalists, tired of the endless years of exile, were open to inducements. Thurloe was in close contact with his friend George Downing, ambassador to the Hague. Downing had once been Cromwell's chief intelligence officer and knew how to recruit agents. Tom Howard, brother of the Earl of Suffolk, was highly regarded among Royalist exiles, but he had a weakness. Downing wrote to Thurloe how Howard 'had a whoor in this country, with which he trusted his secrets and papers: these two afterwards falling out, a person in this town got all the papers from her'. Downing pounced on Howard's fallibility. Although Downing warned Thurloe that 'if it should be known I have given you this account he would endeavour to have me killed', Howard had soon been 'gained'. 'I think I can hardly pitch upon for one a fitter instrument than Tom Howard,' Downing crowed, 'he being master of the horse to the princesse Royal; and I shall endeavour to improve him.' Howard was shortly to ask for a salary of £1,000 as a price for his treachery.

The general air of suspicion and mistrust was indicative of the gradual breakdown of the political process. Hyde's agents probably exaggerated when they reported that a majority of MPs were passive Royalists, but their loyalty to the regime could not be guaranteed. A proposal was made that some peers should be allowed back into the Upper House, which caused consternation, since the readmittance of the hereditary principle would lead inexorably to the idea of restoring the King.

Even the Protector, with his easy familiarity towards all parties, was not immune from suspicion. He was widely perceived to be weak and an instrument in the hands of more ambitious men. Sir Richard Baker, in his *Chronicle of the Kings of England* of 1674, noted that 'the Protector did intend to . . . put the army into the hands of the nobility and gentry of the nation, thereby to bring in the king, and destroy that liberty of the gospel they had so long contended for'. Nehemiah Bourne, an Army sympathiser, considered that Royalist Members of Parliament exercised influence over the Protector, whom they intended 'to dress and set on horsebacke, but to warme the saddle for another whom they loved and liked [the King]'. In fact Charles had instructed Lord Belasyse to approach the Protector but this had been unsuccessful.

The Republican leaders in parliament, hoping to replace Richard Cromwell as the dominant political force, portrayed themselves as the heirs of a great parliamentary tradition who were best placed to defend the interests of Englishmen, both civilian and military. There was another, less high-minded aim to this campaign. By emphasising that they represented legitimate authority, Hesilrige and his colleagues wanted to ensure that all land transactions carried out while they were in office could not be overturned.

Although they strongly objected to Cromwell's reliance on military force, the Rump leaders realised that their best chance of replacing Richard was to form an alliance with the Army grandees. They therefore joined Fleetwood in supporting Col Ashfield, a well-known troublemaker. Monck had advised Thurloe the previous autumn to send Ashfield back to his post in the north, where he would be out of harm's way; but Richard did not take Monck's advice. He had failed to court-martial Ashfield for disobeying orders following a public quarrel with Maj Gen Whalley, one of the Protector's most loyal supporters; and the example of Ashfield's insubordination spread. When a cornet impugned his major for moral lassitude, the Protector rounded on the soldier and, clapping his hand on the shoulder of Col Ingoldsby, a loyal supporter, exclaimed: 'Go thy way, Dick Ingoldsby, thou canst neither preach nor pray, but I will believe thee before I believe twenty of them.'

The breakdown of military discipline reflected the growing confusion in England, a profound disillusionment with the political process. This disenchantment was allied to a growing fear of anarchy. This, in turn, led men to consider the use of violence to defend their beliefs. The normally peaceful Thurloe responded to this climate of fear by spreading rumours of a Cavalier plot to 'presently unite the contending parties, or at least the heads of them'. He was heard to remark 'that the Kingdom would never be quiet till all the royal party's throats were cut'. Henry Burton voiced the opinion of many Republicans: 'how shall 1 be indemnified but by my sword. We will not give the cause away.' These violent remarks were a product of a growing sense of helplessness and the fear that extremists were poised to take over England. In particular, men feared that religious tolerance, championed by Vane and by many soldiers who were members of extreme religious sects, would lead to anarchy. There was increased persecution of the Quakers, who were imprisoned in large numbers. The Quakers' belief in the individual's direct communion with God, their antipathy to an organised Church, their refusal to take oaths and their disruption of church services were regarded with particular horror by most of society.

At meetings in St James's during the spring, the soldiers expressed their increasing dissatisfaction with the Protector, 'unanimously crieing up the good old cause And A Commonwealth, and noe single person', as one observer recorded. One of the more successful propaganda devices of the many Republican tracts published during this period, masterminded by Vane, was that the Rump would be the means of helping the Army to restore the Good Old Cause, frequently referred to in many pamphlets. The two institutions would be joint champions of liberty and freedom. The Good Old Cause was likened to a virgin, a frequently used sexual image, and would no longer be 'mishapen with a strange dresse, we had almost said, with the attire of a harlot'. The soldiers seemed oblivious of the fact that the majority of Englishmen, all too aware of the Army's role in the execution of the King and the dismissal of parliament on several occasions, saw them as the destroyers rather than the preservers of liberty.

The military might have been willing to countenance Richard's reliance on civilians and ex-Royalists if their financial future had been secure, but the Army was now owed almost £1 million. Complaints flooded in. Fairfax, still a highly influential figure in retirement, presented a petition to parliament on 9 April on behalf of 2,500 maimed soldiers and 4,000 widows and orphans, asking for regular payment of their pensions. More worryingly, the senior officers, responding to pressure from their juniors, persuaded Richard to summon the General Council of the Army on 2 April. Fauconberg was dismayed by the way the meeting went, 'for all the rabble were present', applauding the radical Col Lilburne, former deputy to Lambert in the north of England, and the troublesome Col Ashfield. Four days later, these two, together with Col Mason, presented the 'Humble Representation and Petition' to parliament, expressing devotion to the Protector but with an underlying hint of menace. Richard must find some means of satisfying the soldiers' grievances if they were to continue to support the Government, with the threat that this would mean 'plucking the wicked out of their places, wheresoever they may be discovered'. Sir Arthur Annesley, an Irish grandee who had fought for parliament and was a leader of the secluded members, and a prolific pamphleteer, compared the petition to 'lightning before thunder . . . whereof the sword was like to be the interpreter, that the sting was easily visible through the honey'.

The Navy was in as parlous a financial state as the Army. They had an additional grievance, since their officers thought that the backdated pay was being diverted to pay the New Model Army, whose leaders could exert a more effective lobbying campaign from their base in London. In early April Richard was faced with the mass resignation of the Admiralty Commissioners, who were exhausted by 'the incessant clamours from poor men that are creditors of the navy, and with the cries and complaints of seamen and their relations for pay due to them'.

The Commons, meanwhile, had decided to ignore the Army's petition. Instead, on 12 April, the members voted to prosecute Maj Gen Boteler for his earlier, unlawful action in seizing the estate of Holdenby in Northamptonshire. This was a direct attack on the military, since his colleagues, including all the senior commanders in London, would be open to a similar charge of seizing land illegally. Taking up the challenge, at a meeting of the General Council of the Army held two days later, Desborough proposed, as a means of reinforcing the Army's Republican credentials, that all soldiers take an oath that the execution of Charles I was lawful and just. Broghill, strongly opposed to this arbitrary means of imposing control, declared that if it was essential to take an oath, it should be one of loyalty to the Protector.

For a moment it seemed that a compromise might be reached. On 15 April parliament voted the Army three months' pay, but this did little to appease the soldiers' discontent. As a further gesture of defiance, the General Council then elected to its number Col Ashfield. Fleetwood and Desborough were barely in control of the soldiers nominally under their command. Cromwellian loyalists, realising that they were rapidly losing control of events, suggested taking the offensive. Col Charles Howard, commander of the Protector's Lifeguard, offered to get rid of Fleetwood, Vane, Lambert and Desborough. Ingoldsby, even more directly, suggested that he assassinate Lambert. But Richard refused to countenance such drastic actions, claiming that 'Violent counsels suit not with me'.

Instead, on 18 April, the Protector decided that a confrontation with his enemies was the only way to avoid political chaos. He declared that the Army Council was to be prevented from sitting without the permission of the Protector and parliament. With the backing of a vote in the Commons, Richard proceeded to demand the General Council's dissolution and that officers return to their regiments. He hoped that his supporters Maj Gen Whalley and Cols Ingoldsby, Goffe and Howard would rally enough troops to his side to defy the junior officers, followers of Cols Ashfield, Lilburne and Lt Fitch.

Instead, on 20 April Sir Robert Tichborne, representing the views of the more radical soldiers, who had been meeting at the Nag's Head tavern, came to see Richard and urged him to accept the Army's 'advice'. The next day, following a defiant vote in the Commons to turn the Army into a militia under the control of the Protector and parliament, the die was cast. That evening Desborough accosted the Protector and demanded the dissolution of parliament, declaring that, if he did so, in the words of Ludlow, 'the officers would take care of him; but that if he refused to do it, they would do without him, and leave him to shift for himself'. When Richard indignantly refused, backed by Broghill, Fauconberg and Ingoldsby, Desborough withdrew with Fleetwood to St James's, and summoned the soldiers serving in the capital to a general rendezvous. Richard called a rival rendezvous in Whitehall.

The outcome of this trial of strength was almost embarrassingly one-sided. When faced with the choice, the troops preferred to trust the generals under whom they had served in battle, rather than a regime headed by a man who bore the name of Cromwell but who was no soldier and had singularly failed to better their lot. The Protector's troops melted away, even those serving under officers loyal to him. When Desborough roughly repeated his demand, while his soldiers milled around the courtyard in Whitehall 'with considerable licence', the Privy Council advised the Protector to dissolve parliament. All through the night the argument continued. At 5 a.m., Richard capitulated. On the evening of 22 April, after a long and angry debate over this infringement of their liberties, the MPs dispersed through crowds of jeering soldiers, padlocks were placed on the doors of the Chamber and soldiers of the New Model Army stood guard outside. Three days later, Vane, Hesilrige and Ludlow, hoping to benefit from their informal alliance with the Army grandees so as to take over the reins of government, tried to enter the Palace of Westminster, but they too were turned away by the troops.

Opponents of the Protectorate were busy lampooning Richard, whose stay in office had lasted less than eight months. A particularly popular cartoon portrayed him, in a parody of the Great Seal, seated on a horse, with the head of an owl and a pipe in his mouth, and the caption 'His

Highness Hoo, Hoo, Hoo, Lord Protector of Lubberland'. A kinder verdict was provided by Lucy Hutchinson, wife of the regicide Col Hutchinson, who described the Protector as 'pleasant in his nature, yet gentle and virtuous, but became not greatness'. In fact Richard had resisted as long as he could, and was now plunged into despair, suffering an acute feeling of betrayal. 'The world is false,' he wrote to his brother Henry, 'and for myself, those that were my father's friends, pretended ones only were mine . . . they tripped up my heels before I knew them, for though they were relatives they forsook me.' A few days later he was writing again, that it was 'better for me to throw myself in the dust and cry before the Lord', but he added, with great prescience, 'Nothing giveth hope but a clear understanding and good correspondence with General Monck. . . . I believe Fleetwood and Desborough are not long-lived.' In fact Richard was still nominally Protector and it was not until 25 May that he officially resigned.

5

THE RUMP AND THE ARMY

The downfall of Richard Cromwell marked a decisive break in the history of the Interregnum. Despite all the political uncertainty since the execution of Charles I, the dominant figure of Oliver Cromwell had ensured continuity. The fall of Richard, however, marked the end of the Protectorate, a five-year political experiment that had brought victory in wars with Holland and Spain, and maintained a unified England, Ireland and Scotland. During the autumn of 1658 and the following spring, the vast majority of Cromwell's leading followers, both military and civilian, had stayed loyal to his son. Now that he had fallen from power, this loyalty disappeared. Each man was compelled to consider his best interests. Some, such as Monck, were content to see how events would develop. Others, such as Montagu, Broghill and Fauconberg, who had no love for either the Army grandees or the leaders of the Rump, made contact with the Royalists.

The generals, having used brute strength to overthrow the regime, were divided over what to put in its place. Fleetwood and the senior officers wished to retain the Protectorate with Richard, as the figurehead, acting the part of 'a Doge of Venice'. They gathered at Wallingford House to draw up a new constitution, hoping, in the words of one well-wisher, 'to piece and mend up that broken government'. But it was the influential junior officers, keeping 'their council apart at St James's', who were making the running. 'All the inferior officers of the army,' as one contemporary recorded, 'yea whole regiments of soldiers gave in their petitions for it, and almost all persons well affected centred [agreed] therein.'

They had formed an alliance with the leading Rumpers, who orchestrated a propaganda campaign equating the Good Old Cause with the 'Good Old Parliament', i.e. the Rump. A flood of newsletters in the *Faithful Scout*, the Army newspaper, the *Weekly Post* and the *Weekly Intelligencer* espoused their cause in eloquent terms. In one example, dated 3 May 1659, an anonymous author stated: 'The government seems now to be naturally falling into a Commonwealth and free state, and the generall cry of the people is for the Longe Parliament [the Rump] to take possession againe, and this appeares to be the sence of the officers of the army now continuing, and all others out of the army that have bin of the Longe Parliament partie.'

Fleetwood and Desborough, the Army leaders in London, now joined by Lambert, realised the impossibility of raising taxes legally without parliamentary approval and, after holding two meetings with Hesilrige, Vane and Ludlow on 2 and 5 May, agreed to the recall of the Rump. The Rumpers dominated these meetings and offered to grant the Army an indemnity for its past actions, to pay off Richard Cromwell's debts, and to form a government composed of a representative chamber and a senate. Already, there were splits in the fragile alliance between the two sides. It was only with difficulty that Vane managed to persuade Hesilrige not to insist immediately that parliament exert its right to control the military.

Now that they had dismissed Richard Cromwell, the generals nursed their own ambitions, taking careful note of potential rivals. Meanwhile, the rank and file in the Army looked on with suspicion as their ambitious commanders jockeyed for position. As John Barwick, a Royalist agent, reported to Hyde on 2 May: 'Desborough and Fleetwood are now as low as before they were high, being looked upon as self-seekers.' Lambert, who had now fully re-emerged into public life, was seen by Royalists as their most dangerous opponent. As another of Hyde's correspondents, his agent, wrote on May Day: 'Lambert will infallibly reap the benefit of the disorder as to the army, by the ill conduct of Desborough and Fleetwood, the one being too rough and the other contemptibly smooth.' For the moment, Lambert was prepared to work with the Presbyterian-dominated Rump, even though it was known to be hostile to the Independent sects, whom he supported. He realised that the only hope for the survival of the Republic was for the Army and the Rump to combine effectively to exclude Charles II.

Outside London, senior military figures regarded their colleagues' actions with distaste and alarm. Influential figures who had retired, such as Fairfax and Col Hutchinson, one of the most high-minded of the regicides and High Sheriff of Nottinghamshire, were shocked at this blatant overturning of the political process by the military. Their views were shared by numerous commissioned officers, backed by the Independent churches and the common soldiers based in Whitehall, who demanded the restoration of the Republic, presided over by the Rump.

Hyde lamented the alliance between the Royalists' two most militant opponents as 'the most dismal change that could happen, and to pull up all the hopes of the King by the roots'. But the Chancellor judged that, without active service, the soldiers would become ever more disgruntled and more inclined to interfere in politics, which would, in turn, antagonise parliament. He was therefore content merely to encourage underground resistance, and was gratified to hear of the number of anonymous pamphlets advocating the King's restoration. Besides, there was always the hope that he could persuade leading members of the regime to come over to the King. Whatever their role in the destruction of the monarchy and the House of Lords, they were always capable of seeing the error of their ways, especially when they realised the depth of their unpopularity, and that they were viewed by the majority of the population as destroyers rather than upholders of liberty.

The Revd Ralph Josselin, vicar of Earls Colne in Essex, a schoolmaster, book collector and farmer, and former parliamentary chaplain, gave a sorrowful verdict of recent events in the entry into his diary on 30 April: 'Heard a sad account of things at London. Protector: deserted; army divided. This selfe seeking, deceitfull crew, are likely to receive the recompence of their deceits wherin they have sported themselves.'

The high-handedness of the soldiers in treating it as their right to arrest any suspected malcontents and search their houses attracted particular criticism. Even foreign ambassadors were not safe. One Sunday night in May the troops determined to carry out a search throughout London for Royalists and Catholics. Meeting some hesitation at the Danish ambassador's house, 'the soldiers knocked it down with their muskets,' as the incredulous Venetian ambassador Giavarina reported: 'Behaving outrageously in the house they carried off the Danish minister himself. They met him on the stairs clad only in his shirt with a cloak thrown over, having hurried down on hearing the noise at the door. They gave him no time to dress himself, paying no attention to the character he bears or his remonstrances, but covering him with abuse and vile expressions.'

The Rump soon demonstrated that its members were just as arrogant and self-serving as the Army. At their first meeting on 7 May, the privileged few, just forty-two MPs, entered Westminster in pairs like beasts into the Ark, as Sir Arthur Annesley recorded in his tract *England's Confusion*, showed that their prime consideration was to ensure their own survival. Although they voted to fill up numerous vacancies with carefully selected members, increasing their number to 122, they were more concerned to exclude Annesley and the other 212 secluded members, victims of Pride's Purge, who had tried to assert their rights. William Prynne, a vociferous secluded member, had managed to enter the House of Commons unnoticed, and was only ejected with the greatest difficulty, complaining loudly of being deprived of his liberties, worse 'than the beheaded King and his party were ever guilty of'. He was soon hard at work writing pamphlets, ridiculing the constitutional basis of the Government, and castigating 'the confederated Triumvirate of Republicans, Sectaries and Soldiers', all of whom he despised.

Almost immediately, splits appeared between the Rump and the Army. With no military activity to occupy them, and the vexed question of pay unresolved, the soldiers were determined to interfere in politics. On 13 May, within a week of the Rump's return to Westminster, eighteen officers, with Lambert at their head, presented a 'Humble Petition and Address of the Officers of the Army' with the same demands that Richard Cromwell had refused to accept. More controversially, Lambert was now demanding the establishment of a nominated senate with senior generals, appointed for life, holding a veto over acts made by the House of Commons. Hesilrige, Vane and Ludlow agreed to an act of oblivion and optimistically offered payment of the Army's back pay, but their negotiations made no mention of Fleetwood's appointment as commander-in-chief.

Royalists drew heart from these disagreements. Mordaunt wrote to the King on 19 May with news of the Army's readiness to mutiny. A day later an agent of Hyde reported to his master: 'Fleetwood dare not appear on account of their [the soldiers'] threatenings, for they have found godliness not a good paymaster.' The Royalists would have been even more heartened had they known of an alleged meeting held by senior officers on 23 May. Reflecting their deep concern with events, and a lack of a credible alternative, a vote to restore the King was only defeated by six votes.

The fragile alliance between the Rump and the Army was reflected in the composition of the Council of State. The leading generals and Republicans were among its thirty-one members, but the military were in a minority. At least one member, Sir Horatio Townshend, a nephew of Fairfax, was a secret Royalist who had sought and been given permission by the King before taking his seat. Prynne regarded him as 'a gentleman of too great an estate to be hazarded with such a crew'. The President was Sir Archibald Johnston of Wariston, a fanatical Scottish Presbyterian, who had been an inveterate opponent of the Royalists in Scotland throughout the Civil Wars. Johnston was, however, no more than a figurehead, given the job, as a fellow member commented acidly, so that 'they might be rid of his multiloquy and impertinent motions'. The general public openly ridiculed this list of unelected representatives, and insulting pamphlets soon appeared describing them: 'Colonel Thompson, as wooden a head as leg; Mr Wallop, a silent Hampshire gentleman, much in debt, fit indeed to be a councillor, if he could advise the Commonwealth how to get out of debt; Desborough, a country clown, without fear and wit; Berry, the worst of the Major-Generals, except Butler; Josiah Berners, fool of the play etc.'

The more aggressive leaders of the Rump seemed impervious to the low regard in which the majority of the population held their rulers. They were intent on cementing their hold on power. Vane and Ludlow, anxious not to break the fragile alliance with the leading generals, urged caution, but they were overruled by Hesilrige, supported by Henry Neville, a disciple of the political theorist Sir James Harrington, and Algernon Sidney, both staunch Republicans and champions of parliament. The most contentious issue was whether officers should receive their commissions from parliament or from the Army high command. In a vote on 6 June, Hesilrige's arguments in favour of the supremacy of the House of Commons carried the day. Fleetwood was finally appointed commander-in-chief but he was merely one of a committee of seven with the power to commission officers. A majority of these commissioners – Gens Fleetwood, Monck and Ludlow, Cols Walton, Morley and Overton, and Sir Arthur Hesilrige – were members or close allies of the Rump. They retained the right to cashier officers without a court martial, a highly provocative move since it gave the military no redress from any perceived injustice.

The Rumpers were soon busy giving back regiments to committed Republicans, such as Cols Rich and Overton, imprisoned by Richard's father but recently released. Lambert, Hesilrige and Okey were given the regiments formerly commanded by Fauconberg, Howard and Ingoldsby, Cromwellian loyalists who were all soon in communication with the Royalists. Ludlow was another Republican to benefit from the overthrow of the Protectorate. He was made a member of the Council of State and Committee of Safety, and was soon to be appointed lieutenant-general, and commander-in-chief in Ireland.

Meanwhile, Richard Cromwell, who had been given the contemptuous nickname 'Tumble-Down Dick' by Royalists, had all but disappeared from the scene. Without the trappings of office, he was a shadow of his former self, pursued by his creditors. Hyde heard of his plight: 'Poor Richard', he was told, 'dare not stir out of Whitehall, the bailiffs are so active.' On 18 June he moved to the porter's lodge at Hampton Court, where Hyde heard that he had killed a buck, 'for which he was soundly cheaked and the buck sent for'. On 11 July, however, the Rump took pity and authorised that he was to be exempt from arrest and his debts paid.

In a dangerously volatile situation, with the regime increasingly unpopular and a general climate of suspicion, whom could its rulers trust? The regicide Thomas Scot, one of the most aggressive Republicans, had proclaimed boldly his part in Charles I's execution, that he 'did it in the face of God, and of all men'. Scot was constantly on his guard for any suspicion of treason among his colleagues, accusing Bulstrode Whitelocke and Anthony Ashley Cooper, both members of the Council of State, of corresponding with the King. Both protested their innocence, but Ashley Cooper, who had indeed been approached by Hyde, found it difficult to win his colleagues' trust. Whitelocke noted that he refuted the accusation so violently, that 'it bred in some the more suspicion of him'.

Chief Justice Oliver St John, related to the Cromwell family by marriage, gave an indication of the doubt afflicting leading Parliamentarians in a letter to his son-in-law: 'Sell two manors, and transport ten thousand pounds abroad; and for the remainder, run the hazard of a general pardon, for such we may expect, should the King prevail.' John Thurloe, although he had not been reappointed Secretary of State, remained influential behind the scenes. Meanwhile, his under-secretary, Samuel Morland, was risking his life by secretly passing on valuable intelligence to the King. Morland was convinced that Sir Richard Willis, one of the leaders of the Sealed Knot, was a double agent, and had the evidence to prove it. Initially, Charles and Hyde were unwilling to believe that someone who had been privy to their most intimate plans had betrayed them. But gradually they were compelled to accept the evidence. It is still not entirely clear how much danger Morland was in. His reports tended to hyperbole, with urgent entreaties to the King, 'for Christ's sake, to burn all writer's papers as soon as read or he [Morland] will be a dead man'. Morland, who was hopeful of gaining promotion should the restoration occur, kept careful note of his sovereign's gratitude. On 27 June Charles assured him in a letter that he 'will not only give [Morland] the Garter but somewhat else to make him wear it with more delight'.

Lord Broghill, an ex-Cavalier but a staunch Cromwellian for the previous decade, had protested at the Army's interference in the political process and had advised Richard to dissolve the Council of Officers. Now that they had assumed power, he hastened away to the relative safety of his native Ireland, where he persuaded the Commissioners of Irish Affairs in Dublin to let him retire to the province of Munster. From there he was soon in communication with Hyde and the King. In April, Edward Villiers, Charles's agent in Ireland, told Hyde that he had made 'some progress in discoursing at distance with Ld Broghall'. But it was difficult to know who to trust. Thomas Howard, now a double agent in the pay of Downing, also wrote to the King that Broghill wished Charles to come to Ireland, and 'he assures me he will doo all things that may advance your Service'. Hyde agreed and was happy to write that 'the King lookes upon lord Brahall as a Person who may be most instrumentall to doe him service there and he does not beleeve he will have any aversion to it when ye Season shall be prope'.

The position of Henry Cromwell shows how difficult it was to assess the loyalty of the leading figures. In his letter to Villiers, Hyde instructed him to tell Henry that as soon as he declared for Charles, the Royalists would 'send over men, money and Armes'. There was never the prospect of Charles forgiving Oliver Cromwell for the part he had played in his father's execution, but Henry Cromwell was not tainted with the crime of regicide and might yet prove a valuable ally. Henry had called a meeting of his officers, but had failed to persuade them to remain faithful to his brother. He therefore accepted the inevitable and resigned his post as Lord Lieutenant of Ireland, expressing the earnest wish that the Army would acknowledge its fault in dismissing the Rump in 1653, and that it would now 'be the instruments of your defence while you quietly search out the ways of peace'. Fauconberg, now a convinced Royalist, had also approached Henry, and Hyde was later to claim that he had promised to declare for the King but changed his mind at the last moment. However, Henry resisted a more direct approach by Sir Charles Coote and 'pistolled the officer that laid hold of him'. There seems no reason to disbelieve his letter of resignation to the Rump in which he thanked God that he had resisted 'the great temptation, wherewith I have beene assaulted to withdraw my affection from that cause, wherein hee [his father] lived and died'.

Like Broghill and Fauconberg, George Monck in Scotland was a former Royalist who had become a loyal supporter of Cromwell and his son Richard. Fleetwood had sent Monck a disingenuous letter on the Protector's fall, excusing himself: 'I beleive some will very evilly represent us in this action, as if wee had forced the Parliament, though his Highnesse [Richard] by his own authority did dissolve them, in which the army did stand by his Highnesse.' It appeared that Monck accepted this explanation and he had sworn allegiance to the new regime. But Giavarina noted that his letter of submission was ambiguous. He was prepared to accept the Rump's refusal of his request that no changes be made to his command, 'without hearing, without charge and without trial', merely observing: 'Obedience is my greate principle and I have alwaise, and ever shall, reverence the Parliament's resolutions in civill things as infallible and sacred.' This was due to the general's fundamental belief in the supremacy of civil over military authority, 'where soldiers received and observed commands, but gave none'. Optimistic Royalists felt that there was a chance that Monck might revert to his former allegiance to the King. He was known to be dismayed at the political instability and to be strongly opposed to the religious radicals who were so prominent in the English Army. In the words of Hyde, he had 'no fumes of fanaticism to turn his head'.

Edward Montagu, another staunch Cromwellian and commander of the Navy, had been sent by Richard Cromwell with a powerful English fleet to the Baltic in April to try to negotiate a peace between Sweden and Denmark. Montagu formed a close relationship with the Swedish king Charles X and favoured using the English fleet to balance the influence of the Dutch, allied to the Danes. The Rump leaders, however, were anxious to improve relations with the Dutch, whom they regarded as republicans and fellow Protestants, and therefore kindred spirits. First, they needed to secure the allegiance of Montagu, who had heard the news of the Protector's fall with 'feares and sorrow', as he reported to Speaker Lenthall, though he promised to obey parliament's orders.

The only message Montagu sent, pledging his loyalty to the nation, was not well received. In the words of Giavarina, his 'expressions have a double meaning, which leaves them here disturbed and hesitating'. The new regime was taking no chances. A search of the admiral's rooms and a close inspection of his private papers revealed nothing incriminating, but a suspicion hung over him. He was to be deprived of his lodgings in Whitehall and his regiment, with the attendant pay, was given to Col Alured. In addition, he was dropped from the Council of State and his peerage was forfeit.

The Rump had already appointed the Republican John Lawson, a well-known Anabaptist, to command the Channel fleet, 'to balance the power of Montagu's party', in the words of Ludlow, 'who we knew was no friend of the commonwealth'. Lawson was to engage in a holding operation against the Spanish and Flemish ships in the Channel, and to ensure that they were unable to bring a Royalist force over from the Spanish Netherlands. Leading Rumpers such as Vane, and Cols Valentine Walton and Herbert Morley, who had played such a major role in running the Navy under the Commonwealth, were placed once again in control of the Admiralty, and were to approve the appointment of officers.

Now the Council of State decided to ensure Montagu's obedience by sending three commissioners, led by Algernon Sidney, one of their younger and more able members, to the Baltic (their departure was delayed for a fortnight while £2,000 was found to pay for their expenses). The three men arrived off Elsinore in the *Langport*, one of the Republic's newest frigates, on 18 July, and were welcomed aboard Montagu's flagship, the *Naseby*. Sidney was soon busy arbitrating between Sweden and Denmark, an attempt to coerce Sweden into accepting peace. Montagu, however, unwilling to accept this outside interference, out-manoeuvred Sidney by enlisting the support of his captains, claiming that supplies were short and that the fleet must return to England.

Doubts remain whether Montagu made his decision in order to be on hand to further the Royalist revolt planned for the beginning of August. He had certainly been approached by two Royalist agents in the Baltic: Edward Montagu, a cousin of the admiral, and Capt Thomas Whetstone, a renegade Parliamentarian officer and related to Cromwell. Whetstone, who arrived immediately after Algernon Sidney, carried a message for Montagu from Charles II, and news of the impending Royalist rising in England. As one of Hyde's correspondents noted: 'This is the most favourable occasion that ever was to tempt him.' Whetstone's letter from the King offered Montagu an earldom and bountiful reward if he would change sides. But the admiral remained cautious. He was worried that Whetstone might reveal himself, particularly when he met him in a street in Copenhagen in the company of the suspicious Sidney, while the admiral was carrying a letter from the King in his pocket. Thoroughly alarmed, he made a vague reply to Charles's overtures, and Whetstone was only able to report back to Hyde that 'upon any appearance of disorders in England, he might expect a good account' of Montagu. Independently, the admiral complained to Hyde in late July how Whetstone 'was the most unfit the King could have sent. Sent him back as soon as possible.'

Montagu's cousin Edward gave a more accurate analysis of the situation in the Baltic. He ended his letter to Hyde on 27 July quoting his cousin the admiral: 'If there be any divisions or difference in England between the military and civil governors, or any party that will or can stand up for the king, I will venture my interest where it is most effectual.' In other words, Montagu was virtually guaranteeing that he would support a Royalist rising. Another cousin of the admiral, the young and ambitious Samuel Pepys, who was looking after his official lodgings in Whitehall Palace, was later to recount a remark made by Montagu, that his employer's conversion to the Royalist cause 'commenced from his being in the Sound, when he found what usage he was likely to have from the Commonwealth'.

Hyde and the King had less success with leading members of the Government serving on the Continent. Downing, in the Hague, was busy negotiating with the United Provinces over the war in the Baltic. Lockhart, ambassador to France, was trying to ensure that England, still allied to France, was included in the treaty Mazarin was negotiating with Spain. Throughout the late spring he was constantly visiting Paris to try to gain news of the intentions of Cardinal Mazarin. Both Downing and Lockhart kept their distance from Royalists who were allied with Spain, still at war with the government they served.

The differences between the Rump and the Army, however, continued to widen. Lambert's 'Humble Petition' was rejected by the Rump. This was one of several constitutional theories advanced during the late spring. Vane shared Lambert's desire to create a permanent settlement where the select few would have an effective veto on all political activity. But, unlike Lambert, the champion of the Army, he wanted to restrict voters to godly and loyal men, and not to include 'the depraved, corrupted and self-interested will of man, in the great body which we call the people'. Sir James Harrington's *Oceana* was another attempt to produce a constitutional settlement. His proposal of a republic with an extended franchise based on property limitations and a rotating senate, with one-third of the members retiring at each election, was specifically designed to prevent parliament from becoming self-perpetuating. This was something Hesilrige and his fellow Rumpers could never accept.

When the vote for an ambiguous Act of Oblivion was carried on 12 July, Lambert complained to Hesilrige that it was unclear who was to be indemnified. The veteran Parliamentarian replied disdainfully: 'You are only at the mercy of the parliament, who are your good friends', to which Lambert retorted truculently: 'I know not why they should not be at our mercy as well as we at theirs.' The bad blood between the two men dated back to the beginning of the decade, when Hesilrige helped to prevent Lambert from gaining the prestigious and lucrative post of Lord Deputy of Ireland. Hesilrige, in turn, had never forgiven Lambert's prominent role in the dismissal of the Rump Parliament in 1653.

One unexpected result of this wrangling was a growing nostalgia for the ancient constitution and, in particular, for the House of Lords. The peers were seen as 'the great bulwarks and defenders of the liberties of the nation'. All could see what would happen following their restoration. 'It will then as naturally follow', Maj Gen Kelsey exclaimed, 'that Charles Stuart is as rightful King at this day, as the Lords are rightful Lords.' Vane, probably the most intelligent of the Rumpers, was all too aware that the fragile alliance between the Army and the Rump might easily fall apart. He wrote pessimistically: 'The King will, I believe, at one time or another, obtain the crown, for the nation is dissatisfied with any other governement.'

The divisions among the Republicans, and their growing unpopularity, lifted morale among Royalists. As Hyde's agent John Barwick concluded: 'The proceedings at Westminster are so full of distraction, that it is probable they will end in confusion.' The Chancellor intended to exploit these divisions. Hyde hoped to work on Lambert through his cousin Lord Belasyse. In June the Chancellor asked him: 'Is not Lambert, by the charges against him, disposed in any degree to the King? He may promise anything the king can do for him.' A second approach to the general was to be made by Lord Hatton, who shared Lambert's love of botany, a passion he had developed while in retirement in Wimbledon.

The general dissatisfaction with the regime reached the highest level of Government. Johnston of Wariston wrote in his diary on 15 June of the Rump's lack of purpose: 'Alas, this motions of refounding, of disannulling all gifts and settlements maid by the Protector, and of questioning former treatyes and stopping juges and officers to proceed til further order. I feare least thes and uther such lyk things draw unto inconsistency and confusion and universal discontent.' A few days later, he reiterated his fears: 'There is a strange contempt and hatred throughout the nation of this present parliament.'

This contempt for the Government was allied to a fear of religious extremism. A sense of panic gripped the country that summer. There was an increase in trials for witchcraft, always a sign of popular fear. Even more threatening were the activities of the religious sects. The radical beliefs of Quakers and Anabaptists threw into question the very fabric of society. Lord Conway wrote to his brother-in-law Maj Rawdon from Ragley Hall in Worcestershire of the extremists' desire 'to turn out the landlords'. The Fifth Monarchists, with their millennial beliefs, were equally frightening. The appointment of three of their more prominent members, Nathaniel Rich, William Allen and Richard Overton, to command regiments increased this fear. They were now, as a paper in London recorded on 6 June, 'Arm'd, officer'd, and every way in Readiness'. The very next Tuesday, the author continued, they would burn the city and massacre 'all considerable people of all sorts'. William Prynne waxed lyrical on the threat of this 'fresh combination between the Sectaries, Republican, Anabaptistical, Jesuitical, levelling party' out to 'extirpate the Church and ministry of England . . . and demolish all parish churches as antichristian'.

The antiquarian Anthony Wood recorded the panic among the congregation of St Martin's in Oxford on Sunday 31 July when stones were blown from the tower during a service, which falling on the leads of the church, a great alarm and out-cry was among the people in the church. Some cried 'murder!' – at that time a trumpet or trumpets sounding neare the Cross-inne dore, to call soldiers together, because of the present plott, they in the church cried out that the day of judgement was at hand. Some said the anabaptists and quakers were come to cut their throats; while the preacher, Mr. Georg Philips, perceiving their errour, was ready to burst with laughter in the pulpit, to see such a mistaken confusion, and several of the people that were in the galleries hanging at the bottom of them and falling on the heads of the people crowding on the floor to get out of the dores.

Throughout the country there was a deep-seated fear of anarchy. A Cavalier commented on a huge Fifth Monarchist meeting in Sussex: 'We daily expect a massacre.' In Tiverton, on 14 July, the town was roused at midnight by rumours of an imminent attack by 'Fifth Monarchie Men, Anabaptists and Quakers', the usual suspects. Royalist leaders hoped to turn this to their advantage. Sir Edward Hyde, sitting in Brussels, would have been very content if he had heard of the Parliamentarian Col William Parker's remark, that 'before ye Quakers should have their liberty, hee woulde draw his sworde to bring in King Charles'.

6

BOOTH'S REBELLION

All through the summer of 1659, plans continued for a Royalist rising, since, for the first time in many years, it appeared that there was a genuine chance of overthrowing the Commonwealth. Charles, always keener on military action than his Chancellor, wanted to test the resolve of his followers. The problem, as Hyde perceived, was that a Royalist rising might reunite the Rump and the Army, both fiercely republican and still formidable opponents. The Chancellor had warned Mordaunt, in charge of coordinating plans for the uprising, in June: 'Any unseasonable attempt of hot-headed men would gratify Thurloe with a plot, and presently unite the contending parties, at least the heads of them.'

Moreover, there were serious divisions among the Cavaliers. Many of the older Royalists, including leaders of the Sealed Knot, had become 'fatally stupefactive', as Mordaunt observed. They, for their part, regarded the recently ennobled viscount as vain, quarrelsome and tactless, and were constantly complaining about his behaviour to Hyde. Mordaunt disregarded the arguments of Sir Richard Willis, a senior figure in the Sealed Knot and one of his main critics, that many potential supporters would be busy with the harvest, that the rising would be dominated by the Presbyterian faction rather than traditional Anglican Royalists, and that it was to be managed by 'rash, vaine, giddy people'. Since Mordaunt had been trying to engineer an alliance between Anglican Royalists and Presbyterians or Cromwellians who had fought for parliament but had now changed sides, this was a direct attack on his leadership. He felt himself vindicated when Willis, who had forcefully argued for a postponement to the rising, was accused publicly of betraying his

Royalist colleagues in a placard posted by an anonymous Cavalier at the Exchange on 3 July.

The suspicion that one of the Royalist leaders was a traitor was indicative of the general lack of security. At the end of June Hyde was telling Mordaunt how he was 'amazed that their friends, who are frequently mentioned in London streets and letters abroad, are not all cast in prison'. Hyde's difficulty in interpreting the news from the mainland was greatly increased by a delay of at least three days in receiving information, particularly when the situation was changing daily. A long day's journey, either by horse or coach, took a messenger from London to the Channel ports. He continued his journey for another day by boat to Ostend or one of the other Flemish ports, avoiding the hostile English garrison in Dunkirk, and proceeded for a further full day on horseback to Brussels. An alternative line of communication was via Mary Knatchbull, abbess of the Benedictine convent in Ghent, who received a weekly packet of letters, which she forwarded to the Royalist leaders in Brussels. There were a number of hazards to overcome. The roads were often in shocking condition, the myriad potholes filled with mud. Kent was notorious for press gangs, 'so that unless some course be taken, expresses and envoys cannot come or go'. The Channel was little safer, filled with Flemish privateers.

Hyde was right to be worried about poor security. Government activity appeared to confirm fears that it was well aware of its opponents' plans. Arms were distributed from the Tower to the London militia, regiments brought up to strength, artillery at St James's made fit for service, householders required to submit lists of lodgers, known Cavaliers ordered to leave the capital, and travellers without passes arrested. Throughout the country, local militia commanders were instructed to search inns, and disband race meetings, bull-baiting and cock-fights, which attracted large numbers of spectators and might be used to ferment disorder. Troops were moved into danger areas such as Kent, a likely landing point for invading forces. Chichester, Arundel and Chepstow, thought to be Royalist targets, were secured. Vice Adm Lawson, a firm Republican, was stationed off the Flemish coast, with instructions to intercept and search any vessel likely to be bringing exiled Cavaliers back to England. Messages were sent to Scotland, Ireland and Dunkirk summoning additional troops. Bulstrode Whitelocke recorded how the Council sat 'all day and almost all night for a good while together', the members sleeping in Whitehall and snatching their meals whenever they could. Orders were issued for the arrest of leading Cavaliers.

Despite all these setbacks, Mordaunt determined on action and fixed 1 August as the date for the rising. Much hope was placed in Sir Edward Massey, who was to take Bristol and Gloucester, the very town he had defended so stoutly for parliament in the First Civil War. Massey was to be helped by Alexander Popham, who made extravagant claims about the support he could raise. He promised 20,000 troops, provided that the King appeared in person with 500 men; otherwise, he would do nothing. Further west, Sir John Grenville was to take command in Cornwall. In north Wales, Sir Thomas Middleton, Governor of Chirk Castle, pledged to support Sir George Booth, who had volunteered to raise Cheshire and Lancashire. Across the Pennines, Lord Belasyse, a founder of the Sealed Knot, and the Earl of Manchester, would lead the Royalist rising in Yorkshire. Lord Byron, a dashing commander of the Royalist cavalry, undertook to capture Newark and the Trent crossing, in Nottinghamshire.

Further south, Henry, Lord Falkland, the dissolute son of the noble Lucius Cary, Hyde's closest friend, promised support for the King in Oxfordshire. To the east, Edward Rossiter, formerly a colonel in the New Model Army, was active in Lincolnshire, while Sir Horatio Townshend had offered to secure King's Lynn, giving the King the chance of landing in the port. South of London, Mordaunt attempted to coordinate activities with Lord Willoughby of Parham, a former Parliamentary commander and the most active Royalist among the Presbyterian peers, Sir John Boys and Sir Thomas Peyton. They had a particularly important role, since Charles had decided to move to Calais, and he or his brother

James were most likely to cross the Channel to Kent or Sussex on receiving favourable news of the rising.

The royal brothers had at their command an army of exiled Royalist troops but, even if they managed to cross the Channel, it was unlikely that their forces would pose much of a threat to the New Model Army. A number of regiments had been formed under the command of the Duke of York, who had proved an able pupil while serving under the great French Marshal Turenne in the early 1650s, but chronic shortage of funds meant that they were rarely paid and their discipline suffered accordingly. As the Commonwealth broadsheet *Mercurius Politicus* put it: 'This country [Flanders] is full of Charles Stuart's soldiers, better versed in the art of begging than fighting; all ragged, miserable creatures.' The value of these troops, sometimes numbering 6,000 men and the nucleus of the Grenadier Guards formed after the Restoration, lay in the disquiet they caused the English government.

The result bore out the Sealed Knot leaders' pessimism. Even the weather seemed to be conspiring against the Cavaliers. High winds and excessive rain on 31 July hampered those struggling to make a rendezvous. Little was achieved in the south-west, a traditional bastion of Royalism. Massey was captured on the eve of the rising but, as he was riding behind a trooper en route for prison on 31 July, 'as they were going downe a hill in the evening of this stormy day,' as Anthony Wood recorded, 'the horse fell, and gave the colonel an opportunity to shove the trooper forward, and to make an escape into an adjoining wood at night', where he evaded the pursuing bloodhounds. Grenville, who had only just been released on parole, claimed that he could do nothing until he had news, either that Bristol and Gloucester had been seized, or that the King or the Duke of York had crossed the Channel. In Oxfordshire, Lord Falkland called off his participation. In Wiltshire, it was a similar story, with the cancellation of a projected rendezvous at Stonehenge.

The story in the Home Counties was equally depressing. Even Mordaunt, who had promised so much, and managed to escape the

Rump's order for his arrest, cancelled the rising he was to lead in Surrey, although he was to try again ten days later. The quantity of government troops in Kent deterred any attempt on the Channel ports. Lord De La Warr, leader of the Hampshire Cavaliers, was caught attempting to jump a ditch and sent to the Tower. In London, despite the plans of Maj Gen Browne, the flood of broadsheets calling on the populace to rise, and the support of Presbyterian ministers, who preached virulent sermons against the Government, no serious rising occurred. The procrastination of the Sealed Knot meant that there was negligible activity in East Anglia, home of most of its leaders. In the Midlands there was little action on 1 August. The north of England demonstrated the efficiency of the Government, who rounded up the likely suspects, including Lord Belasyse, during the first week of August. Indeed, so many suspects were arrested throughout the country that part of the old archbishop's palace at Lambeth was commandeered to house them.

The atrocious weather had one benefit. The King had travelled secretly to Calais with his physician, Dr Quartermaine; his brother James, meanwhile, was at Boulogne. Now, together with 2,000 French troops supplied by Turenne, they were stranded on the Continent. If Charles had crossed the Channel, his opponents would have been ready and waiting. Samuel Morland gave a graphic account, probably fictitious, in his *Autobiography*, written many years later, of how Sir Richard Willis had planned the King's assassination. According to Morland, Willis hired Weston Hanger in Kent, where 'there were several thousands of chosen men Arm'd Cap-a-pied, who had instructions to place themselves round about in woods and as privately as was possible, and upon the Watchword given that the King was enter'd into the said House, to rush in and murder Him and all his followers in a hurry'.

The sole, unexpected success was in Cheshire, where Sir George Booth, 'a man we never dreamt of', as one of Hyde's contacts recorded, raised the flag of revolt. A firm Presbyterian and former Parliamentarian, Booth had fought under Fairfax at the battle of Nantwich in 1644, where they had captured Monck. Booth, like so many Presbyterian MPs, had been among those expelled by Col Pride in 1648. Like most of his co-religionists, however, he would only countenance the restoration of Charles II on conditions favouring Presbyterianism. On 1 August, unaware that the Sealed Knot had postponed the rising, 500 men, including the influential Earl of Derby, whose father had been executed for his support of the King at the battle of Worcester, appeared at the rendezvous he had called. The next day, the gates of Chester opened to the Royalists, although Thomas Croxton in the castle, with a substantial armoury, defied the rebels.

Booth sent Maj Gen Egerton to Chirk Castle, where he was received enthusiastically by Sir Thomas Middleton. Further north, Derby took over Preston, and Col Gilbert Ireland occupied Liverpool. There was, however, little consensus among the insurgents. Some were outright Royalists, like Middleton, who had proceeded from Chirk Castle to the neighbouring town of Wrexham, which he entered, 'waving his sword about his head, [and] caused Charles Stuart to be proclaimed King in the market-place'. Booth, on the other hand, was more cautious. He had been eager to capitalise on his success, and had, with the full support of the local Presbyterian clergy, published a number of manifestos, stressing the illegal actions taken by the Rump and the Army, and advocating a free parliament. The Government was 'subjecting us under the meanest and fanatic spirits of the nation, under pretence of protection'. These appeals for support, written in studiously moderate language, omitted any mention of Charles II. The response to his attempt to play on Englishmen and women's fear of the sects was lukewarm. People feared the renewed outbreak of civil war even more. They also knew that they could expect little mercy from the New Model Army, which had enjoyed two of its greatest victories nearby at Preston and Worcester.

The delayed rising in the Midlands was of brief duration. On 12 August Lord Byron and Col Charles White led a force of 100 cavalry out of Sherwood Forest. Although Byron's men were soon scattered when confronted with the militia at Southwell, White pressed on to Derby, where his horsemen created havoc in the marketplace, crying out for the King and a free parliament. Their spirits rose still higher when the militia appeared and changed sides. But then Col Mitchell, one of Lambert's officers, remonstrated with the rebels for 'their base ingratitude to the Parliament'. Next morning, when reinforcements did not arrive, the 'pale-faced' rebels dispersed. Mordaunt attempted to revive the revolt in Surrey but, after spending three nights in the woods near Chelsham waiting vainly for support, his motley force dispersed, and by 15 August he was in hiding in London.

The Council of State's major concern was whom to send against Booth. Hesilrige and his colleagues were all too aware of the power a victory would give to the triumphant general. As a contemporary recorded: 'If Lambert can beat them this disorder will contribute much to the establishment of the Republic; but if he were beaten, great changes will happen.' It was tempting to send Fleetwood, whom they regarded as a weak and malleable character, but his military reputation was inferior to that of Lambert. Owing to the gravity of the situation, they opted for the latter, who was authorised on 5 August to lead a force from London to Cheshire. He was to be assisted by 1,500 troops sent over from Ireland by Ludlow, who had taken over from Henry Cromwell, three regiments from Lockhart's garrison in Dunkirk, and by forces commanded by Col Lilburne in Yorkshire and Maj Creed in Shrewsbury. The county militia was summoned and all horses within the vicinity of London requisitioned. Ships were dispatched to prevent supplies reaching the rebels.

Despite the usual problem over lack of pay, which led to the outbreak of two minor mutinies, with the cavalry and infantry coming to blows, Lambert led his troops north, leaving Fleetwood 'to shuffle the cards' in London, as one Cavalier noted. Although he was held up temporarily by floods near Stafford, Lambert reached Nantwich on 15 August, where he was joined by reinforcements from the northern and eastern counties.

Lambert had under his command some 1,200 horse and 3,000 foot. Four days later, having spurned the offer of negotiation, he met Booth's force, drawn up in broken ground by the River Weaver in front of Northwich. The maze of small fields bordered by hedges was unsuitable terrain for cavalry, so Lambert sent in the infantry under Col Hewson, who drove Booth's men back over Winnington Bridge. Booth's amateurs were no match for Hewson's seasoned veterans and the contest was soon over, the infantry 'leaping over the hedges, and hiding themselves'. Mordaunt wrote bitterly of the engagement, that the infantry 'had no match, others no ball, the horse trotted away, which is the civilest term'. Lambert's cavalry pursued the scattered Royalists as far as Warrington and Manchester, but casualties were light. The general had little desire to crush such poor opponents, commenting: 'Alas! Poore men, these are forced and hired.'

The next day Lambert entered Chester. Then Liverpool and Manchester were also occupied without resistance. When Middleton surrendered Chirk Castle on 24 August, the rising was over. Booth himself was caught days later at Newport Pagnell, disguised as a woman, when the innkeeper became suspicious after his female guest asked for a razor. 'He acted the Woman's part not so well,' as a Government newsletter drily remarked, and was sent to the Tower. Under questioning from Hesilrige and Vane, he admitted to meeting Mordaunt, but denied any direct correspondence with the King. For the first time in fifteen years, minimal retribution was taken against the losing side. It was as if the Government, like the rest of the population, had grown tired of bloodshed. When Grenville was interrogated, rather than defending his Royalist principles, he resorted 'to complain of my hard usage and sufferings by old Cromwell', something that appealed strongly to Vane, who ordered his release.

Meanwhile, Montagu appeared to have made a serious miscalculation. The Government was deeply suspicious when he decided, against the express wishes of its commissioners in the Baltic, to sail back to

England, ostensibly to replenish his supplies. He set sail on 24 August before news of the failure of Booth's rising had arrived. Barwick was in no doubt. 'Lord Mountagu', he wrote to the King, 'intended really your service when he set sail from the Sound, having heard of the party up in Cheshire. His return was opposed and protested against by the Plenipotentiaries; and the contest grew so hot, as [Algernon] Sydney told him, he knew his errand, and your Majesty was in his heart.' Barwick thought that he intended to block up the Thames with a squadron, a manoeuvre Lawson was to carry out very successfully a few months later.

News of the failure of Booth's Rebellion reached Montagu at the end of the month just off the English coast. As soon as he anchored in Southwold Bay, three commissioners sent by parliament, including an old adversary, Col Walton, hastened on board the *Naseby* to question him. Sidney had already sent a hostile report, accusing Montagu of interfering in his negotiations with the Dutch. The Government's suspicions were heightened by wild rumours that the admiral had held a secret meeting with the King at Flushing and that the Duke of York had travelled incognito to meet him in the Baltic. It was widely thought that 'Charles Stewart was ready by the waterside, and Mountagu was engaged to bring him over'. He was summoned to attend the Council of State, where he was examined, and parliament debated his actions. But Montagu was a first-class conspirator and had covered his tracks. No evidence of his correspondence with the King, carrying with it the sentence of death, came to light, nor was the Council aware of a letter from Montagu to Robert Barnwell, his steward at Hinchingbrooke, on 19 August, the day of Booth's defeat, asking him to be in touch with the admiral's friends and tenants, presumably to support the rising. The Rump, unwilling to make him a martyr, was content for Montagu to resign his commission and retire to his estate in Huntingdonshire.

Monck's position was equally dangerous. He was very aggrieved at the Government's high-handed removal of some of his best officers for political reasons during the summer. Their substitution by Lt Col Pierson and Mason, both known Anabaptists, and therefore representative of the religious anarchy he so much dreaded, had been particularly inappropriate. He protested in a 'Letter to the House' and urged all those cashiered officers to go south and fight their cases in London, where they could 'sollicit their own concernments, and as much as they could obstruct and retard the proceedings of the committee', while he delayed carrying out the Rump's orders for as long as possible. Monck's sense of injustice at the treatment he had received was exacerbated by the fact that two of the commissioners who had authorised this action were his fellow generals Lambert and Fleetwood. This was to contribute to the stand he was to take later in the autumn. And he knew he could rely on the support of the cashiered officers whom he had supported.

Monck's anger at his treatment at the hands of the Rump coincided with the arrival of his brother Nicholas, a clergyman, later to become Provost of Eton and Bishop of Hereford, who had, ostensibly, come to celebrate the engagement of his daughter Mary, who was staying with her uncle and aunt in Scotland. In fact, Nicholas had been selected by his kinsman Sir John Grenville, who had given him a benefice at Kilkhampton in Devon, to deliver a message from the King to his brother. Arriving in Scotland at the beginning of August, and having committed the contents of Charles's letter to memory, he confided in John Price, the general's chaplain and an Anglican Royalist, who encouraged him that Monck 'would be willing to close with any fair overture to redeem his country from the slavery of the army under which it groaned'. Encouraged by the chaplain's sentiments, Nicholas delivered the contents of the King's letter to his brother. It was couched in general terms, declaring: 'I cannot think you wish me ill, nor have reason to do so; and the good I expect from you will bring so great a benefit to your country and to yourself, that I cannot think you will decline my interest. The person who gives or sends this to you, has authority to say much more to you from me: and if you once resolve to take my interest to heart,

I will leave the way and manner of declaring it entirely to your judgement, and will comply with the advice you shall give me. It is in your power to make me as kind to you as you can desire, and to have me always, your affectionate friend, C.R.'

Nicholas Monck arrived at his brother's headquarters at the very moment that Booth raised the standard of revolt. As Price recorded, the general had refused to offer any encouragement to Col Jonathan Atkins, a messenger from Booth, with whom Monck had served in Ireland. At the same time, he declined to send any troops to Lambert's aid, claiming that he needed his full quota of troops to control Scotland, still strongly Royalist. The memory of his humiliation at Lambert's hands nine years earlier must also still have rankled. When Cromwell had appointed Monck to command Col Bright's regiment, the soldiers were asked 'if they would have Colonel Monk? "Colonel Monk!" said one of them, "What! to betray us? We took him, not long since, at Namptwick, prisoner: we'll have none of him." The next day the colonels came again, and propounded the case afresh, and asked if they would have Major-General Lambert to be their colonel? At which they all threw up their hats, and shouted a Lambert! A Lambert!"'

Although Monck appeared to be keeping his options open and waiting on events, he had instructed his closest confidants to draft a letter of protest to parliament. Edinburgh and Leith were to be secured, and Monck's officers invited to sign the letter. But the plan was to be put on hold until they had definite news of the success of Booth. Monck's caution was fully rewarded. No sooner had John Price and Thomas Gumble, a Presbyterian Parliamentarian and, like Price, a chaplain to Monck, both of whom were to write biographies of the general, set to work on the letter of protest than news arrived of Lambert's victory and all hope of an immediate challenge to the Government was shelved. As if nothing had happened, Monck reverted to his customary impenetrable taciturnity. Price recorded the news of Booth's defeat at the celebratory dinner that night:

Good news fly apace, and by noon severall officers (and those the most considerable of the sectarian sort) came to rejoyce, and dine with the general; but his ordinary table served for a thanksgiving-dinner for them. Mr Monk, Mr Gumble, and Adjutant Smith, had the good fortune to dine abroad; but my duty was to be at the general's table, where I heard the expressions of joy that passed from officer to officer, for the total defeating of General Booth . . . that it was apparent that Booth and his confederates, would have brought in Charles Stuart. Upon this the general gave them the complement of a thanksgiving-day, that he could wish that the parliament would make a law, that whoever should but mention the restoring of him [Charles II] should presently be hanged. I had reason to think that he was but in jest; otherwise, I could guess where the hanging lay.

Feeling powerless to influence events, and resentful of the Rump's continuing interference in his command, including the order to cashier Col Daniel, one of his most faithful officers, Monck tendered a letter of resignation to Speaker Lenthall on 3 September. It was only the intervention of his brother-in-law Thomas Clarges, who was tipped off by Nicholas Monck, that prevented the letter from being read out in parliament.

The failure of Booth's Rebellion was due to a number of circumstances. Royalist disorganisation, efficient Government intelligence, the inexperience of Booth and the bad weather all played a part. More importantly, too many senior figures held back. Traditional Royalist grandees such as the Earl of Southampton and the Marquis of Hertford had too much to lose; they 'industriously declined any conversation or commerce with any who were known to correspond with the king'. The leading Presbyterians were split. Booth was willing to declare openly for the King. Others, such as Lord Willoughby of Parham, Maj Gen Browne and Sir William Waller, were Royalist sympathisers but failed to rise.

Fairfax and the Earl of Manchester, important Civil War commanders, had made no response to Royalist overtures and were sitting firmly on the fence. Manchester spoke for many people when he expressed his fear 'of his Majesties restoration by tumult'. It was the lesser gentry, with 'more honour than inheritance', in the words of Maj Gen Berry, who were willing to rise in revolt.

The failure had another longer-term effect of great consequence. Once again the Royalists had shown that they were no match for the republican Army. A restoration would only occur when the King's enemies fell out among themselves. As a result, Charles and his ministers focused their attentions more closely on winning over their major opponents. It was to be these turncoats, not the die-hard Cavaliers, who were to effect the Restoration and benefit most from it.

7

A SPLIT IN THE ARMY

Booth's Rebellion had achieved what the Royalists most dreaded: a union between the Rump and the Army. The Army had proved that it still possessed the power to impose order, while the Rump represented legitimacy by maintaining a direct link with the Long Parliament elected in 1640. And its leaders were extremely efficient. Throughout the summer of 1659, despite the Royalist threat, the Government was busy issuing edicts, corresponding with its representatives throughout the country and abroad. Local government continued to function well, courts were held in the counties and Booth's rising did not prevent taxes from being collected. The key question was whether the Rump could maintain its fragile alliance with the Army. The aftermath of the rising provided some hope for opponents of the regime. Although some of the leading rebels had been imprisoned, they were soon released and little attempt was made to impose fines on them, despite the Government's pressing need for money.

The morale of the King, who had been waiting impatiently for the chance to cross the Channel, was at a low ebb. Once again, as in 1655, what had appeared to be a promising Royalist rising had ended in total failure, the declarations of support from the many Cavaliers throughout the country disappearing as soon as they were required to risk their lives or their livelihood. The cautious Mazarin had refused to commit French troops to the Stuart cause until a sufficient number of Royalists in England publicly declared their support. Mazarin's greatest general, Turenne, had been more encouraging, offering to transport Charles and James from Boulogne to England.

Charles had been prepared to accept Hyde's view that it was Englishmen who must effect his restoration, but now decided that he must look further afield. Tired of waiting on the Channel coast, he set off for the Pyrenees, where the French and Spanish governments were negotiating an end to a generation of warfare. The King chose as his companions Ormonde, the rakish Daniel O'Neill and the mercurial George Digby, Earl of Bristol on the journey south. He demonstrated his remarkable powers of recovery. Charles's letters as he travelled through France were light-hearted and full of humour, joking to Hyde, sitting hungry in Brussels, surrounded by Cavaliers full of bitter recriminations: 'God keep you, and send you to eat as good mutton as we have every meal.' At Fuenterrabía, however, Charles realised how low his stock had fallen among the major European powers. Mazarin refused to meet him, and although Don Luís de Haro, the Spanish minister, paid the King every courtesy, he could offer no positive help. Fortunately for the Royalist cause, the English Government had missed a golden opportunity to participate in this momentous event. Sir William Lockhart, although he enjoyed a good relationship with Mazarin, had received no definite instructions from parliament since July. He travelled south to Fuenterrabía but was too late to exercise any influence on the treaty.

In England, Lambert, flushed with victory, was now the supreme power in the land, his reputation much enhanced. Barely a fortnight earlier he had led his men out of London in a semi-mutinous condition. Now, his written report to parliament on 20 August was written in Cromwellian style, calling on 'God that he will direct your counsels to such things as may be for His glory'. The Rump waited anxiously for the return of the triumphant general to the capital. They knew full well that the underlying problems facing the Government were as serious as ever, and their fears were fully justified. No sooner had Lambert's troops finished celebrating their victory than their grievances resurfaced, exacerbated by the deepening financial crisis. Increasingly, the troops were taking the law into their own hands. There were numerous incidents of common soldiers seizing commissioners of the militia until they raised enough money to pay for them to go home. They ignored the growing hatred of the civil population for the military, expressed by Alice Thornton, a devout Anglican, who begged to be delivered from 'the raige, rapine, and destruction from the soldiery'.

Rather than altering its ways, the Army turned to the triumphant Lambert, the one general capable of facing down the backlash if the military interfered yet again in the political process. Few had much faith in Fleetwood, who was despised for his reliance on divine providence. It was widely felt that it was only a matter of time before Lambert made his bid for supreme power. The perceptive Francesco Giavarina observed that 'the chief object of the army was to raise Lambert to the post of generalissimo and then by degrees to that enjoyed by Oliver'. Hyde analysed the relationship between Lambert and Fleetwood: 'Lambert knew well he could govern him as Cromwell had done Fayrefax, and then in like manner lay him aside.'

Lambert's ambition, however, had offended many of his fellow officers. Fairfax, also a Yorkshireman and once Lambert's commander, feared for the destruction of the parliamentary process. Col Hutchinson's wife Lucy recorded: 'Lambert was exceedingly puffed up with his cheap victory, and cajoled his soldiers; and, before he returned to London, set on foot among them their old insolent way of prescribing to the parliament by way of petition.' Monck, still in command in Scotland after his near involvement in Booth's Rebellion and his attempt to resign his post, commented with his usual perspicacity: 'I see now that I shall have a better game to play than I had before; I know Lambert so well, that I am sure he will not let those people at Westminster sit till Christmas-day.'

There was a further mark against Lambert. Not only was he accused by many of overweening personal ambition, but it was also feared that he was intent on undermining the social order by his alliance with the extreme religious sects whose activities had provoked such widespread panic in the summer. People were still consumed with fear. Richard

Baxter, the prominent Presbyterian minister, gave a typically muddled description in October of his antipathy to the Quakers, with their reliance on foreign aid and 'swarmes of Fryers and Jesuits at their backs'.

The Rump gave little indication that it would heed Lambert's wishes. Instead, the impetuous and obstinate Hesilrige, determined to control the military, vetoed Lambert's promotion to the rank of major-general on 21 August, the day after parliament received his report on his victory. This blatant rebuff was very ill received. Lambert refused to attend meetings of the Council for the next month. He was not placated when Hesilrige doubled the money voted to him by parliament for his win, using the increase of £1,000 to bolster his popularity by distributing it among his grateful soldiers.

Relations between the Rump and the Army deteriorated further in September. The Derby petition, drafted by Cols Mitchell and Sankey, and Maj Creed, was a direct involvement of the military in politics. It advocated the permanent appointment of Fleetwood as commander-in-chief, with Lambert as his second in command, Desborough in charge of the cavalry, and Monck of the infantry. No officer was to be cashiered without a court martial and the Army retained the right to punish those who had given false information against it, 'thereby creating jealousies, and casting scandalous imputations upon them'. Lambert and his men arrived in London late in the month, 'a little flushed' with their victory, and the general and his senior officers were soon holding regular meetings with Fleetwood and Desborough at Wallingford House. The Army in England was united but, ominously, in Scotland Monck stated that he had always opposed petitions to parliament and refused to let his officers sign the Derby petition.

Hesilrige regarded the Derby petition as a direct attack on the authority of parliament. He had been shown a copy privately by Fleetwood, and immediately attacked its legality in parliament on 22 September, proposing that Lambert be sent to the Tower. When tempers had cooled, a less provocative measure was passed, admonishing the officers who had presented the petition for their irregular conduct. Hesilrige and his colleagues were, however, determined to exert control over the issue of commissioning officers in the armed forces, an interference guaranteed to irritate the Army high command. The Rumpers were deaf to the soldiers' opinions, now expressed in the oft-repeated cry of 'God save the Army', whereas they had formerly cried 'Hurrah for Parliament'.

The generals were further annoyed by the Rump's proposal to create a militia in the counties, under the control of trustworthy officers. For the regular troops, this appeared the first step towards their disbanding. Whitelocke, by nature a trimmer, saw the danger in this provocative policy. He thought it highly inopportune 'to exasperate those who had so lately done so great a service to the Commonwealth, by denying them a matter not of great consequence'. His views were, however, ignored. The Rumpers were more interested in working out ways of raising money to pay off these troublesome soldiers. Fines on Royalists for delinquency had proved insufficient. Raising taxes was certain to arouse the hatred of the population. A third option was to approach the City for a loan. On 26 September the Rump had voted that Sir John Ireton, an Anabaptist known to be sympathetic to its views, and brother of Henry Ireton, Cromwell's son-in-law and close associate, should continue as mayor. It feared that a free vote by the City Council would elect a hostile or even a Royalist candidate. A fortnight later, the Rumpers, realising the need to placate the City, changed their mind and allowed the Council to vote in Alderman Sir Thomas Allen.

The political situation became more confused. On 5 October Desborough, the most aggressive of the generals, presented a second petition to parliament, with the sinister proviso that anyone casting aspersions in parliament against the Army should be punished. There was also news that Lambert and other senior officers were canvassing for additional signatures to the petition among troops stationed throughout Britain. At first the Rump intended to make a conciliatory reply, but the members' opinion changed on receiving a letter of support from Monck, authorising his brother-in-law Thomas Clarges to acquaint the leading members that 'if they would assert their own authority, he would march into England, to justify it against any opposition'. Fearing that they were about to be forcibly dissolved, the Rumpers rushed through a bill on 11 October declaring it high treason to levy a tax without the consent of parliament. Moreover, in a direct snub to the Army, all acts passed since the Rump's dismissal in April 1653 were declared void.

The next day, in a measure bound to provoke a response, the commissions of the chief culprits, including Lambert and Desborough, were revoked. Lambert himself was to be arrested and taken to the Tower. Fleetwood was a more ambiguous figure. As commander-in-chief he was, in theory, the leader of the Rump's opponents, but in practice he was a much less resolute figure than either Lambert or Desborough. At this crucial juncture he seems to have been ignored by Hesilrige and his colleagues. In defence of these provocative decisions, the regiments commanded by Cols Morley, Okey and Moss, deemed to be loyal to the Rump, were ordered to stand outside Westminster Hall, with loaded muskets.

Lambert took up the challenge immediately, relying on his reputation as the Army's most charismatic general. He determined to issue a direct appeal to the troops loyal to the Rump to change sides. Although Morley and Moss refused to let him pass, their men hesitated to oppose one 'who had so often spent their blood for them and with them'. Maj Arthur Evelyn, guarding Palace Yard, submitted as soon as Lambert approached. Even though the general was on foot, he marched straight up to the mounted major. In the words of Bulstrode Whitelocke: 'Lambert commanded Evelyn to dismount who thought it safest to obey, & though Lambert were on foot, & none with him, yett Evelyn in the head of his troups dismounted att his command, & his troupe also obeyed Lambert.' Lambert now proceeded to form a ring round the troops loyal to the Rump. No one was allowed to break the cordon, although the Rumpers were permitted some supplies of bread and cheese.

When Speaker Lenthall tried to enter Palace Yard, he was stopped by an officer. Undaunted, he commanded the soldier: 'Then know, I am your General, and return unto your duty.' But the soldier replied that 'they knew no such thing; that if he had marched before them over Winnington-bridge, they should have known him'. Hyde heard from an agent that Lambert told the Speaker 'hee was a foolish, impertinent fellow, and bid him get home'. This riposte sums up the Army's inability to accept its place in the civilian hierarchy. Lenthall was just as unsuccessful when he tried to enter Wallingford House.

Throughout 13 October the troops faced each other, former comrades now on opposing sides but extremely reluctant to open fire. Occasionally, the silence was broken by the boldest on either side urging his opponents to desert. In the Council of State Lambert and Desborough faced their opponents Hesilrige and Morley. The key issue was identified by Johnston of Wariston: 'I found at the Counsel', he wrote, 'some asserting the Parliaments absolut authority, some that it was limited [so as] not to be prejudicial to the cause.' The two views had proved utterly irreconcilable.

Pressure grew on the members, isolated in the House of Commons, to leave Westminster before the soldiers forced them to. John Bradshaw, chief judge at the trial of Charles I and a firm champion of parliament over the Army, was one of the few to attack the 'despicable behaviour' of the military, calling Lambert a rebel and a traitor. At last, parliament yielded, and the Council ordered all troops to return to their quarters. Both bodies of soldiers marched away. As they disbanded, Lambert rode through Moss's regiment, and the troopers, supposedly loyal to the Rump, saluted him with volleys of shot 'in the acknowledgement of so brave a soldier'. Whitelocke, like many fellow members, returned home from Westminster full of trepidation and proceeded to lock the doors and close the shutters. He was concerned for the safety of his wife, Mary, and their week-old son. But his family slept undisturbed that night, despite the sound of the more exuberant troops firing their muskets.

The Rump had been forcibly dissolved again, as it had been in April 1653. To show his domination, Lambert left some of his men behind to guard Westminster. The rest of the troops around the capital soon declared for him, realising that he was the general most likely to secure them their pay. Perhaps, as Ludlow suggested, they had little wish to return to civilian life.

On 14 October the Army Council suspended officers, including Col Morley, who had supported the Rump. Fleetwood was nominated commander-in-chief, his authority no longer controlled by a commission, but few had confidence in his leadership. Johnston of Wariston described his vacillating character: 'No good friend and no ill foe; slow to come to a determination and suddenly to break it; and doe things by privat suggestions.' It was clear to all that Lambert wielded ultimate power. The new government was to consist of a Committee of Safety, of whom the key figures were the chief generals in England – Fleetwood, Lambert and Desborough – and Sir Henry Vane, the only senior Rumper willing to work with the Army. He justified his action by claiming that cutting a deal with the Army was the only way to preserve the principle of religious toleration in which he believed so deeply and which was anathema to the Presbyterian-dominated Rump. Bulstrode Whitelocke, a more practical politician who had served under Cromwell throughout the 1650s, was another civilian willing to serve, although he was dismissed by Dr Moore, writing to Hyde, as a trimmer someone who 'plays his game so well that he always rises on the right side'.

The general feeling among the population was that those willing to support the coup were acting for selfish reasons. Many Royalists thought that Lambert was distrustful and jealous of Fleetwood, who was thought to be inclined to their cause. Republicans were saddened that ideals for which they had fought so hard seemed to have disappeared. John Milton, Cromwell's Latin secretary and a keen supporter of the Army in its struggle with parliament a decade earlier, was thoroughly disillusioned. He regarded the Army's behaviour as 'most illegal and scandalous, I fear me barbarous and or scarce to be exampled among any barbarians, that a paid army should, for no other cause, thus subdue the supreme power that set them up. This, I say, other nations will judge to the sad dishonour of that army, lately so renowned for the civilest and best-ordered in the world, and by us here for the most conscientious.' He awaited 'the Heavy Judgement of God', punishment for 'these Hypocrisies, Violations of Truth and Holiness'.

The majority of Londoners, however, dulled by the constant political instability and conscious of the Army's seeming indifference to their concerns, were considerably more sanguine than Milton. Hyde's agent Samborne reported on the following day: 'What government we shall have next is not yet known, but the people are prepared for any, for in all the hurly burly the streets were full, every one going about their business as if not at all concerned, and when Parliament sent unto the city to relieve them, they answered they would not meddle with the dispute, but endeavour to preserve the peace of the city.'

8

LAMBERT VERSUS MONCK

Lambert had earned the loyalty of the majority of the troops in England. His main threat came from Monck in Scotland, who received news of the *coup d'état* on 17 October 1659. Acting with great decisiveness, Monck summoned his closest advisers, including Cols Wilkes and Clobery. They decided to declare for parliament at once, and determined to gain the support of the two infantry regiments based in Edinburgh, those of Col Talbot and Monck himself. Fortunately, Talbot, who was soon to throw in his lot with Lambert, was absent in England, but his deputy, Maj Hubblethorne, was confident of the men's loyalty to Monck. The general deemed the troops to be more loyal than his own regiment, where the English Government had insisted on replacing several of his officers with its own appointments, against his wishes, during the summer.

Monck therefore marched into the Scottish capital the next morning and ordered a review of the two regiments. Having first ensured the loyalty of Talbot's regiment, he addressed his own men in the High Street and explained the reasons for his decision:

The army in England has broken up the Parliament, out of a restless and ambitious humour to govern themselves, and to hinder the settlement of the nation. Their next practice will be to impose their insolent extravagances upon the army in Scotland, which is neither inferior nor subordinate to them. For my part, I think myself obliged, by the duty of my place, to keep the military power in obedience to the civil; and since you have received your pay and commission from Parliament, it is your duty to defend it. In this,

I expect the ready obedience of you all; but if any declare their dissent to my resolution, they shall have their liberty to leave the service, and may take their passes to be gone.

The general was taking no chances. To back up his words, he had ordered Talbot's regiment to parade in battle order with lighted powder, matches and bullets, with Capt Johnson and a troop of horse in reserve. His own regiment, in contrast, had no powder for their muskets. The loyal troops greeted this speech with shouts and volleys of shot, and while they stood guard, Monck purged all suspects in his regiment on the spot. Including those absent and later deserters, these amounted to the lieutenant-colonel, a major, sixteen other officers and nine non-commissioned officers. A further 150 officers from other Scottish regiments were cashiered, including religious extremists, and held in Tantallon Castle before being sent back to England.

Monck was particularly keen to prevent potentially hostile officers sent from the south having the chance to address his troops. Capt Johnson marched south to Berwick, strategically situated on the English border, where he was to assist the governor of the town. He arrived just in time to apprehend Col Cobbet, who had been sent north by the Army grandees in London on 19 October with a letter for Monck and to take command of a regiment in Scotland. Johnson recorded how Cobbet was 'brought with a guard to Edinburgh Castle and kept there, the General being much incensed against him, upon private advice that he had instructions to have seized him, if he had not agreed to the army's action in England'. Monck took immediate action to secure Cobbet's regiment based in Glasgow. Maj Barret and Capt Dean, who had been sent over from Ireland by Ludlow, a supporter of Fleetwood and Lambert, were 'sent away from Scotland with a severe rebuke'. Regiments of dubious loyalty were dispatched to distant posts.

There was a strong divergence of opinion between Monck and his counterparts in England. Monck was a Presbyterian and a traditionalist who believed strongly in the maintenance of the old social order, and the supremacy of parliament. He feared the religious extremists who had served so prominently in the New Model Army. His opponent, Lambert, on the other hand, favoured the Independent sects and was known to be sympathetic to the Quakers. He had resolutely defended James Nayler, a prominent Quaker, formerly in his regiment, despite his extraordinary entry into Bristol in 1656. This was a re-creation of Christ's entry into Jerusalem, an event regarded with horror by the vast majority of Englishmen. Col Robert Lilburne, who had preceded Monck as commander of the Commonwealth forces in Scotland, and now in charge of the English forces in York, shared Lambert's support for the Independent sects. He established a garrison in Newcastle in order to defend the north of England against a potential invasion from Scotland. Col Overton, a well-known Anabaptist, who commanded the important military arsenal at Hull, had been implicated in a plot to replace Monck as supreme commander in Scotland in 1654.

Monck was intensely suspicious of these religious radicals. They, in their turn, were hostile to the split Monck had introduced in the New Model Army. His challenge to the Army grandees had shattered the unified *esprit de corps* that had made it such a formidable fighting machine. Overton's troops were unwilling to march against their comrades in the south, with whom they had 'prayed together, took counsel together, fought together, obtained victories together, and rejoiced so often together'. Lilburne expressed the opinion of many soldiers, on receiving news of Lambert's coup, that 'he hoped never a true Englishman would name the Parliament again, and that he would have the house pulled down where they sat for fear it should be infectious'.

As the commander of a much smaller force than his opponents in England, it was vital for Monck to secure his men's loyalty. He therefore set about educating them. At a number of meetings of all commissioned officers, the general defended the Rump but encouraged his men to air their opinions. Monck's chaplain, Price, summed up the contempt with which the army in Scotland held the generals in London, 'that it could not enter the thoughts of the men at Wallingford House [Fleetwood's residence], that soldiers should love their country better than their pay'.

The debates among Monck's soldiers were published in a weekly gazette, edited by an officer 'who was guilty of a little wit', and distributed throughout Scotland and, where possible, in England. Monck made his men offers of promotion, and used a considerable war chest carefully built up over the previous months to gain their support. He was shrewd enough to realise that the appearance of the Scots under his banner was likely to unite his opponents in England and he was anxious to play down any accusations of his latent Royalist sympathies. Most Scots were seen as supporters of the Stuart Restoration and Lambert had already accused his rival of increasing the likelihood that Scotland 'will fall into the hands of the late King's party there'.

A fierce propaganda war now commenced between the two sides. Monck's agents posted three letters to Fleetwood, Lambert and Speaker Lenthall in Edinburgh and London, all dated 20 October. In them he accused Lambert of naked ambition, chided Fleetwood for participating in 'an action of such a dangerous and destructive consequence', and assured Lenthall, Speaker of the Rump, that he was determined to uphold the supremacy of parliament. He wrote further letters to the commanders of the Irish army, the chief captains of the fleet, many of whom were old colleagues from his time as general-at-sea under Blake, and the governors of the key towns in England. Having made his decision, Monck was determined not to suffer the fate of Booth, whose rising had been confined to Cheshire.

On 1 November Col John Pearson wrote from Northallerton in Yorkshire: 'We have apprehended a person that had two letters from General Monck sewed in his doublet. . . . The substance was to invite them to an insurrection in the West, and to seize upon Exeter as a place to make head in; and tells them that when the greatest part of the army was drawn to oppose him, then London would rise and destroy the rest;

so that you may see, here is the second part of [sequel to] Sir George Booth. The letter was written by Sir William Clark, and signed by Monck's own hand: I saw it.'

Both sides realised that the longer they remained divided, the more likely Royalist fortunes were to revive. Lambert wrote to Monck, emphasising the terrible danger he was putting them into by splitting the Army. He made no attempt to justify the dismissal of parliament or the introduction of arbitrary rule, backed by naked force, 'that intollerable slavery of a sword government' that had so incensed Monck. Nor was there any mention of any possibility of an election, now or in the future. The Navy was also divided. Lawson's second in command, William Goodson, and twenty-one senior officers sent a letter to Monck in early November, reproaching him for dividing the military against itself, but the vice-admiral himself remained aloof and refused to sign the letter.

The Committee of Safety, which had replaced the old Council of State, still hoped that it could bring the errant general to heel without a battle. In order to avoid interception, a message was sent to Col Thomas Wilkes by normal, rather than special, post, ordering him to arrest the general and to take him back to London, by frigate. But Monck, from his base at Dalkeith, ordered the interception of the letter at Leith, where the London packet docked. He opened the letter before it reached Wilkes, who soon found himself under close arrest in Edinburgh Castle.

The generals in London, equally conscious of the need for maintaining unity, removed a number of senior officers suspected of disloyalty from their posts. They were alarmed to discover that five colonels and four other officers publicly protested that 'all authority is now devolved upon and resides in the army . . . and our government must be a sword government'. They ended their protest with the ringing words: 'Is England's dear-bought freedom come to this?' These sentiments exactly echoed those uttered by Monck.

It was too late to compromise. Fleetwood and Lambert ordered Cols Okey, Morley and Alured, all veterans of the New Model Army but suspected of sympathising with Monck, to be cashiered. Fleetwood also sent officers to Scotland and Ireland to maintain unity, but Cobbet, as already recorded, was intercepted at Berwick, and Col Barrow found the army in Ireland disunited, despite efforts by Ludlow to cashier many of the officers loyal to his predecessor Henry Cromwell. Morale among the soldiers in England continued to deteriorate due to lack of pay. Lucy Hutchinson expressed the widely held view of the coup's leaders: 'They there began their arbitrary reign, to the joy of all the vanquished enemies of the parliament and to the amazement & terror of all men that had any honest interest.'

In the provinces there was a sense of bewilderment as the two factions of the New Model Army lined up against each other. With the Courts of Justice now closed, local government, which had continued through all the political upheavals, and even during Booth's Rebellion, was close to collapse. An officer, writing to Fleetwood from Montgomery in Wales on 16 October, expressed the prevailing lack of purpose or direction. Nobody had 'received the last express or account from any public person since the dissolution or interruption of the late Parliament. I have been at a meeting for the sequestration and the militia, and there was but one person to join with me. The commissioners of the militia were loath to meddle in it, being themselves unconcerned; and the commissioners for sequestration are also loath to raise moneys, they know not for whom, nor for what end.' He ended his letter by lamenting the breakdown of government: 'The army heretofore declared their repentance for their former interruption of the Parliament; we know not but they may please to repent for this also, or else the former repentance is to be repented of.'

In Scotland, there was a similar sense of confusion. The majority of the population was either actively or passively Royalist, and had little sympathy for either faction of the New Model Army. Johnston of

Wariston lamented the situation in his native land: 'In the meantyme,' he wrote, 'poor Scotland lyes desolate without law, justice, gouvernment or settlement of publick or privat interest, religious or civil.'

As the breach between the two branches of the Army became public, Royalists felt hope stirring. John Evelyn published *An Apology for the Royal Party* on 27 October, a bold move as the Commonwealth regarded any acknowledgement of the House of Stuart as treason. Evelyn lambasted the Scots for betraying Charles I to parliament, and for abandoning Charles II during his expedition of 1650–1. He then directed his attack at Cromwell, a particular figure of opprobrium, 'the most infamous hypocrite and proflegate Atheist of all the Usurpers that ever any age produc'd'. Evelyn, a devout Anglican, was harshly critical of Presbyterians and Independents. There was but one way out of the present impasse: to recall the King. Evelyn was not arrested, a sign that the Government was losing some of its aggressive efficiency. The Royalists were further heartened by the release of several prominent Cavaliers, arrested after Booth's Rebellion.

With the split in the Republican ranks growing wider, the high-minded principles that had persuaded men to take up arms in the First Civil War were now seen as irrelevant. Mordaunt was busy trying to re-create an alliance between Anglicans and Presbyterians, but for most individuals, there were more personal concerns. If they were to change allegiance, they looked for some reward. As Alan Brodrick reported to Hyde in December: 'Religion, though the sacred pretext to the earlier part of the War, they lay aside . . . treating of single interests. Can [the King] comply with each, whilst perhaps two (or it may be three) aim at the same Office, Forest, Chase etc?'

The number of inveterate opponents making overtures was growing. Col Richard Ingoldsby, a regicide (although he had not attended the trial) and one of the most popular officers in the Army, had offered his allegiance to Charles in June, hoping that the King would be prepared to forgive him for signing his father's death warrant. In early November

Mordaunt wrote to the King that Henry Cromwell was willing to serve him. Hyde was looking for other opportunities to persuade opponents to switch allegiance. Evelyn, a friend of Mordaunt, had approached Col Herbert Morley, MP for Sussex, and appointed one of the seven commissioners of the Army in October. More importantly, Sir John Pettus, related by marriage to Fleetwood, was hoping to win over the general. On 14 October he received a letter, appealing to his self-importance: 'I beseech you make good use of this happy opportunity, & consider how great you may make yourself, & how glorious you will be to posterity, if you be the means of laying the government on the shoulders of him who ought to bear it, which will in an instant restore a happy peace & settlement to this distracted nation.' But Fleetwood made no reply to this eloquent overture.

Mordaunt was trying to coordinate Royalist activity in England, but his reputation had been tarnished by the failure of Booth's Rebellion, and his arrogance continued to offend many of his fellow Cavaliers. There was much confusion when it was discovered that he and the Duke of York were making independent attempts to secure Dunkirk, a key target. Royalist expectations were higher in Ireland. Lord Broghill, who had retired to Munster following the fall of Richard Cromwell, now favoured the restoration of the King, and he was in close contact with three of the main military figures, Sir Charles Coote, Sir Hardress Waller and Sir Theophilus Jones. Their commander, Edmund Ludlow, returned to England in October, hoping to help to engineer some form of compromise between the Army and the Rump in order to save the Republic.

Royalists were also contemplating how to approach Lambert. A member of the Yorkshire gentry and a natural leader, he had enjoyed the trappings of power and high office. The French ambassador, Bordeaux, reported how 'he is, therefore, greatly caressed by the Royalists, whom he has latterly treated with great consideration'. Some Cavaliers even mooted the idea that the Duke of York or the King himself might be matched off with Lambert's daughter. But the prospect of such a match would have fatally compromised Charles with all of Lambert's enemies, while James was busy carrying on a clandestine liaison with Anne, daughter of Sir Edward Hyde. The affair was to lead to their scandalous marriage in September 1660, when Anne confessed to being in the latter stages of pregnancy. Moreover, the royal brothers shared the general view that Lambert was a die-hard Republican who was 'bewitched, with an itch of having all', in the words of John Barwick. As the Duke of York put it to Mordaunt: 'If neither Monck nor Lambert could be won for the King, it will be best for his friends to remain passive until actual fighting between the two generals begins.'

The Army grandees in London were all too aware of the threat posed by Monck's condemnation of their *coup d'état*. The Committee of Safety, determined to justify its position, made plans to 'prepare a form of government to be settled over three nations in the way of a free state and Commonwealth'. Numerous letters were dispatched, hoping to reassure Monck's soldiers, or to convince them of the error of their commander. Six commissioners, comprising Gens Whalley and Goffe, three ministers and Maj Dean, a special envoy of Fleetwood's, headed for Scotland. In an attempt to show the breadth of the new Government, two prominent Parliamentarians, Vane and Whitelocke, were given command of regiments. Monck's brother-in-law Thomas Clarges and Col Talbot, whose regiment Monck had recently taken over, both of whom happened to be in London, were sent north with messages intended to effect a reconciliation. They were received politely, but without changing the general's mind. Privately, Clarges reported to Monck the discontent of the civilian population in London with their rulers.

Monck realised that the longer he could delay a confrontation, the weaker his opponents would become, reliant solely on the military for their authority. In addition, their commander, Fleetwood, was prone to prevarication and had no wish for conflict, as Hyde had noted on 10 October: 'The character which we have always received of this man, is not such as makes him equal to any notable design, or to be much relied on to-morrow for what in truth he resolved to do yesterday.'

Lambert, however, was determined on action and left London on 3 November with 12,000 men, intending to bring his old rival to heel. Although he had a reputation as a fighter, an onlooker commented to one of the departing soldiers that he did not look as if he meant to hurt Monck, to which the man replied: 'Noe, Sir, you may swear it.' The New Model Army, once full of crusading zeal, was now no more than a tool in the hands of its ambitious commanders. The inability to propose any form of government to replace the Rump had deeply affected morale, and it now possessed no other purpose than to perpetuate its own rule.

As yet, there had been no major mutiny, but the lack of pay and collapsing morale had led to a general outbreak of lawlessness. Soldiers billeted on civilians demanded sustenance, and when this was not forthcoming, seized what they regarded as their due. With increasing numbers of Englishmen refusing to pay their taxes, and officers no longer firmly in control of their men, soldiers used threats to try to raise revenue. One of the most effective, and most unpopular, as Bordeaux reported to Mazarin, was to billet troops on those who refused to pay their taxes. Sir Thomas Wroth summed up the widespread contempt for the military: 'It is said the soldiers have ventured their lives, they were well paid for it.'

Lucy Hutchinson recounted how her husband stood up to the bullying of the soldiers who appeared at their house. When 'six of Lambert's troopers came to gather money', the colonel was outraged at their insulting remarks about parliament. On being asked by whose authority they came to his house, they laid their hands on their swords and replied: 'That was their authority.' Hutchinson, a staunch Parliamentarian and senior officer of the New Model Army, and precisely the sort of man whose support Lambert needed, drew his own sword and, despite their 'cocked pistols', succeeded in locking them into his great hall. As the colonel commented to the soldiers he had arrested, their behaviour 'would bring back the Stewarts'.

Lack of pay was also causing serious unrest in the Navy. Lawson, the senior admiral, and his men stationed in the Downs, watched angrily as funds desperately needed for the sailors' wages were diverted to pay the Army. There were a number of mutinies during the autumn, and Royalists drew heart from reports they received that angry sailors were declaring that 'if they cannot have it at home, they have another master to go to'. The Duke of York, always interested in naval matters, and shortly to command the Navy, hoped that his agents might 'feel the pulses of those which commanded the English ships, if by money or by any other means they may be reduced to their obedience'. But the sailors showed little enthusiasm to declare for the Royalist cause, and Lawson remained impervious to overtures from the King's agent Arnold Braemes. He was 'a sea-Fairfax [who had also rejected numerous overtures, though this was shortly to change], so sullen, so senseless, of so obstinate a courage, and so wayward obstinacy'.

The senior Cavaliers in exile explored the possibility of recruiting foreign aid. But the prospect of a Catholic army landing on English soil, with the exiled King at its head, was likely to antagonise the strongly Protestant majority in England, brought up on the memory of the Spanish Armada and the Gunpowder Plot. However, to Pepys, writing to Montagu on 22 October, it appeared a real possibility: 'People talke now very boldly of the resolucion the Kings of ffrance and Spain have taken to assist the King of Scotts.' In fact, Charles, in the Pyrenees, had failed to elicit any positive response from the French and Spanish ministers preoccupied with negotiating their own peace treaty.

By the middle of November, disaffection had spread to the capital. Both sides were seeking the allegiance of the City, hoping to elicit its financial support. Monck appealed to Londoners' fear of disorder, epitomised by the more radical members of the Army. He appeared to have succeeded, and Bordeaux reported to Mazarin 'that those Sectaries, against whom the people are greatly enraged, shall no longer be employed to guard the town'. On the other side, Fleetwood, Desborough and Whitelocke were running out of options, fully conscious that discontent was rising in the counties, with numerous threats to refuse to pay taxes without the necessary legislation passed by Act of Parliament. On 8 November they went to the Guildhall, hoping to secure a loan from the City of London for £30,000. Each spoke very much in character, Fleetwood emphasising the disinterestedness of the Army, while Whitelocke, ever the politician, stressed the Committee of Safety's desire for unity and peace. The more blunt Desborough, however, vowed 'that the army would never put itself in a position of dependence upon those whom it had conquered, and that it would rather support the Sectaries than suffer any resolution to its prejudice'.

The Lord Mayor, Thomas Allen, the aldermen and the Common Council of the City, on hearing these words, with minimal justification for the *coup d'état*, had little hesitation in rejecting the request for a loan. Monck had also sent a letter to the Council explaining his actions, but the councillors were unwilling to reply, for fear of antagonising the Army grandees in the capital. As a further measure, Monck dispatched Thomas Clarges to London to find a writer who would put forward his point of view. His choice, Henry Muddiman, was to become the most influential journalist of the Restoration era. A flurry of pamphlets appeared, protesting against the 'interruption' of parliament and lamenting the oppression suffered by all freeborn Englishmen.

To counter this propaganda, the Army leaders now invited Monck to send three representatives or commissioners to London; he himself chose Cols Clobery and Knight, and allowed his officers to select Col Wilkes. Barwick was gratified that his good friend Col Clobery, now a committed Royalist, was given such an important post. The commissioners were stopped by Lambert in Yorkshire, but insisted that they were only to negotiate with Fleetwood. On their arrival in London on 12 November, they were subjected to the most persuasive proponents of the Army's cause. The key issue was the restoration of parliament, and the commissioners were soon persuaded by the Army leaders to concede that the General Council of the Army should exercise a veto over the constitution of the new parliament. Moreover, all the changes Monck had carried out to his officer corps during the autumn were called into question. Hesilrige and Ashley Cooper, strong opponents of the Army grandees, held a meeting with Monck's commissioners in the Fleece tavern in Covent Garden the next day, urging them to stand their ground, but they had already signed the agreement.

Fleetwood and Desborough immediately sent two of their own commissioners, Capts Wallington and Lloyd, north with the news. They were joined on their journey by Lambert's representative, Capt Cambridge. The three men arrived at Haddington, outside Edinburgh, on 18 November with a copy of the treaty that Monck's men had signed. Monck and his inner circle were very downcast on receiving the news, but the general swore to stick by his men if they would stand by him. They knew that they would not easily be forgiven by their counterparts in England for this display of disloyalty. Returning to Edinburgh the next day, Monck found his men full of indignation at the terms his representatives had agreed in London. This was exacerbated by the behaviour of Fleetwood's commissioners, who, despite Monck's efforts to prevent them, had been able to approach his troops. One of them was heard to proclaim, when passing in front of a company of infantry: 'My Lord Lambert is coming upon you, and all Monk's army will not be enough for breakfast for him.' But the soldiers refuted him. 'Lambert has a very good stomach this cold weather,' one remarked, 'if he can eat pikes and swallow bullets.'

Monck was anxious to play for time and avoid an open breach. He therefore sent messages to London that his representatives had misunderstood the message they were to deliver and were to receive fresh instructions. He was alarmed by the arrival of Lambert's superior forces at Newcastle on 23 November, where they were joined by a troop of deserters from among his own men, led by Capt Robinson. Monck's chaplain, Gumble, had kept his friend and leading Rumper Thomas Scot informed of events in Scotland. Anxious to reward the general for his support, Scot and his colleagues on the old Council of State, led by Hesilrige, had appointed him commander-in-chief of all forces in England and Scotland. He was to destroy the Rump's enemies, either in England or wherever they were to be found. But there was an important caveat: he was to be answerable to parliament, the nine members of the Council of State or a commission of five, comprising Hesilrige, Walton, Morley, Overton and himself.

These protracted negotiations increased pressure on Lambert, whose men were growing increasingly restless over lack of pay. Their commander, worried that Fleetwood and Desborough might do a deal with Monck behind his back, and nervous of the possibility of Fairfax declaring for the Rump, sent Col Zanchy to Berwick, where Monck had established his headquarters. He was well received, but this changed when news arrived on 7 December that Lambert, anxious to force the issue, had advanced to Chillingham Castle near the border. Preparing for combat, Monck arrested Zanchy and ordered his men to advance to Coldstream on the River Tweed, 'a place for good Christians to perish in', as his soldiers grumbled. The general then made a careful inspection of the fords across the river. The two opposing armies were of roughly equal strength, Monck commanding 6,000 infantry and 1,800 cavalry, while Lambert had 4,000 foot and 3,500 horse. The weather was very cold, hindering the chance of an attack by Lambert's men through the snow.

Monck had earned his troops' loyalty by his willingness to endure privation alongside them. Gumble described his headquarters at Coldstream:

The General's Palace was a little smoky cottage that had two great dunghills at the door; an hall or entry as dark and narrow as a man could not turn in it; the rooms were worse than I can describe; he ate and lodged in the same; and I think his secretary was his chamber-fellow, or else he must have lain upon the snow and ice: his bed was like a bird's nest, into which he was forced to creep; but yet it had so much state, as to have a canopy of boards over it: curtains and vallens were things never heard of in this place; and glass-windows were as precious as crystal at Edinburgh.

Price noted that the general's bed was so uncomfortable that he found him, on one occasion, asleep on two stools, his head resting on the side of the bed. The chapel at the headquarters was a cow-stall with dung up to the top of the men's boots. Despite the usual grumbling about the 'lean mutton and bad poultry', and beer 'accounted stale and only fit for officers', morale was high. With £20,000 in his war chest, Monck was confident that his men would receive adequate pay, and to encourage his troops he handed out promotions to key officers and men.

However, Monck was taking no chances and was determined to protect his rear before contemplating an invasion of England. The general had already summoned a meeting of commissioners from every shire and borough before leaving Edinburgh on 15 November, where their decision to elect as their president the Earl of Glencairn, leader of a Royalist rebellion against the Commonwealth five years earlier, was a sign of the strength of the Stuart cause among the Scots. Now Monck summoned them to a further meeting at Berwick on 12 December. The most important decision was how to secure his base. The general was nervous of leaving in his rear a substantial force of former opponents, commanded by officers with strong Royalist sympathies, but was prepared to authorise a few trustworthy noblemen and gentry to carry weapons, providing they took an oath that they would not act against the Commonwealth or 'in favour of Charles Stuart's interests'. In exchange Glencairn guaranteed that the assessment would be paid early, thus ensuring Monck's troops much needed revenue. But the general tactfully turned down an offer of active support when he entered England, stating privately: 'The Scots I dare not trust in any measure.'

More importantly, his fellow countrymen had come to detest their northern neighbours for their persistent intervention in England during the Civil Wars.

Having secured his base, Monck could concentrate on pressurising Lambert by securing allies in his rear. His excellent intelligence service meant that the general was kept abreast of events in London and in Ireland, where he was in contact with Lord Broghill, now President of the province of Munster, and the 'proud and avaricious' Sir Charles Coote, President of Connaught. Monck had also made contact with Fairfax, living quietly at Nun Appleton in Yorkshire. The former commander of the New Model Army had held aloof from politics throughout the 1650s, but had finally quarrelled with Cromwell when the Protector had arrested his son-in-law Buckingham in 1658. Despite efforts by the King to contact him via his nephew Sir Horatio Townshend, the old general had kept his counsel and had played no part in Booth's rising in August.

Maj Gen Thomas Morgan, second in command of the victorious English forces in Flanders, and now appointed deputy to Monck in Scotland, had come north to York, where he was being treated for gout by Dr John Troutbeck. The small, irascible Welshman who spoke 'as though he had been castrated' was an excellent soldier with a high regard for both Fairfax and Monck, under whom he had served in Scotland in the early 1650s. Lambert, realising his importance as an intermediary, came to see him in York. Morgan was instructed to go north to try and persuade Monck to avoid the coming conflict. Little did Lambert realise that Morgan had also been in communication with his old commander Fairfax. Having delivered Lambert's message to Monck, Morgan returned to York with a letter from Monck to Fairfax, vowing to restore parliament. According to his cousin Brian Fairfax, the old general 'approved of it, but added withall that if Generall Monk had any other designe than to restore Parliaments to Government Hee would Oppose him, but otherwise Hee would hartely Joyne with him'.

In addition, Edward Bowles, 'Lord Fairfax's Chaplain, Counsellor, and Agitator', insinuated that Fairfax would support the return of the secluded members, of which he was one. Monck, much encouraged by Fairfax's offer of support, sent Thomas Clarges, who had returned from London, down to York to coordinate plans for a rising. After consulting Buckingham, Maj Smithson, his nephew by marriage, and his former subordinate Col Hugh Bethell, Fairfax agreed to lead an insurrection in January. The veteran general was risking all in a confrontation with his former protégé and fellow Yorkshireman Lambert, and Col Robert Lilburne, who commanded a total of 12,000 men. But he needed to know exactly when Monck was making his move before raising his home county.

Fairfax's first messenger to Monck, Capt Bacon, was captured, but his cousin Brian Fairfax, disguised by Buckingham as a 'yong Contry clowne', made an epic ride across the fells of Westmorland and Cumberland, bluffing his way past Lambert's troopers. He reached Coldstream on Christmas Day and told Monck to take advantage, should Lambert's troops fall back into Yorkshire. Monck hastened to reassure him that he would watch his opponent as a cat watches a mouse. Fairfax made the hazardous return ride successfully, bringing heartening news that Lambert's men had decamped from Brampton when they heard that Fairfax was coming against them, 'for as Mr Bowles used to say of my Lord ff: hee was like a great Bull, long a raysing, but being up, he made a great noyse'.

With the Army split down the middle, it was vital to know where soldiers' allegiance lay. Fairfax was encouraged to hear that there were supporters of parliament in other parts of England: Col Nathaniel Whetham, Governor of Portsmouth and a Presbyterian friend of Monck's, Sir Arthur Hesilrige, and Cols Hacker and Rossiter in the Midlands, and Col Okey in London. But it was by no means certain, even with his great reputation, that Fairfax could secure Yorkshire. Col Overton, commanding the important garrison in Hull, had been approached but had been unwilling to commit his forces, and remained neutral, preferring to wait on events.

With little of the radical fervour that had inspired the original soldiers of the New Model Army, and a fear of renewed civil war, the decisive element in many troops' minds was their pay. Lambert's men had not been paid since they left London, and their morale was low. One of his soldiers put the case forcibly in a pamphlet to 'his loving fellow soldiers':

> Did not most of those officers (by God's mercy now cashiered the army) purchase your debentures (the price of blood) from two shillings to a noble in the pound to enrich themselves and perpetuate your slavery? And through their cruelty many of our fellow soldiers, who were wounded in battle and made unserviceable, with wives and children starved in the streets for want of bread, while they lorded over you tyrant like. Now examine yourselves whether when you have demanded your pay, you were not had before Court martials and hanged to all your shames, while they robbed you and the Commonwealth of your dues.

John Owen, a Puritan divine who had championed the Independent sects, urged Monck to maintain the unity of the Army in order to preserve the rule of the saints, even if this meant a military dictatorship. One of the few politicians still prepared to work with the Army leaders was Sir Henry Vane. Driven by his religious beliefs, he hoped that he could use the Army to inaugurate rule by a godly elect, 'an introduction to the glorious appearance of the kingdom of God'. Vane, however, was regarded with deep suspicion on all sides. His enemies saw his support of the Army as the best way to exert power, using the purported marriage of his son to Lambert's daughter as a means of cementing the alliance between the two men. In fact Vane was still searching for some constitutional support for Lambert's *coup d'état*. He spent hours in fruitless debate in November with Johnston of Wariston on who was eligible to vote for a non-existent parliament. It was to prove a fatal waste of time.

Hesilrige, together with Morley and Walton, entered Portsmouth on 3 December, where they were welcomed by Governor Whetham. The naval base, with its important arsenal, was an excellent point from which to defy the Army in London, and supporters from the southern counties were soon flocking to join Hesilrige. He had obtained private declarations of support from Sir Charles Coote in Ireland, Fairfax in Yorkshire and Vice Adm Lawson moored in the Thames, who offered to blockade London. The capital had a population of almost 400,000, ten times greater than any other city in England, and possessed a large percentage of its wealth. All factions agreed that whoever controlled London controlled the destiny of the nation and that it was the failure to recapture the capital that had ensured the ultimate defeat of Charles I in the First Civil War.

The Rumpers hoped to harness the dissatisfaction of Londoners with the Army to their own cause, but the political tide was flowing against them. It was the Royalists who were gaining in popularity as the group untainted by the political failures of recent years. During December the City showed its antipathy for the Commonwealth leaders, both civil and military, by electing a number of Royalists as aldermen. Numerous pamphlets appeared, voicing increasing disillusionment with the Government, out of touch with the needs of the population. As the *Unhappy Marksman* put it, the most pressing question was whether it could feed 'the poor people with bread and porridge'. The author launched into an attack on the arrogance and self-interest of the rulers, 'such as are resolved to raise themselves by the ruin of others, making religion a stalking horse to policy, and the people a stirrup to mount themselves into the saddle of their so much desired greatness, in these tottering, deplorable, groaning and rolling times'. A growing number of

Londoners were openly showing their dissent by singing the popular song, composed during the Civil War, 'When the King Enjoys His Own Again'. Whitelocke recorded the collapse of the Army's power as their support fell away: 'The King's party was very, very active and every man was guided by his own fancy and interest.'

On 2 December the Lord Mayor ordered a general fast, but this did little to deter the rising chorus of dissent. Samuel Pepys, clerk to George Downing, temporarily returned from his post as ambassador in the Hague, kept his kinsman Montagu, still in retirement at Hinchingbrooke in Huntingdonshire, informed of the news. He recorded fears in London of a projected rising when the impoverished apprentices, 'young men that were newly out of their times', hard hit by the slump in trade due to the political uncertainty, delivered their petition to the Lord Mayor on 5 December. They were resentful of the oppressive presence of large numbers of troops in the capital, and were encouraged to defy them, well aware that Lambert and the best soldiers had marched north to confront Monck. The apprentices' action was a deliberate affront to the Committee of Safety, which had banned all petitions, ironically the very means used by the Army to oust the Rump. Pepys's prognosis was correct: the discontent was too widespread to be contained. The day began ominously with shops shuttered and a large number of apprentices, scornful of 'the Committee of Shifty', milling around. When the sergeant-at-arms attempted to post a note forbidding petitions at the Exchange, the apprentices rioted.

Pepys gave a vivid impression of Londoners' hatred of the troops brought up to impose order. They were commanded by the one-eyed Col Hewson, a former cobbler, whose statue out of snow in St Paul's churchyard, with one eye and a halter round his neck, had attracted much ribaldry. Hewson was in no mood for such mockery and his men were unused to the way that they were treated by the apprentices, as Pepys recorded:

the souldiers as they marcht were hooted at all along the streets, and where any stragled from the whole body, the boys flung stones, tiles, turnups & c. at them with all the affronts they could give them; and when Huson came in the head of his Regiment they shouted all along a Cobler a Cobler; in some places the apprentices would gett a football (it being a hard frost) and drive it among the souldiers on purpose, and they either darst not (or prudently would not) interrupt them; in fine, many souldiers were hurt with stones, and one I see was very neare having his braines knockt out with a brick batt flung from the top of an house at him. On the other side, the souldiers proclaimed the proclamation against any subscripcions [petitions], which the boys shouted at with contempt, which some could not beare but lett fly theyr musquets and killed in severall places (whereof I see one in Cornhill shott through the head) 6 or 7 and severall wounded.

Hewson, enraged by the apprentices' cries of 'old blind cobbler', ordered the troops to fire into the crowd. The onlookers sullenly dispersed but, ominously for the soldiers, Pepys recorded the antipathy of the trained bands, the city militia brought in to support the regulars: 'Nothing passed between the souldiers and them but sowre looks.'

That evening Fleetwood agreed to withdraw his troops if the magistrates would do their best to restore order. Desborough, forceful as ever, knew only one way to act. He marched 'at the head of three companies of cavalry, with drawn swords and pistols in hand, went to the Mayor to request him to order the people to retire, which was immediately done'. Not surprisingly, this did little to diminish the widespread ill feeling of the citizens. On 6 December a Londoner recorded: 'The soldiers here are so vilified, scorned, and hissed that they are ashamed to march; and many officers when they go into the City dare not even wear their swords for fear of affronts; and thus God hath blasted them and they are become vile in the eyes of the people.' An inquest was held on the events of 3 December, with the verdict that Hewson and his soldiers were guilty of murder.

In the face of this hostility, the General Council of Officers resolved on 10 December that a new parliament was to be summoned before February. Ludlow had left his post as commander-in-chief in Ireland to try to arbitrate between the Rump and the Army, and to reconcile Vane with Hesilrige. But his recording how the Council insisted 'that the army should not be diminished, their conduct altered, nor their pay lessened without the consent of the major part of the Conservators', whom they were to choose, reinforced the view that the Army was only really interested in self-preservation. Civilian pressure on the military continued to mount, with the circulation of more petitions, and rumours that the troops guarding the City were accumulating 'guns, bombs and other artificial fires'. In fact, they were making a last-ditch attempt to retain control as law and order seemed to be at the point of collapse. Hesilrige had left his able colleague Ashley Cooper in charge of the Rump's cause in London. He was already renowned for his political skill and, although few could read him, he was marked out as a man of the future. Ashley Cooper was hard at work trying to turn the soldiers in the capital against their commanding officers. Ludlow mistrusted his 'smooth tongue and insinuating carriage', but there was no denying his energy in maintaining 'a great correspondence and interest with the inferior officers and common soldiers of every troop and company'.

John Evelyn had already unsuccessfully attempted to persuade Col Morley, Lieutenant-Governor of the Tower of London, to declare for the King. Morley preferred, however, to join Hesilrige in Portsmouth. His replacement, Lt Fitch, proved equally suspect and, on 12 December, Desborough only just managed to prevent him from handing over the Tower to troops led by Col Okey, who was in collaboration with Scot and Ashley Cooper. Montagu had been summoned to appear before the General Council of Officers and, fearful of the consequences, was planning to move his possessions out of his lodgings in Whitehall.

Ashley Cooper, with an eye to the main chance, was preparing to move in, but Montagu, who had been alerted by Pepys's letters to the grave problems of the Government, gave an indeterminate answer to the summons and delayed his move.

Following a letter from the senior naval officers to Monck in November, the Army grandees invited representatives of the English, Scottish and Irish navies to come to London to help to draw up a new constitution and summon parliament. Lawson, however, who had heard of the Rump's control of Portsmouth, the chief naval base in southern England, from his friend Col Rich, who controlled the troops in the town, turned down the invitation, as did Montagu, still in retirement in the country. On 9 December the vice-admiral informed Fleetwood that he ought to recall the Rump. Four days later, having given refuge to Scot and Okey, both men wanted by the Army for their part in the attempt to seize the Tower, Lawson sent a letter to the Lord Mayor, aldermen and councillors of the City of London from his flagship anchored at the mouth of the Thames, demanding the restoration of the Rump. His proclamation also included a far-ranging programme of social reforms, including an indemnity, religious freedom, the abolition of tithes, legal reform, encouragement of trade, relief for the poor and unemployed, and the end of pressing men. Despite their wish to secure him as an ally, Lawson's radical agenda and his known republicanism received a cold reception from the City, many of whose aldermen were Royalists. Undaunted, the vice-admiral prepared to set sail up the Thames.

The Committee of Safety realised that Lawson's move was more serious than either the opposition of Monck or the defection of the Portsmouth garrison. If his twenty-two ships decided to blockade the Thames, either London would be starved into surrender, or the populace, as the apprentices had shown barely a week earlier, would rise in revolt. In Hyde's eloquent phrase, it was Lawson's action that 'brake the heart of the Committee of Safety'. Sir Henry Vane, known for his persuasiveness, and Maj Richard Salwey were dispatched forthwith to try to win the admiral over. They boarded the *Bristol* at Tilbury on 17 December and sailed downstream, but were dismayed to find Scot and Okey on board Lawson's flagship, both of whom urged the vice-admiral to arrest the two newcomers.

Vane was anxious for Lawson to keep the fleet at anchor while a decision was reached; but the vice-admiral was determined to sail on, so the two sides had no option but to engage in debate on board as he sailed upriver. Vane argued that a parliament called by the Committee of Safety would be better able to serve England than the Rump, but Lawson was adamant that it would be no more than a puppet of the military, 'who have nothing to do with giving laws to the nation'. This 'sham-Parliament' would be 'a mask to the army's tyranny'. His officers were unanimous in offering their support to the Rump. A dejected Vane returned to a London rife with rumours of plots and talk of insurrection. A number of arrests were made, but feeling continued to rise against the Army. 'The Final Protest and Sense of the City', a petition, accused the Army of using the threat of Royalist conspiracies as an excuse that suspected Cavaliers' houses 'must be searched and disarmed, and their throats cut, to preserve the City'. Royalist ex-soldiers were to be spared, but their officers were to be shown no mercy.

Meanwhile, on 16 December, a deputation from the Rump led by Ashley Cooper went to see Fleetwood with 'The Remonstrance and Protestation of the Well-Affected People of the Cities of London and Westminster, and Other the Cities and Places within the Commonwealth of England', signed by 450 notables, including Monck, Fairfax, Lawson, and the Lord Mayor and Council of London. They immediately confronted the general 'with the breach of faith to the parliament, from whom you received your commission; with the ruin you have brought upon your native country; and with the misery you have led the poor soldiers into who, instead of being the instruments of receiving and settling the peace and liberty of these nations, enjoying the honour and quiet thereof, their arrears fully paid, future pay and advancement settled and established in order and with the blessing of their countrymen, are now become the instruments of 9 men's [the Council of State] ambition'. The 'Remonstrance' contrasted Fleetwood's abuse of 'all laws and privileges' with Monck, whom it regarded as a divinely sent deliverer.

Three days before this dramatic meeting, the Rump's allies in the Irish army had seized Dublin Castle and arrested Ludlow's deputy, Col John Jones, a strong supporter of the Army leaders in London. He was replaced by Sir Hardress Waller, a Republican and a regicide, who immediately issued a declaration in favour of the restoration of the Rump, and sent letters of support to Monck, Hesilrige and Lawson. The two dominant characters in the rising outside Dublin were Broghill and Coote. Although rivals, they were united by their hatred of Ludlow, absent in England. As a measure of the complexity of the situation, both men were already in secret communication with the Royalists but declared publicly for Monck. The Rump, anxious to retain their loyalty, hastened to send them a letter of congratulation. Ludlow himself, hearing that Ireland had declared for parliament, hastened back to find that the new leaders of the Irish army had voted not to allow his return unless his command was approved by parliament.

Even at this late stage, with the Government visibly collapsing, the Royalists mounted no proper challenge. Despite overtures to all the main players, Charles had failed to elicit public offers of support from major military or political figures, such as Hesilrige, Lambert or Vane, all staunch Republicans. Fairfax and Monck had failed to respond to various messages from the King. And yet, the Royalist cause continued to prosper as people contrasted it with the Government's moral and political bankruptcy. As Hyde had predicted, the strength of the tradition that the King stood for would ultimately triumph, but only when England had exhausted all other constitutional possibilities. Samuel Tuke, writing to his sovereign, gave a succinct analysis of the situation: 'The King's friends, fearing the consequences of a conquest by foreigners, generally desire his restoration by a Parliament, which is certain if they may vote with freedom. Though Presbyterians for their own security may desire to limit his powers, Royalists believe they will find that their own preservation depends upon the strength of his prerogative. Therefore believes that the King must wait for the Parliament, unless he has substantial aid from abroad.'

Tuke's acute assessment of the political situation was of little immediate use to Charles, who remained detached from events across the Channel as he travelled north through France in leisurely fashion during November. Hyde, watching events in trepidation in Brussels, anxiously awaited the arrival of the King. Charles, however, was making amends for years of disagreement with his mother. He arrived at Colombes, outside Paris, on 5 December, where Henrietta Maria was residing with her youngest daughter, Henrietta Anne. The King was pleased to be reunited with his family, as Sir George Carteret, who had fought so hard to maintain the Royalist cause from his home in Jersey, recorded: 'All unkindnesses are forgotten between the mother and the son, and I hope that goodwill go through all the royal family.' Although he was pleased to see his mother, Charles was even more delighted at meeting once again with his sister, whom he had not seen for five years, and who had now been transformed into a charming and gifted 15-year-old. Henrietta Anne, whom he nicknamed Minette, had captivated all at the French Court with her gaiety, elegance and intelligence. Her older brother, touched at the hero-worship with which he was treated, was so smitten that he could hardly bear for Minette to be out of his sight. The fortnight they spent together was to form the basis of a lifelong love. But the pressure of events meant that he was unable to tarry longer and he left for Brussels before Christmas.

Meanwhile, Charles's supporters had been active in London but an attempted Cavalier rising on the night of 18 December suffered the same fate as so many of its predecessors, as *Mercurius Politicus* reported:

This night discovery being made of a design which the Cavaliers had to rise this night, and of places where many of them were to meet, search was made accordingly; and at the White-horse near Moorgate (whereabout a strong party of horse was appointed to embody) about twenty horse, with warlike furniture in the stable were surprised, and made prize by the soldiery; and fourteen gentlemen, ready armed, back, breast and head-pieces, were taken; the number had been far greater, had not the soldiery come so soon. Also at the Golden Griffin in Shearlane ten more in arms were taken; and in Temple Garden were more, many of which had run away upon hearing the discovery; only six remained behind, and were apprehended, having newly put off their arms, and hid them in the garden among the bushes. In Thames Street, about the Three Cranes, a great company of foot were to gather, of which eighty met, but escaped all save two, who are in custody, and give an account of the intent of the rest. Divers others were met in the streets in small companies, and pickt up as they were going to their confederates. Towards morning intelligence being brought, that a number of them were drawn forth in equipage in Greenwich Park, under one Col. Culpeper a Kentish man, a party of horse was immediately sent thither; which the Cavaliers (being about eighty horse) having notice of, immediately fled, and only one Mr. Dancer, a cornet, was taken.

Despite the failure of the Royalist rising, opposition to the Government was gathering strength, although it was by no means united. On 21 December news came that the troops sent to Portsmouth had deserted and joined the Rumpers marching on London. The City, with its financial and political muscle, was assuming an increasingly important political role. Twenty-one of Lawson's captains had delivered a second letter to the Common Council, reiterating the admiral's earlier demands, and Lawson had followed this up by insisting that the Rump be recalled, and demanding that the City leaders disavow the King. This the Council refused to do, sending commissioners instead to confer with Hesilrige,

Morley and Lawson regarding the calling of a free parliament, i.e. one hostile to the Rump. The general discontent had spread throughout England. Sir Henry Yelverton in Northampton and Sir John Boys in Kent were preparing for action. Maj Robert Huntingdon was at the head of 1,200 men in Oxfordshire, but had not declared his allegiance.

Fleetwood needed to take decisive action if his position in London was not to become untenable. Bulstrode Whitelocke, who had supported the Army's coup in October and had been appointed keeper of the Great Seal, was approached by Lord Willoughby of Parham and Maj Gen Browne, two leading Presbyterians turned Royalists, and agreed to try to bring Fleetwood over. On 22 December Whitelocke urged Fleetwood either to go to the Tower in person and rally the troops who would be needed to confront the six regiments of trained bands called out by the City Council, or, failing that, to send Whitelocke himself across the Channel to negotiate with the King. Fleetwood agreed to the latter course, after much praying on his knees, only to change his mind when Vane, who had appeared with Desborough and Berry, persuaded the vacillating general to delay taking a decision until he had consulted Lambert. Lamenting to Whitelocke, 'I cannot do it, I cannot do it', Fleetwood acknowledged his defeat. Brodrick wrote dismissively to Hyde: 'Fleetwood weeps and prays, prays and weeps again.'

The next day the Council of Officers dissolved itself. On Christmas Eve, a general rendezvous was held in Lincoln's Inn Fields, where the troops were reviewed by Cols Alured and Okey, both firm supporters of the Rump. The same men who had participated in the ousting of the Rump just two months earlier now proclaimed their resolve 'to live and die with the Parliament', as *Mercurius Politicus* reported. 'After this,' the writer continued, 'they marched in good order down Chancery-lane; at the Speaker's [William Lenthall, Speaker of the Long Parliament since 1641] door they made a stand, and several of the principal commanders sending in word that they attended to know his pleasure, his lordship came down to them in his gown to the gate in the street, where standing, the officers as they passed with the forces made speeches to him, signifying in the name of themselves and the whole soldiery, their hearty sorrow for the great defection in this late interruption, with their absolute purpose of a firm adherence in the future.' There could be no argument with this emphatic restoration of the old order. On the evening of Boxing Day, Lenthall led a quorum of forty members of the Rump from Whitehall to Westminster, and entered the House of Commons by torchlight, applauded by scattered groups of soldiers.

Fleetwood bowed to the inevitable and resigned, uttering the memorable words: 'The Lord had blasted their counsels and spit in their faces.' Johnston of Wariston, who had lost his position as President of the Council of State, was equally bitter, lamenting in his diary: 'And hereupon some heavy, bitter words of my wifes to me for my meddling with this Committee, and my passionate repart[ee] that I found her often a miserable comforter to me in the day of my calamity; my heart was like to break and burst with grief and anguish.' Maj Miller, Governor of the Tower, offered his submission to the Rump. Col Richard Ingoldsby approached Whitelocke and urged him to deliver the Great Seal to the King, but the veteran Parliamentarian, despite his recent attempt to persuade Fleetwood to send him as an emissary to Brussels, refused. Instead, fearing vengeance from his former colleagues in the Rump who accused him of being a turncoat, he burnt his papers, put on a disguise and slipped out of the capital on 30 December.

Desborough, the toughest of the generals, remained defiant and left London, hoping to join Lambert in the north. But his colleague, isolated in Northumberland, faced equally severe problems. His men, worried by the chaotic news from the south, and unpaid, had shown little inclination to march through the snow to confront Monck's troops at Coldstream. They were also extremely unpopular for insisting on taking 'free quarters' wherever they were based. Hearing of the restoration of the Rump, and that Fairfax was preparing a rising in Yorkshire, Lambert turned south, hoping to assist his lieutenant Lilburne, sending ahead instructions that he was to dispatch 500 picked cavalry to seize Fairfax and secure York. Fairfax, however, in the words of Monck's chaplain Price, 'was too politick to be napping', and escaped to Selby, where he decided to bring forward the date of the rising. He was a sick man, suffering acutely from gout and the stone, but he dared not stay at Nun Appleton; jolting in his coach through deep snow, he avoided Lilburne's troops and reached Arthington, where he took to his bed. Still determined to avoid capture, Fairfax was greatly heartened by the arrival of an Irish officer offering the service of 1,200 men sent over the previous summer by Ludlow to help suppress Booth's Rebellion. They were heading for Marston Moor, scene of Fairfax and Cromwell's famous victory in 1644, where they would receive the general's orders.

9

MONCK'S MARCH ON LONDON

A brilliant frost covered the village of Coldstream, perched on the Scottish bank of the River Tweed, on the morning of New Year's Day 1660, as the 6,000 troops stationed in the vicinity prepared to move out. Under the watchful eye of their general, George Monck, his seasoned soldiers descended the gentle slope to the water's edge and waded into the water. John Price was impressed at the stalwart way in which they faced the icy current, happy to endure hardship in order to regain a foothold on English soil. 'The frost was great,' he recorded, 'and the snow greater; and I do not remember that we ever trod upon plain earth from Edinburgh to London. The air this day was so very clear too, that we could distinguish the very colours of the pebbles of the Tweed.'

Monck was leading his troops south in defiance of 'that intolerable slavery of a sword government' in order to reinstate parliament. To counter Lambert's superiority in numbers, Monck had increased the number of pikemen and turned many of his dragoons into cavalry, but his caution proved unnecessary; the opposition, underpaid and underfed, were deserting daily. The morale of those facing Monck on the border was further undermined when they received a letter from Speaker Lenthall commanding them to disband. Lambert himself had turned south to meet the threat posed by Fairfax in his rear, abandoning his headquarters at Newcastle to Monck's colleague Col Knight. Lambert tried to keep his supporters together but, by the time he reached Northallerton, he was accompanied by no more than fifty horsemen. Thomas Gumble, although impressed by Lambert's personal qualities, summed up why he had failed: 'He was a person of great parts & good courage, as fit for the Protectorship as Oliver, & some think fitter, but that foolish comedy was not to be acted upon again.'

In contrast to numerous invasions from Scotland during the Civil Wars, Monck was leading an English army of occupation home. His veterans of the New Model Army were used to physical hardship and waded confidently through snowdrifts up to their knees. At Wooler in Northumberland, their first halting-place, they were confronted by a messenger bearing a letter from Lenthall informing them that parliament had been reinstated. In contrast to the Speaker's instructions to Lambert to disband, the letter suggested that Monck proceed southwards with a reduced force of 500 men, rather than a force of almost 6,000. But, unlike Lambert's ill-disciplined troops, these hardened and well-paid soldiers had no intention of disbanding. After the contents had been read out at the head of each regiment, the men were unanimous in their desire to continue their march towards London. Two days later, Monck was greeted at Morpeth by William Man, sword-bearer of the City of London, bearing a declaration in favour of readmitting the secluded members who were bitter opponents of the Rump. Monck gave an equivocal answer to the declaration, unwilling to commit himself until he had gauged the mood of the civilian population. When Man returned to London, he was accompanied by Gumble, with letters from his commander asserting his loyalty to the recently restored parliament and the Council of State. Meanwhile, the general continued his steady march south, greeted with great enthusiasm at Newcastle and Durham, where his non-committal reply to every question about his intentions was that 'his endeavour should never be wanting for the good and welfare of his country'.

Further south, Fairfax, marching via Marston Moor, reached the city of York on New Year's Day. Col Lilburne, defending the city, offered free entry to anyone who would subscribe to a declaration for the Rump and against 'a King or any Single Person whatsoever'. Many of the soldiers from the Irish army under Fairfax's command were happy to comply, but the general refused, tearing up the declaration as soon as he had read it, and remained outside the walls. For a moment it appeared that the two sides would come to blows. Fairfax 'went to the head of his troops', in the words of his cousin Brian, and seemed to become 'another man, his motions so quick, his eyes so sparkling, giving the word of command like a general'. Next morning, however, when reinforcements appeared, Lilburne accepted the inevitable and opened the gates. He realised that he could expect no help from Lambert, who had slipped away south, sending a submissive letter to parliament.

The situation in London at the beginning of the year was one of utter confusion. On 1 January 1660 Samuel Pepys began his secret diary. Walking about the busy streets of London, complaining of the cold and his swollen nose, Pepys tried to make sense of the political situation. His entry for 4 January recorded: 'Strange, the difference of men's talk: some say that Lambert must of necessity give up; others, that he is very strong.' But the very next day he was speculating on the lodgings in Whitehall to be provided for Lambert's enemy Monck when he arrived in the capital. The astute Francesco Giavarina was equally in the dark. His weekly report to the Venetian government, trying to keep abreast of the chaotic political developments, had predicted 'terrible and tragic change' as the likelihood of a renewed civil war grew stronger. On 6 January he wrote: 'Everything is uncertain, in this inconstant country, which must amaze the world by the extraordinary things which are seen here daily.'

Pepys and Giavarina, like so many others, were bewildered by the propaganda war being waged in an ever-growing number of unlicensed tracts and broadsides. Pepys, always anxious for the most up-to-date information, met Henry Muddiman, Monck's most effective propagandist, on 9 January, and retired with him to discuss the situation over a cup of coffee, the fashionable drink that had just been introduced to England. Their chosen venue, the Turk's Head coffee shop in New Palace Yard, was the home of the short-lived Rota Club, devoted to discussions of political theory. The founder of the Rota was Sir James Harrington, whose radical book *Oceana* had been much discussed.

Meanwhile, Gumble had arrived in London and immediately met
Lenthall, who invited him to address parliament so that the Rump could
ascertain Monck's intentions. With considerable boldness Gumble
expressed his commander's sincere hope that they would approve of his
actions, particularly cashiering troublesome officers 'to put some stop to
their haste in their remodelling of the army with persons who had been
confederates of Lambert and Fleetwood'. The Rumpers were little
reassured by the confidence of Gumble's tone and he was summoned to
explain himself by the Council of State later the same night. The
chaplain, however, stood his ground and refused to accept the Council's
assertion 'that General Monck was for the King', answering that this was
merely 'a suggestion of their own fears and jealousies'.

Although the Rumpers had failed to bring Gumble to heel, they
realised that they were in no position to antagonise Monck, who was
elected to the Council of State on 2 January and a recommendation was
made to the provost and fellows of Eton College to elect Gumble to the
first vacant fellowship. Gumble, however, was cautious over the extent of
the Rump's support for Monck; his conclusion was: 'Do not trust to those
persons with whom you correspond; in the times of danger, to provide
security for themselves, many have kept a secret correspondence with your
enemies. The prevailing and governing influence in the Parliament is
reduced into the hands of a few and inconsiderable persons – either hare-
brained and hot-headed fools, or obscure and disregarded knaves. . . .
Besides, these scraps of a Parliament are much divided among themselves.
. . . But you must keep your forces near you, or else you are in great
danger.' Gumble understood that the Rump's distrust of Monck's
intentions would resurface once the military threat had disappeared.

Lawson, whose support for the Rump had proved so critical in
December, was also elected to the Council of State, given a vote of thanks
by parliament, awarded land worth £500 and offered Lambert's quarters
in Whitehall. But there was again a suspicion that the Rump wanted to
curb his power. Pepys noted in his diary, 'a picture hung up at the

Exchange, of a great pair of buttocks shitting of a turd into Lawson's mouth, and over it was writ "The thanks of the House"'.

The Rumpers wanted to widen their basis of support by utilising the civilian population's hatred of the military, and to punish those who had expelled them in October. The generals offered little resistance. Fleetwood was a broken man, sitting 'peaking in his chamber at Wallingford House, as if it were moulting-time', as Samuel Morland recorded. Lambert had been deserted by his troops on his march south, and had sent his submission to parliament on 4 January, but a motion was passed debarring him from the capital. Desborough had left London and was in hiding. Maj Salwey spent four days in the Tower before being expelled from London after making an abject apology for his misdemeanours, 'his tears, sighs, supplications, confessions of all secret practices, and humbling his mouth in the dust, mitigating in some measure his eager prosecution', as Brodrick reported with considerable satisfaction to Hyde. Hesilrige, Walton and Morley, appointed Governor of the Tower, who had all returned to London from Portsmouth, had been given the key job of appointing officers, and were soon busy cashiering those suspected of disloyalty. They were joined by Ashley Cooper, as Mordaunt recorded: 'Cooper yet hath his tongue well hung and works at will, and employs his rhetoric to cashier all officers, civil as well as military, that sided with Fleetwood and Lambert.' As a reward for his efforts, Ashley Cooper was entrusted with command of Fleetwood's regiment of horse. Other loyalists such as Cols Howard and Ingoldsby, who had seized Windsor Castle, were similarly rewarded.

Not content with punishing the soldiers who had ousted them, the 'hare-brained and hot-headed fools' in the Rump were determined to take revenge on their former colleagues who had supported the Army. Sir Henry Vane was dismissed from parliament on 9 January and ordered to retire to his home at Raby. Bulstrode Whitelocke, still keeper of the Great Seal, who was in hiding, heard that Scot had issued a threat: 'that I should be hanged with the great seal about my neck'. Meanwhile, parliament was busy passing acts that would ensure that it maintained its status as the sole constitutional authority in England. As sitting members of the House of Commons, the Rumpers had the legal right to raise taxes, which they contrasted with the blatant illegality of the Army's efforts since Lambert's coup in October. They further undermined the Army's position by asserting the right to appoint officers to the militia, which they intended to replace the costly and unpopular standing army, and dismissed John Ireland and Sir Robert Tichborne, both regarded as extreme members of the New Model Army.

Outside the capital, however, it was apparent that the Rump was just as unpopular as the Army. The political confusion of the previous nine months since the fall of the Protectorate meant that there was a growing desire for change. Hull, Plymouth, Portsmouth and other towns declared for a free parliament or for the return of the secluded members. Northumberland and Newcastle were now controlled by Sir William Fenwick and Allison, both secluded members. For the moment, however, the Rump leaders felt strong enough to resist declarations or petitions for a free parliament, and individuals such as Sir Robert Pye, former colonel in the New Model Army, who had the temerity to present one, were dispatched forthwith to the Tower. The London lodgings of Montagu, still living in Huntingdonshire but thought to be in communication with the King, were thoroughly searched once more. Loyalty to the regime was rigorously enforced. A measure was passed that all those eligible to sit on the Council of State or in Parliament must swear an oath 'to renounce the pretended title or titles of Charles Stuart'. But so many members objected that, after protracted discussion, the Commons agreed on a simpler oath of fidelity to the Commonwealth, omitting any mention of the King.

The fundamental weakness in the Rump's position was the chronic shortage of money. With income from taxes much reduced, the City's financial importance increased as a source of loans. Although the Lord Mayor was authorised to seize 'treasonable, seditious, and scandalous papers and pamphlets', no action was taken against a City committee demanding free elections to parliament. Royalists were encouraged by the Rump's leniency to the City and by the appointment of Aldermen Wale and Robinson, known for their Royalist sympathies, to the militia. In December Evelyn had urged Col Morley to hand over the Tower. Now he tried again, writing to him on 12 January, and adding a note that Morley 'was absolute master of the city, there being very few of the rebel army any way near it, save at Somerset House a trifling garrison'. But the colonel proved 'wavering and so irresolute' that the chance was lost. De Vaux, one of Mazarin's ministers, writing to his agent du Chastel in London, delivered a more measured and objective verdict on the chaotic political developments of the past few months: 'The existing Parliament is convoked in opposition to all the laws of England. . . . The late sources of revenue are exhausted, commerce ruined, and new taxes not to be thought of. . . . [There is] weariness of the constant changes; a monarchy is most in keeping with the genius and laws of the English.'

In Ireland, Ludlow had failed to reassert his authority and had barely escaped arrest by soldiers formerly under his command. He had retreated to the fort at Duncannon, the only part of the country still loyal to the English Army. A vote of high treason was taken by the Rump against him and Ludlow returned to London to face his accusers. He was in no mood to submit tamely, writing with great bitterness: 'The Irish officers presented him [Monck] with a pair of spurs, and a hilt of a sword, together with a rich hatband and an embroidered belt, to manifest their acknowledgement and acceptance of his good service in betraying the public cause.' The commissioners who had taken over from Ludlow were, however, divided. Sir Hardress Waller was a strong supporter of the Rump, while Sir Charles Coote and Lord Broghill were now in contact with the King.

The exiled Court in Brussels found it almost impossible to keep up with the rapidly changing situation. The King arrived back from his travels in France at the end of December to find that even the perspicacious Hyde, on whom Charles relied so heavily, was unable to guess Monck's intentions. The Chancellor had little sympathy for the general, despising his early career as a mercenary on the Continent, practising 'that devouring profession', and his decision to change sides in 1646. Hyde was deeply unhappy that the destiny of the Royalist cause lay in the hands of a man he regarded as uncouth and untrustworthy, and expressed his anguish in a letter to Sir Henry Bennet: 'I believe if you did, at this instant, receive twenty letters from London of the same date with our last, you would receive so many several opinions of the state of affairs there . . . and it was never harder for me to make a judgement of the state there than now.' His agents in England were equally confused. 'Monck is so dark a man,' Mordaunt observed, 'no perspective can looke through him, and it will be like the last sceane of some excellent play, which the most juditious cannot positively say how it will end.'

Ormonde was clearer sighted and expressed his hopes in a letter to Henrietta Maria's favourite, and possible lover, Lord Jermyn in Paris:

> Though the submission to the parliament [Rump] seems universal and hearty in all those that have any military or civil authority in the three kingdoms; and though I conceive the appearance of its being so, and the drawing of the Army towards London, reason enough to stop the King if he were ready to embark with a force that a month since in the judgement of all men would have done his work; yet you may take it for a certain truth, that many of those who pretended to secure places for the parliament, and possessed themselves accordingly of them, did it with a purpose of making use of them in the end to the King's advantage, if the contest had been kept up a little longer. Of this we have good evidence, besides the known inclination of many of the persons that acted.

The leading Royalists' doubts about Monck were part of the widespread confusion over which members of the Commonwealth they could

Oliver Cromwell. *(By kind permission of the Duke of Grafton)*

Richard Cromwell by an unknown artist.
(National Portrait Gallery, London)

John Lambert by an unknown artist.
(National Portrait Gallery, London)

Thomas Fairfax, 3rd Baron Fairfax of Cameron by
William Faithorne. *(National Portrait Gallery,
London)*

Charles Fleetwood by Jacobus Houbraken.
(National Portrait Gallery, London)

George Monck, 1st Duke of Albemarle by
David Loggan. *(National Portrait Gallery,
London)*

Edward Montagu, 1st Earl of Sandwich by an unknown artist. *(National Portrait Gallery, London)*

Sir Arthur Hesilrige by an unknown artist. *(National Portrait Gallery, London)*

Charles II by Philippe de Champaigne. (*By kind permission of the Duke of Grafton*)

Edward Hyde, 1st Earl of Clarendon by David Loggan. *(National Portrait Gallery, London)*

James Butler, Duke of Ormonde by Sir Peter Lely.
(By kind permission of the Duke of Grafton)

Cornelius Johnson's depiction of the ball at the Hague the night before Charles II's departure for England. Charles II is dancing with his sister Mary, Princess of Orange. *(By kind permission of the Duke of Grafton)*

Barbara Villiers, Duchess of Cleveland holding the infant 1st Duke of Grafton by Sir Peter Lely. *(By kind permission of the Duke of Grafton)*

Charles II by Sir Peter Lely. *(By kind permission of the Duke of Grafton)*

trust. Letters were frequently intercepted. The Government was increasingly anxious to prevent Royalists entering England. Dr Richard Allestree, who had been negotiating with Col Clobery, a close associate of Monck, was arrested at Dover on his return from Brussels. Fortunately, he managed to conceal the letters he was carrying from the King. The zealous Col John Dixon sent an account to the Council of State on 19 January: 'Two gentlemen landed at Dover from Ostend; believes they are persons of quality though they pretend to be merchants. Amongst their luggage were maps of Kent and other counties, and geometrical instruments. Has placed them in this castle. If they are to be sent up asks for a party of horse to send with them and that Charles Stuart's chaplain and another detained here be included in the order. The flocking over of those dangerous persons indicates a sudden design. None will pass this port.'

There is no record of Charles's reaction when he heard of Monck's advance, but he must have appreciated the irony of looking to Scotland for his deliverance. His Scottish expedition of 1650–1, shortly after his father's execution, had been a disaster. Although he had been crowned King at Scone, the invading army he led into England had been utterly defeated by Cromwell at the battle of Worcester. Nevertheless, the King had learnt from his experiences in Scotland and his mood of self-controlled detachment was ideally suited to coping with the rapidly changing situation developing on the mainland.

News spread across England that Monck had dined privately with Fairfax on his arrival at York on 11 January. It was widely felt, in the words of one Gower, that Fairfax had an unique opportunity, not only 'to make himself great, and the nation quiet by a free Parliament; it is most certain he might have done what he list; Lambert's army disbanded and melted, only by the fame of his rising.' But the older general felt that he had done his part in overthrowing Lambert and preferred to retire again to Nun Appleton, although he dined privately with Monck on several occasions during the four days the younger commander spent in York. It was later claimed that Fairfax urged Monck to declare for the King, but it seems more likely that he tried to persuade him to support a free parliament, where Englishmen would once again be able to choose who was to govern them.

The Rump Parliament, concerned at the meeting of the two generals, dispatched two commissioners, Thomas Scot and Luke Robinson, to monitor Monck's movements, the former an acknowledged regicide, and therefore bitterly opposed to a return of the monarchy. On 16 January Monck headed south, having sent back to Scotland Col Clarke's regiment of foot and Maj Gen Morgan's regiment of horse, some 1,500 men. It was vital to secure his rear, in case of the need to retreat, and Monck had absolute confidence in Morgan. Gumble gave his master's verdict: 'This little man', he wrote, 'is of more worth at that time than the seventeen score officers who had deserted the service.' A further infantry regiment under Col Charles Fairfax was left behind to garrison York and keep watch on Overton in Hull. The troops left behind in the north also showed that Monck was leading a respectable, but not too threatening, force of 4,000 foot and 1,800 horse, towards London. Unlike the previous autumn in Scotland, when Monck had allowed his men to discuss the political situation and whether they should support parliament against the Army, there were now no meetings. Discipline was rigorously enforced, the men following the orders of their general. But the enthusiastic welcome they received from every town and village they passed through helped to maintain their high morale.

On 18 January Monck met Gumble, returning from London, at Mansfield. He reported his meetings with leading figures in parliament and the City, who had indicated their support for the general. The same day in Westminster the Rump were holding a heated debate over the vexed question of whether to abjure Charles Stuart. The fact that such a staunch Republican body was in disagreement was a sure sign that change was in the air. One of the leading members unwilling to take the oath was Ashley Cooper, who thus demonstrated his disagreement with Hesilrige, as Mordaunt noted. It seems that he now favoured the return of the secluded members.

The following day Clarges arrived in Nottingham to greet Monck with news from the capital. In Clarges's opinion, despite the growing calls for free elections to parliament, a large number of the lower orders still favoured Lambert, now back in London. More importantly, Clarges had used his friendship with Quartermaster Gen Butler to procure a list of the troops stationed in and around London, and where they were quartered. Of the senior officers commanding a total of 8,000 infantry and 2,000 horse, just three colonels, Ashley Cooper, Morley and Fagg, were likely supporters; the rest were almost certainly hostile. Clarges advised Monck: 'Except you can get all these horse and foot out of London, and disperse them into several quarters, you can never expect to do any good for your country. Your best way will be to write a letter to the Parliament to this purpose – that you conceive it not for their service that those soldiers now in London, lately in rebellion against them, should mingle with your approved faithful regiments, till their officers have by discipline reduced them to a more assured obedience.' Monck agreed with this cogent advice, but, until they were nearer the capital, there was to be no mention of this key issue.

The next day saw the arrival at Leicester of Scot and Robinson, the parliamentary commissioners. The general greeted them with the greatest respect, dismounting from his horse in order to join them in their carriage, and ordering his troops to fire a volley in their honour. Scot was reassured by Monck's bland protestations of loyalty. The general was adept at turning aside any awkward questions. On being asked whether he would take an oath abjuring the monarchy, Monck, on Clarges's advice, tactfully replied that he would defer taking any decision until he had reached London, when he could judge the arguments of both sides. The commissioners never left the general's side, sharing his lodgings and his meals, and even, according to Price, boring holes in the walls of his room to spy on him. They were, however, alarmed at the way that his march had now acquired the aspect of a triumphal progress, 'exalted to the skies', in the words of Giavarina, and greeted everywhere with applause and the peeling of bells.

Monck was bombarded with letters and petitions, expressing disgust with the present regime and demanding a free parliament. But his response was muted, 'consisting in a nod, a frown, or the rubbing of his forehead if the speech were too long', in the words of one observer. The general's words were equally obtuse, stressing, 'I am but a servant to the Parliament in a military capacity, and these things, of great and civil concernment, must be left to the judgement of the Parliament.' Despite his recent meetings with Fairfax, Monck gave no indication of support to a declaration from Yorkshire, signed by the most influential gentry, including Fairfax, the High Sheriff and the Lord Mayor of York, demanding the readmission of the secluded members, and threatening to refuse to pay their taxes if they were to be denied their fundamental rights as Englishmen and to be forbidden elected representatives.

The general's response was still less favourable to declarations that appeared to be overtly Royalist. A letter from the gentlemen of Devon, Monck's home county, stressed that, 'since the death of the King, we have been governed by tumult; bandied from one faction to the other; this party up today, that to-morrow – but still the nation under, and a prey to the strongest.' Monck's reply contained a stern injunction that 'Monarchy cannot possibly be admitted for the future in these nations, because its support is taken away', that the admittance of the secluded members would 'obstruct our peace and continue our war', and that they were therefore 'to desist from your petition, and submit to the proceedings of Parliament'. The Devonians remained unhappy with this answer, but Scot and Robinson, much heartened, sent a copy of the general's letter to their colleagues in London.

Although Monck's troops were content to obey parliament, they could see, from the reaction of the towns through which they passed, that the Rump was regarded with widespread contempt. Monck was also aware that, despite Englishmen's detestation of the present regime, they were still more concerned about peace and security. Although many people, even a majority, might be passive Royalists, they were as reluctant to take up arms in the cause as they had been the previous summer. As the Parliamentarian Ralph Josselin observed on 25 January, if there was to be a restoration, it would be when all other options had been exhausted, 'the nacion looking more to Charles Stuart, out of love to themselves, not him'.

Scot and Robinson, seemingly oblivious to the growing hostility to the Rump, were keen to show that they were in charge. When the City, anxious to know the general's intentions, sent four of their aldermen to greet him at Market Harborough, it was the commissioners who took the initiative. Scot, well aware of the growing chorus of dissent in the City, rebuked the aldermen: 'having already given our judgement in the case of the secluded members, it does not become you to insist on their re-admission', and refused to heed Alderman Fowke's riposte, that 'it is unreasonable that we should be governed by a Parliament in which we are not represented'. Monck supported the commissioners in public but sent Clarges privately to assure the aldermen of his good intentions. At St Albans, Scot dealt even more aggressively when Sir Richard Temple, later to be a minister under Charles II, made a similar request when presenting an address from the gentlemen of Hertfordshire. The Rumper exploded: 'My age might excuse me from taking up arms; yet, old as I am, before the present Parliament shall be entangled by restoring the secluded members or by new elections, I will gird on my sword again, and keep the door against them.'

The two commissioners had little idea that the ground was being cut beneath them. At Dunstable Monck sent Col Lydcott with a letter to parliament, following the advice Clarges had given in Nottingham. He requested the removal of some of the troops stationed in London, including four regiments of horse and six of foot. These men were to be scattered in widely separated quarters in order to minimise the threat of mutiny. Only those commanded by Cols Morley and Fagg, of whose loyalty he was sure, were to be permitted to remain. With military thoroughness, the letter included lists stipulating where Monck's forces were to be quartered on their arrival in the capital, and ended with the request for an early reply, so that 'I may send the Quartermasters to make provision for the men'. Although there was a fierce debate in parliament over this thinly veiled demand, none dared to defy openly his wishes and all the general's proposals were accepted. The same day, the Rump received a further rebuff when the gentlemen of Norfolk presented an address declaring that unless the secluded members were readmitted, the people of England were under no obligation to pay their taxes.

Despite the surge of Royalist activity in December, notably in London, there was little action against the regime in January, apart from brief outbreaks of violence in Shrewsbury and Bristol. The Cavaliers, like everyone else, waited in trepidation for Monck to declare his intentions. Some even dared to hope that their enemies in the Rump might be changing their allegiance. John Shaw, a merchant based in Antwerp, wrote to Sir Edward Nicholas on 26 January: 'Our English letters import something of comfort, and I begin to believe the same Parliament that destroyed us may restore us.' He noted the Rump's decision to fill London with troops 'as if they designed to possess themselves of the city before his [Monck's] coming'.

The cold that winter was intense; the North Sea froze off Ostend. The harsh weather exacerbated the feeling of deprivation among the impoverished exiles, desperately waiting on events across the Channel. For the King, the main concern was to find enough money to survive, since royal debts amounted to £80,000. Charles's despairing laundress, Dorothy Chiffinch, submitted a backdated account for 4,103 guilders for over four years' work with no realistic hope of payment. Mary Knatchbull, the abbess of the English Convent at Ghent, described the position of Ormonde's brother Col Richard Butler to Hyde. For five months this brave soldier had been in debt for his 'diet, washing, and all manner of necessaries, without a penny in his power to pay for a letter or mending a pair of shoes'.

The Chancellor was conscious of the need for the King and his senior ministers to keep up appearances. 'The worst of poverty,' he wrote mournfully, 'depressing as it is, is that it makes men look ridiculous.' But for Hyde, like everyone else, it had become a question of mere survival. 'I am sure the penury is not to be imagined,' he declared. 'It is very true I do not know that any man is yet dead for want of bread, which really I wonder at; I am sure the King owes for all he has eaten since April and I am not acquainted with one servant of his who hath a pistole in his pocket; five or six of us owe for God knows how many weeks to the poor woman who feeds us.' For once, Hyde's stoicism disappeared as he lamented all those 'born and bred in those corrupt times, "when there was no king in Israel"'.

What would the King, eating his solitary daily meal off a pewter plate, have given to change places with Pepys, still no more than a junior clerk in London. Despite financial problems that led him to borrow money from whoever would lend it, Pepys ended a busy day on 26 January with a dinner party in the lodgings in Whitehall of his kinsman and soon-to-be employer, Sir Edward Montagu. He provided a full description of the menu: 'A dish of marrow-bones. A leg of mutton. A dish of fowl, three pullets, and two dozen of larks, all in a dish. A great tart. A neat's tongue. A dish of anchovies. A dish of prawns, and cheese.' Four days later Pepys's singing of his song 'Great, good and just' suddenly reminded him that it was the anniversary of an event he had attended when he absconded from school, 'the fatal day, now ten years since, his Majesty died' on a scaffold outside the Banqueting Hall of Whitehall Palace.

131

10

THE FALL OF THE RUMP

The beginning of February 1660 saw Monck based at St Albans within a day's march of London. He sat in silence while the fiery Hugh Peters, soon to be tried and executed for his militant republicanism, preached a sermon on the journey of the Israelites to the Promised Land. Whether or not the audience understood the general to be a latter-day Moses, come to deliver his people, the general was extremely sensitive to any talk of the King's restoration. An officer who suggested it openly was caned in public for his pains. Monck welcomed Lawson and twenty of his senior officers but tried to play down the admiral's suggestion that the general use his forces to protect the Rump from the City and from the Army.

Monck's caution was justified by events in the capital, where political uncertainty was about to erupt into violence. With their pay more than three months in arrears, the soldiers in London showed no inclination to obey the Rump's order for them to disperse outside the capital. When an officer, attempting to exert his authority over an insolent trooper, knocked him senseless with the butt end of a musket in St James's Fields, the troops mutinied. The mutiny soon spread to the regiments stationed at Somerset House and Salisbury Court. With shouts of 'let us hang up our officers', they threatened to strip their commanders. There was little unity to their protests, some soldiers shouting for a free parliament, a few for King Charles II. The only point of agreement, as Pepys witnessed, was that they 'swore they would not go without money; and that if they [the officers] would not give it to them, they would go where they might have it, and that was the City'. Once they were convinced that their pay was forthcoming, due to Hesilrige's swift action in borrowing £30,000, the mutiny subsided. Pepys, however, was to run across numerous discontented soldiers in the days that followed, and some companies at Gravesend, on being told they were to go to Dunkirk, mutinied once more. The apprentices who had hoped to use the mutiny to provoke an uprising were brutally ridden down by troops loyal to the Rump in the streets around Leadenhall. A fortnight later two of the leading mutineers were hanged at Charing Cross, and a further seven men given a lashing on their bare backs. The mutiny reinforced civilian dislike of the military, seen as answerable to no one but themselves and no respecter of law and order.

Monck, showing his characteristic composure, refused to alter his plans, despite being woken in the middle of the night by a semi-hysterical Scot in 'his night-gown, cap and slippers', begging him to march immediately to the aid of the Rump and suppress the mutineers. The general, however, had no intention of slipping into London at dead of night, so went back to bed. He wanted his troops to create the maximum impact when they entered the capital. Accordingly, the next day, Friday 3 February, Monck rode into London at the head of his men, 'gallantly mounted, with his Trumpets richly habited before him'. His soldiers were equally well turned out, his officers smartly attired with 'red and white favours in their hats, and his trumpeters and foot-boys bore a red livery, laced with silver lace', as one witness noted. The troops, in their characteristic red coats, soon to be adopted as the normal uniform of the British Army, marched down Gray's Inn Road and Chancery Lane, watched by a silent, apprehensive populace, in marked contrast to the welcome they had received throughout their journey from the Scottish border. With relations strained between the Rump and the City, the citizens wondered which side Monck was going to take. The apprehension of Londoners was expressed in a song, published as 'The Rump dock't' on 21 January:

> Till it be understood
> What is under Monck's hood,
> The City dare not show its horns.

Till ten days be out,
The Speaker's sick of the gout,
And the Rump doth sit upon thorns.

Monck, anxious to appear the servant of the state, greeted Speaker
Lenthall with due ceremony near Somerset House in the Strand, before
proceeding to his apartments in Whitehall. The following Monday, still
attended by Scot and Robinson, who continued to monitor his movements,
he reported to the Council of State. The Rump, still suspicious, requested
that the general take an oath abjuring Charles II, but Monck refused to
commit himself, claiming that he needed to consult his troops on such a
vital matter. It rankled with the general that the Rump insisted on
referring to him as Commissioner-General, one of seven appointed by
parliament on 12 October, immediately preceding Lambert's coup, rather
than as commander-in-chief. Hesilrige, with his usual lack of tact, had
even declared that Monck 'was no more General than he was'.

The following Monday, Monck went to Westminster to address the
Rump. He delivered a modest and submissive speech, standing behind
the chair, resembling a throne, that had been prepared for him, his head
uncovered. The members were, however, alarmed by the impression
Monck gave of the mood of the country: 'As I marched from Scotland
hither, I observed the people in most counties in great and earnest
expectations of settlement; and they made several applications to me,
with numerous inscriptions. The chiefest heads of their desires were for a
full and free Parliament.' He added ominously, 'And for admittance of
the members secluded before 1649, without any previous oath or
engagement.' Both sides were displeased with the meeting: the Rumpers
disapproved of Monck expressing himself so freely, while Monck was
annoyed that they had not ratified his post as commander-in-chief.

The members were keen to emphasise their authority. Their mood was
not improved by the noise in the streets, where Londoners, angry that the
City members had not been allowed to take their seats, were everywhere

crying out for 'a free parliament', or, as Pepys recorded: 'Boys do now cry "Kiss my Parliament" instead of "Kiss my arse", so great and general a contempt is the Rump come to among all men, good and bad.' Apprentices in Bristol were equally demonstrative, taking to the streets to express their enthusiasm for the cause. In a vain attempt to counter their unpopularity, the Rump recruited the journalist Henry Muddiman, even though he was suspected of supporting Monck. He was ordered to issue a newsbook every Monday in defence of the regime. The newsbooks were widely read but the populace were not fooled by these efforts; people wanted change and held the opinion that 'Rump Major begins to smell as rank as Rump Minor'.

To prevent this popular discontent degenerating into anarchy, Monck ordered his troops to keep the peace. Before marching into England, he had purged his army of Quakers, and when Pepys went to Westminster Palace on 7 February, he saw 'Monk's soldiers abuse Billing [a prominent Quaker] and all the Quakers that were at a meeting-place there'. Interestingly, Pepys, sharing the general civilian fear of the military, took the Quakers' side, 'and indeed the soldiers did use them very roughly and were to blame'. The next day the political crisis deepened when the City voted to refrain from levying taxes until there were free elections and proceeded to shut its gates. Hesilrige and his colleagues decided to test Monck's loyalty. He was ordered to march into the City, arrest eleven members of the Council and dismantle its gates and portcullises. It was a clever move. The general must choose between disobeying his legitimate superiors or infuriating the population and upsetting his own troops, whose sympathies lay with opponents of the Rump. Despite intense speculation, nobody knew for sure what Monck's intentions were. In the following days Vane's analysis that 'Monck had yet several masques to pull off' was to prove entirely accurate.

On 9 February the general ordered his troops to set to work, despite protests from senior officers who refused to supervise the work and offered to resign. Pepys recorded how 'the City looks mighty blank, and cannot tell what in the world to do'. The citizens, full of consternation, queued up to complain at the behaviour of Monck's soldiers. The vehemence of their protests appeared to register with the general, who remained at his base at the Three Tuns in Guildhall yard, listening in silence with knitted brows and chewing tobacco. But so lacklustre were the troops' efforts, 'both merry and angry at this odious drudgery', in the words of Price, that by nightfall only the chains and posts had been removed. Monck sent a letter to the Speaker, requesting that work might cease, but was commanded that the destruction of the gates and portcullises must continue. Furthermore, the City Council, increasingly critical of the Rump's rule, was to be dissolved. Hesilrige was exultant and was heard to exclaim: 'Now, George, we have thee for ever, body and soul.'

Work continued the next day, but in a markedly different atmosphere, with the soldiers expressing open indignation at their role. Monck was bolstered by offers of support from Col Morley, Governor of the Tower. In the evening, Clarges, who had been urging his brother-in-law to declare for a free parliament, came to visit the general with some of his senior officers, all of whom expressed dissatisfaction at the events of the past two days. After a prolonged discussion, Monck took the momentous decision to authorise the readmittance of the secluded MPs.

This was perhaps the most crucial moment in the whole story of the Restoration. Monck was making clear that he wanted to reinstate the Government that had been in office before the execution of Charles I. The secluded members represented a legitimate part of the age-old trinity of King, Lords and Commons. Their dismissal in December 1648 had ushered in a decade of radical political change that had led to near anarchy. Now was the moment to start to put the clock back, a process that was to lead inexorably to the restoration of the monarchy.

There has been much discussion to what extent this decisive move was Monck's doing, unprompted. His chaplain, Price, convinced of Monck's Royalist inclinations, recorded the general's words: 'This was a trick you knew not of, and I assure you I could not have done my business so soon without it, and possibly not at all.' The probability is that, as a professional soldier all his life, one who had relied absolutely on the loyalty of the men under his command, Monck knew that he could not risk a direct challenge to the Rump until he was sure, not only of the support of the civilian population, but of his own troops. At all events, the general and his closest supporters drafted a letter to this effect that very night, to be delivered to parliament in the morning. It required the issue of writs for new elections to fill up the House by Friday 17 February, and free elections for the whole House, not merely for the vacant seats, as the Rump wanted, were to be held on 25 April.

Monck drew up his forces in Finsbury Fields on the morning of 11 February and marched at their head back into the City. The Lord Mayor was considerably put out by Monck's behaviour during the previous two days, but was eventually won round by his offer, on the advice of Clarges, that he restore the Common Council of the City which had been suspended by the Rump. The meaning was clear to all. As Evelyn recorded in his diary, Monck, 'perceiving how infamous and wretched a pack of knaves would have still usurped the supreme power, and having intelligence that they intended to take away his commission, repenting of what he had done to the City . . . marches to Whitehall, dissipates that nest of robbers'. The Puritan Richard Baxter, soon to be a royal chaplain, put it more succinctly: 'And this in truth was the Act that turned the Scales and brought in the King.'

Meanwhile, Monck's letter had been delivered to parliament. Pepys was in Westminster Hall when it was brought in: 'At noon I walked in the Hall where I heard the news of a letter from Monk, who is now gone into the City again, and did resolve to stand for the sudden filling up of the House, and it was all very strange how the countenance of men in the Hall was changed with joy in half an hour's time. So I went up to the lobby, where I saw the Speaker reading of the letter; and after it was read, Sir A. Haslerigg came out very angry, and Billing (a Quaker) standing by the door took him by the arm, and cried, "Thou man, will thy beast carry thee no longer! Thou must fall."' Hesilrige, however, was not ready to yield, and reiterated that Monck was merely one of five commissioners, including himself, originally appointed by the Rump the previous autumn, in charge of the Army.

The Rumpers realised further that they must act immediately to stop Monck in his tracks. Their best chance was to send Scot and Robinson to persuade him to change his mind. They arrived while the general was dining with the Lord Mayor and the aldermen of the City. The meal was interrupted by their attempt to convince him that it was essential that he come at once to Westminster to explain his actions. Used to issuing commands, the commissioners were astounded to find themselves subjected to insults and reproaches from Monck's officers, who urged them 'to consult for their own safeties'. Monck calmed his officers down, and told the departing commissioners: 'All will be well, if you strictly observe the advice of the letter, and issue writs on Friday next for filling up your House.'

Growing in confidence, and heartened by the enthusiastic demonstrations of support, Monck attended a packed meeting of the City corporations at the Guildhall, where he sought to justify his behaviour, stating: 'I am resolved to quarter my army in your city, and to continue myself among you [his headquarters was now at the Bull's Head tavern in Cheapside], till I see how the contents of this letter [from Monck and his officers to the Rump, drawn up the previous evening], and the desires of the city and nation, are performed.' Loud cheers greeted these words, and crowds of exuberant apprentices pelted with mud every coach they suspected of containing the Rump's commissioners, including that of Monck's chaplains Price and Gumble. Shaken, Price repaired to the Three Tuns, where he found the locals 'transported with joy' when they learnt of the change of heart of Monck's troops. Ashley Cooper and Alexander Popham, a leading Presbyterian turned Royalist, were returning from the City when a mob surrounded their coach, shouting: 'Down with the Rump.' Demonstrating his usual quickness of mind, Ashley Cooper pulled down the window and replied: 'What, gentlemen, not one good piece in a rump?' a joke that appealed greatly to the crowd.

Pepys had already left the Three Tuns, 'not liking the wine', but had the fortune to meet Monck coming out of the Guildhall, greeted by 'such a shout I never heard in all my life, crying out "God bless your Excellence!"' The diarist witnessed the extraordinary celebrations as news spread of the general's change of heart:

In Cheapside there was a great many bonefires, and Bow bells and all the bells in all the churches as we went home were a-ringing. Hence we went homewards, it being about 10 o'clock. But the common joy that was everywhere to be seen! The number of bonefires – there being fourteen between St Dunstan's and Temple bar. And at Strand bridge I could at one view tell 31 fires. In King streete, seven or eight; and all along burning and roasting and drinking for rumps – there being rumps tied upon sticks and carried up and down. The butchers at the maypole in the Strand rang a peal upon their knifes when they were going to sacrifice their rump. On Ludgate hill there was one turning of the spit, that had a rump tied upon it, and another basting of it. Indeed it was past imagination, both the greatness and suddenness of it. At one end of the street, you would think there was a whole lane of fire, and so hot that we were fain to keep still on the further side merely for the heat. Thence home, and my wife and I went out again to show her the fires; and after walking as far as the Exchange, we returned and to bed.

A correspondent of Hyde's compared the situation in London that morning to a deflowered virgin lamenting the rape committed on her, whereas in the afternoon she was transformed into a bride attending her wedding. Outside London, the reaction to the fall of the Rump was equally enthusiastic. In Oxford, Anthony Wood recorded how rumps were 'flung in a bonfire at Queen's College'. The crowd, emboldened, was no respecter of authority: 'Dr John Palmer, a great rumper, warden of Allsouls College . . . had a rump throwne up from the street at his windowes.'

Outside London, from Yarmouth to Bristol, rumps had been burnt in celebration, accompanied by cries of 'a free parliament', interspersed with more muted calls for 'a King'. The gentlemen of Yorkshire, only the day before, had signed a declaration that they were under no obligation to pay taxes until the secluded members were readmitted.

Across the Channel, even the acute cold could not prevent the rise in Royalists' hopes as they strove to keep abreast of the dramatic news on the mainland. On 3 February Percy Church wrote to Sir Edward Nicholas: 'All is in a mist and at a stand until the arrival of Monk with his army.' But there was little consensus as to the intentions of the enigmatic general. Hyde was nervous that the general might set up a Commonwealth based on the Dutch model, where Monck had fought during the Thirty Years War, 'and that himself might enjoy the authority and place which the Prince of Orange possessed in that government'. Dr George Morley, who had been sent back to England by the Chancellor to negotiate with the Presbyterians, wrote to Dr John Cosin, future Bishop of Durham, in Paris of the difficulty of reading the general, 'unless Monk be a much more artificial dissembler than those that know him best do take him to be'. Mordaunt considered him to be a republican. John Shaw, the merchant in Antwerp who had loaned the Royalists vital sums of money, expressed the widespread fear that Monck's move might lead to anarchy: 'I have no hopes of Monk, who will shortly be outed again by the sectaries, and you will find that Vane, Hasilrigg, Lambert, and the rest of that party will compass their animosities to effect that work.'

When news reached Brussels that Monck had submitted to the Rump and sent his men to knock down the City of London's defences, Charles fell into despair and, as Hyde recorded, 'all the little remainder of his hopes was extinguished, and he had nothing left before his eyes but a perpetual exile'. The Chancellor shared his master's despondency: 'And a greater consternation and dejection of mind cannot be imagined than at that time covered the whole court of the king.' Hyde's emotive prose shows clearly the strain that both he and the King were suffering. The two men had striven so hard to engineer the restoration. Now they were dependent on events outside their control. But both the King and his minister had gained strength through adversity. Hyde may have grumbled that his former pupil 'did not enough delight in his business' during the long years of exile, but at this crucial time he could not fault his master's determination. Having regained their composure, they planned to take whatever advantage they could from any split between Monck and the Rump. They shared their thoughts with the Marquis of Ormonde, the closest ally of the Chancellor among the senior Royalists, who was greatly admired for his steadfast refusal to countenance defeat. Sir Edward Nicholas described his character: 'In my life I never knew a worthier person than my lord of Ormond, nor more impossible to be swayed or guided by any but public and noble rules, and to the best ends.'

Charles's greatest achievement in the spring of 1660 was not to be seduced into bartering away his inheritance. This is in marked contrast with the nature of the offers the King had made to his allies in earlier years. He had been prepared to negotiate away all the conquests Cromwell had made in the war with Spain, including the island of Jamaica, and had even stated that the Prince of Conde, who was commanding an army against France, his native country, would be given Ireland. Since the prospect of a restoration was almost non-existent when these offers were made, Charles set little store by them.

The Marquis of Newcastle, now living in Antwerp, was one of many Royalists anxious that the King should only countenance a restoration with his powers intact. As the former governor of the young Prince of Wales, presiding over his household in St James's Palace, he had an intimate knowledge of Charles. Newcastle had exerted a strong influence over his charge, inspiring the Prince with his numerous interests, ranging from horses to music and chemistry. Although an ardent monarchist and a great believer in court ceremonial, instructing the Prince to eat his meals alone, seated beneath a canopy with his hat on, attended by pages on bended knee, the Marquis had taught Charles to use his charm: 'sometimes the raising of a hat or a smile in a tight place will advantage you', sage advice the King was never to forget. Newcastle had, however, witnessed Charles's negotiations at Breda in 1650, when he had delivered himself into the hands of the Scottish Covenanters for little palpable gain. Now he wrote to Sir Edward Nicholas on 28 February: 'That the King will be called in is probable, but on what conditions the Lord knows. I am not of the opinion to come in on any terms, and be trammelled and made a Duke of Venice of, which is but Lord Mayor during his life.' But his pupil had learnt from his mistakes and was not about to repeat them.

The longer Charles waited without committing himself, the more favourable the eventual outcome appeared to be. At the beginning of February Sir Charles Coote's emissary Sir Arthur Forbes arrived in Brussels with encouraging news that Ireland would declare for the King should he set foot there. But Charles favoured a more cautious approach, arguing that it was England that held the key to the restoration and that Ireland should wait on events across the Irish Channel. Then an officer named Baily, who had served under the Marquis of Ormonde in Ireland, crossed the Channel post-haste from Dover to Ostend, claiming to have witnessed the bonfires, the burning of rump steaks and the King's health being drunk openly. Scarcely able to believe the news, Ormonde brought Baily to Hyde's lodgings but his 'discourse was so strange and extravagant' that the two senior Royalists decided that the King must judge the news for himself. Although they agreed that there must be some truth in Baily's account, confirmed in a note he carried written in London by Sir John Stephens, a well-known Royalist, their hopes had been dashed so often that Charles counselled caution. But the good news spread rapidly among the exiled Cavaliers, as Hyde recorded: 'They thought all their suffering over, and laid in a stock of such vast hopes, as would have been hard for any success to procure satisfaction for.'

As the prospect of a restoration suddenly seemed a real possibility, even Henrietta Maria, whose militant Catholicism and belief in absolutism had undermined Hyde's championship of the Church of England and the English constitution, made overtures to her old enemy. In a rare fit of magnanimity, she assured Hyde that 'he will find her his very good friend'. The Chancellor, however, had greater worries to consider than the attitude of the Queen Mother. His main concern was the basis on which the King could be restored.

The sangfroid that the King was displaying in Brussels contrasted with the wild celebrations that Pepys and his wife had witnessed in London. Yet, astonishingly, the leaders of the Rump, still inhabiting a world of make-believe, seemed oblivious of the momentous change that was obvious to the rest of the population. To placate the Army, large sums were voted to the troops, but with no indication where the money would come from. An oath of fidelity to the Commonwealth was to be enforced, and Lambert was summoned to justify his conduct. With a blind disregard for the sea-change in political opinion, Hesilrige and the Rump were busy planning the election to the vacant seats of members, selected by the sitting members, a method of preventing the return of the secluded members. But when a vote was taken to issue writs to fill up the vacant seats, the Speaker, William Lenthall, worried that he would be sued by the secluded members if he defied Monck's order for them to be readmitted, refused to sign the bill, a clear indication of the Rump's declining power.

The behaviour of Monck was more inscrutable than ever in the week following the delivery of his letter to the Rump. Although the letter stated clearly that the secluded members were to be readmitted and free elections to be held in April, the general still seemed anxious to placate the leading Rumpers. Hesilrige accepted at face value a letter of 13 February sent by Monck from the house of the Royalist Alderman William Wale in Throckmorton Street, where he was residing, emphasising how the two men shared a belief in the Commonwealth. Ludlow recorded a conversation between the general and Hesilrige where Monck,

'putting his hand within Sir Arthur's', stated his determination to 'oppose
to the utmost the setting up of Charles Stuart, a single person, or a House
of Peers'. He refused, however, to take an oath abjuring the Stuarts in the
Council of State. Having given these assurances, the general hoped that he
could reconcile the Rumpers with the secluded members. On 18 February
Monck presided over a meeting between Hesilrige and Sir Arthur
Annesley. No agreement was reached but, afterwards, Hesilrige was
reassured by Monck's statement that he would double the guards on the
doors of the House of Commons to prevent the return of the secluded
members.

At a meeting in the evening two days later, however, Monck was
visited by Clarges and Cols Clobery and Knight, two of his senior
officers. After a long conversation he changed his mind, and decided on
the readmittance of the secluded members the very next morning.
Ashley Cooper, who also attended this crucial meeting, later claimed
responsibility for persuading the general to alter his thinking. During
the remainder of the night Monck's supporters hastily summoned as
many of the secluded members as they could find, to meet at 6 a.m. next
morning at Annesley's house in Drury Lane.

Pepys, who had been attending the final meeting of the Rota Club,
hastened to Westminster on 21 February to witness the re-entry of the
secluded members. Monck handled this crucial act with great subtlety.
The members of the Rump, as Pepys recorded, 'heard nothing of all this,
till they found them in the House, insomuch that the soldiers that stood
there to let in the Secluded members, they took for such as they had
ordered to stand there to hinder their coming in. Mr Prynne [the prolific
pamphleteer William Prynne] came in with an old baskethilt sword on,
and had a great many shouts [of support] at his going into the Hall.' The
antiquarian John Aubrey, author of *Brief Lives*, recorded the sequel: 'As
he went into the House, W. Prynne's long sword got between Sir W.
Waller's [the Parliamentarian general] short legs and threw him down,
which caused laughter.'

Sir Arthur Hesilrige, known as 'the hot-headed knight', was furious at being duped by Monck, and stormed out of the House. As he passed Ashley Cooper, his former colleague, who had commanded the troops escorting the secluded members to Westminster, he exclaimed: 'This is your doing, but it shall cost blood', to which Cooper coolly replied: 'Your own, if you please.' Hesilrige swept on without retort, but was to be seen outside, acting 'the raging Turk in Westminster Hall'. Outside Westminster Londoners reacted with universal rejoicing to the demise of the Rump. Throughout the City the event was celebrated 'with a glory about it, so high was the light of the Bonfires . . . and the bells rang everywhere'.

The same day, Monck, anxious to ensure the loyalty of his troops, sent a letter of explanation to the regiments in all three kingdoms calling for their support in readmitting the secluded members and protesting his devotion to the Republic. He pointed out that the enlarged parliament, comprising the survivors of the original Long Parliament, was in a much stronger legal position to authorise the raising of taxes that would be used to pay the troops. Monck hoped that this argument would prevent militant Republicans, such as Col Okey, from contemplating mutiny. For the moment the soldiers remained quiet and the Republicans were reassured by the manner he welcomed the secluded members with 'a bitter speech against monarchy', much to the horror of Royalists. Lawson had shown himself a strong supporter of the Rump, and was a friend of Col Rich and other disaffected officers; a Royalist agent reported that he had threatened to turn his guns on the Tower, but, in the event, he failed to stir. As a sign of the rise in Royalist fortunes, he even offered a safe conduct to Mordaunt, still wanted for arrest by the Rump.

In Ireland, Sir Hardress Waller had declared against the admission of the secluded members, and had attempted to arrest his opponents and imprison them in Dublin Castle. His plan had been thwarted and, on 15 February, Coote and Sir Theophilus Jones, followed by a cheering crowd, rode through the streets of Dublin calling for a free parliament.

145

After a brief siege, Waller was persuaded to surrender the castle, and he, and twenty-eight fellow officers, deemed to be potential troublemakers, were sent off to confinement in Athlone. Coote and his allies proceeded to summon a convention of representatives of the Irish counties and towns to meet on 27 February, hoping to secure nationwide assent for their actions.

Monck now moved from Whitehall to St James's Palace and installed himself in the apartments used by Charles II as a boy. This had been where the Prince presided over a Court in miniature, under the tuition of his governor, the Marquis of Newcastle. This privileged lifestyle had been brought to an abrupt end in January 1642, when Charles had fled London with his father after Charles I's abortive attempt to seize his leading opponents, including Hesilrige, in the House of Commons, an act that was to lead directly to the First Civil War.

Throughout the country, the return of the secluded members gave people the opportunity to express their Royalist sentiments. The citizens of Bury St Edmunds celebrated by calling openly for the return of Charles II, ignoring threats from the local commander. The Government ordered the release of Matthew Wren, Bishop of Ely and a close follower of Archbishop Laud, who had been in prison for almost twenty years. Sir George Booth, fortunate to escape with his life after leading the rebellion of the previous summer, and John Maitland, 2nd Earl of Lauderdale, soon to become the King's chief minister in Scotland, who had been imprisoned in the Tower since the battle of Worcester in 1651, also regained their freedom. Sir Arthur Annesley, elected President of the Council of State on the return of the secluded members, had already made contact with the King, and Lady Willoughby of Parham had written confidently to Hyde on 17 February: 'Fairfax and a great party with him are for the King.' Nine days later, one of the secluded members declared in the House of Commons 'the necessity of the King's restoration by this present Parliament'.

11

MONCK'S GREAT DECISION

Despite the upsurge in Royalist support and the downfall of the Rump, the situation at the beginning of March 1660 was still unresolved, with the name of Richard Cromwell re-emerging as an alternative to Monck and the King. Thurloe, a former key supporter of Richard, had been reappointed Secretary of State. Bordeaux, the French ambassador, gave an accurate analysis of Monck's unfathomable behaviour as he continued to tread a political tightrope. He reported back to his master Mazarin that the general's 'conduct and words still continue to be opposed to each other'. Dr Barwick, keeping careful watch of Monck, advised Hyde that it was still too early for the King to write to the general. The Chancellor was pessimistic, writing on Shrove Tuesday to one of his agents that he had 'no great hope of Monck'.

There was no question, however, that the general was the supreme power in the land. He was elected captain-general of all the land forces of England, Scotland and Ireland, while his deputy Morgan was made commander-in-chief in Scotland. Monck was now responsible for tackling the Army's enormous debt, which was becoming ever more critical. A further £60,000 had been added to the total for the months of January–March, with an additional £30,000 spent solely to maintain the garrison of Dunkirk. With the memory of the mutiny at the beginning of February fresh in everyone's minds, great care needed to be taken to placate the soldiers. In theory the Council was still issuing orders to the general; in practice these were increasingly taking the form of requests for his troops 'to have an eye upon the peace of the city'. On 20 February the Council's concern was 'the great straits' of the forces in Exeter 'for want of provision'. A day later it was 'the great necessities and wants of the Ludlow garrison'. A report published on 1 March stated that revenues for hospitals for sick soldiers were now forty-nine weeks in arrears, so that the patients were 'likely to perish, through imprisonment, hunger, cold, and nakedness'.

The general feeling of unrest convinced Monck of the need to continue treading cautiously. His friends in the City came forward with the proposal for a loan of £60,000. In exchange Monck authorised the restoration of their franchises, and the re-erection of the gates and chains his soldiers had torn down so recently. More importantly, the aldermen of the City were given control of the militia, one of the key disputes leading to the First Civil War. This reorganisation was repeated all over England, with the old landed families and country gentlemen beginning to reassert their control over local affairs. Once the militia was established, the sensitive but essential step over disbanding the regular troops could begin. Not only would this reduce the enormous expense incurred by paying the military, but it would also diminish the republican threat posed by the standing Army. As an indication of the changing political scene, Booth was appointed one of the commissioners of the new militia bill. Monck continued to try to placate the leading Rumpers, who seemed oblivious to the growing number of their former allies making contact with the King.

Monck was also in charge of the Navy, appointed joint general-at-sea with the restored Montagu, who was also made a Commissioner of the Admiralty and a member of the Council of State. The Rump may have regarded Montagu as a check to Monck, since it was widely known, as Hyde and Ludlow recorded from different perspectives, that he bore little love towards Monck, whose wife he referred to slightingly as 'the veryest slut and drudge'. Pepys also benefited from his kinsman's rising importance. On Shrove Tuesday Montagu invited his cousin to accompany him for a private walk in the garden of his London house. The admiral informed Pepys that he wished to employ him at sea as his secretary. The budding diarist still did not know of his new employer's extensive correspondence with the King, although he was well aware of the upsurge in Royalist sentiment. The day before, he had been to the house of his friend Mr Pinkny, 'where he showed me how he hath alway kept the Lion and Unicorne in the back of his chimney bright, in expectation of the King's coming again'.

Pepys was also learning fast how the Navy operated. His diary entries for this period record his busy preparations for his embarkation on the *Naseby*. Commissioner Peter Pett offered Montagu his old flagship on 8 March, 'as a small present, and testimony of a grateful mind for those many great and undeserved favours so plentifully vouchsafed to me and mine'. In exchange the commissioner 'craved leave to recommend Lieut. Rainborrow, for his employment in the *Speaker*, if not disposed of'. Ten days later Pepys gave Capt Williamson his commission to command the *Harpe*, whereupon Williamson 'gave me a piece of gold and 20s. in silver'. The growing corruption was to become one of the hallmarks of the Restoration age.

With Monck busy in dealing with the Army and parliament, it fell to Montagu to deal with the problem of commanding the Navy. His most immediate concern was to ensure the loyalty of Lawson, the highly popular commander and a renowned Republican, whom he had replaced. Fortunately, Lawson appeared to accept his new position below Monck and Montagu. Of greater long-term importance, the naval commanders were faced by a desperate financial position. No money at all had come from the Exchequer since October. Their debts amounted to £690,000, with a further £760,000 for maintaining 20,000 sailors for the past eight months, the price for Cromwell's war with Spain. Britain was still at war, ships must be fitted out and provisioned, and convoys mounted and defended, particularly against the predatory Flemish privateers based in Ostend, the main port of the Spanish Netherlands.

Above all, the demoralised sailors and their dependants must be paid. Not only were they receiving no pay, but there was little food, salt water was used for cooking and disease was rife. Victuallers were increasingly reluctant to provide supplies without ready payment. At Yarmouth the contractor William Burton, a committed radical, stated bluntly that he 'would not trust the state for one penny, for here was one state today and another tomorrow'. Capt Heaton wrote despairingly from Plymouth to Robert Blackthorne on 6 March: 'It would pity any man's heart to hear the cries of poor butchers, bakers, coopers, pursers. . . . One cries, "For God's sake spare me £20 to keep me out of prison", another begs for money to buy his family meat to eat, and to-day I saw a poor woman beg of Mr. Addiss 10s. of her due to buy her 4 poor children bread, as for alms.' Blackthorne was a troublesome character and a Republican who had condemned Lawson as 'the greatest hypocrite in the world' for submitting to the new regime.

There were more prominent Republicans still prepared to defend the cause. John Milton's *Readie and Easie way to establish a free Commonwealth* advocated the restoration of the Rump with unlimited powers, and lambasted the growing number of those who wanted to return to 'their once abjured and detested thraldom of kingship'. Milton was particularly hard on Presbyterians recently converted to Royalism, whom he referred to as 'zealous backsliders'. Although his tract possessed none of the power of his magisterial *The Tenure of Kings and Magistrates*, a justification of the execution of Charles I, it provoked a furious response. 'You have slandered the dead,' in the words of one scandalised Royalist, 'worse than envy itself, and thrown your dirty outrage on the memory of a murthered Prince, as if the hangman were but your usher.'

Marchamont Nedham, the principal propagandist of the Common-wealth, supported Milton's efforts to defend the Republican cause. His forged *Newes from Brussels, in a letter from a neer attendant on his Majesties Person*, published on 23 March, was a subtle attempt to split traditional Anglican Royalists from Presbyterians recently converted to the cause. The supposed author, a Cavalier bent on retribution, writes: 'Hug them you cannot hang, at least until you can.' Nedham was, however, soon captured, and his fictitious letter was immediately refuted by John

Evelyn, whose admiration for his sovereign knew no bounds: 'His person so lovely, amiable and gracefull . . . so meek, gentle, and sweet of Behaviour; so firm, constant, and obliging in his Friendships . . . but above all, so firmly and irremovably fixed, to the profession of the true Protestant religion.'

In parliament the Presbyterian party seemed to be in the ascendancy. The leading members were confident that they could secure a conditional restoration based on the terms of the Treaty of Newport in 1648, whereby England would remain Presbyterian for three years, and parliament would control the militia. The Commons passed a motion on 5 March ordering that the Covenant should be put up in all churches and that it should be read out to congregations once a year. The Royalists, however, were increasingly confident that there was growing support for an unconditional restoration. Hyde confided to John Barwick that 'all discourses of the Treaty at the Isle of Wight [Newport] trouble me little'. One of the City aldermen wrote optimistically to the King that the Presbyterians 'begin to flag a little now, and fear the settlement of Episcopacy and that your Majesty will slip in without conditions'.

Monck appeared to favour Presbyterianism and held regular meetings with prominent ministers, such as Calamy and Reynolds, who replaced Dr John Owen, a prominent Independent minister, as dean of Christ Church, Oxford. But the general was not as committed as fellow Puritans liked to believe. His Anglican chaplain, Price, recorded a conversation one evening in February on the subject of bishops, anathema to strict Presbyterians. Although Monck thought that it would be impossible to reintroduce episcopacy, Price persuaded him that he should stay his hand until he had gauged the mood of the nation, and the general ended the conversation by stating: 'Well, then, so much I will promise you, that I will not be engaged against bishops.'

The Presbyterian peers were waiting to see if they could resume their seats. The Earl of Northumberland wrote to the Earl of Manchester, advising caution. 'For the Lords to go about at present asserting their rights', he declared, 'would, I think, be ill-timed, especially seeing no part of the nation but ourselves have as yet any desire that we should return to the exercise of our duties in parliament; and all in power or authority have either openly or impliedly declared against us.' His analysis was correct and when the Earl of Strafford, an impetuous character like his father, Charles I's great minister, presented himself at the doors of parliament, he was ordered away by Maj Miller under instructions from Monck, who was anxious not to be seen to act unconstitutionally and wished to wait for the newly elected parliament to take this important decision.

Despite this rebuff, the Republicans seemed to be everywhere in retreat. The Council of State formed by the Rump had been disbanded, and Scot had been deprived of his post as Secretary of State, with control over foreign policy and internal security. Lambert had remained in hiding in London since the proclamation for his arrest had been issued the previous month, hoping for an opportunity to lead the resistance to Monck. Now, seeing the Army's submission to parliament, he gave himself up on 5 March and was immediately confined to the Tower.

Monck was aware of the need to tighten his grip on the Army, intending to give the regiments controlled by Cols Okey, Alured and Walton, all ardent Republicans, to Lord Fauconberg, and Cols Howard and Rossiter, men he trusted. Col Ingoldsby, rated by the Royalists as the most important figure in the Army after Monck himself, had already replaced Col Rich and had suppressed a mutiny by a number of Rich's men, sent from London to posts throughout East Anglia. On 6 March news reached Monck that Overton, still commanding the important garrison at Hull, was circulating a letter reminding his fellow soldiers of their devotion to the 'Good Old Cause'. The general was swift to act; an agent of Charles II's Secretary Nicholas reported a few days later: 'Overton had submitted, and surrendered Hull to Col. Chas. Fairfax, nephew of Lord Fairfax. Okey's men in the west desert him daily, and in most counties the fanatic party are as much out of power as of credit.'

But some soldiers were still not biddable. A group of officers drew up a declaration for Monck to sign, pledging the Army to declare for a free Commonwealth, and against the setting up of a single person. On 7 March the general called a general meeting of officers at St James's. Okey, a regicide, argued forcibly against a restoration, and that there should be 'some security' for the Good Old Cause, the clear implication being that the Army should maintain it, if necessary, by force of arms. But he was refuted, first by Clarges, who argued that parliament would never condone such interference, and then by Monck, who reassured the soldiers that nobody who had borne arms against parliament was eligible in the forthcoming election. He ended by stressing the supremacy of parliament, declaring that 'he brought them not out of Scotland for his or the Parliament's council; that for his part he should obey the Parliament, and expected they should do the same'. At a further conference between ten officers and ten leading MPs, the civilians attempted to reassure the military that their fears over an indemnity, over pay and over the militia would be dealt with by the new parliament. But to ensure obedience, officers in all regiments in England and Scotland were to sign an engagement acquiescing in any act of the new parliament. Those who refused to sign were effectively handing in their resignations.

The leading military opponents of Monck were members of the Independent sects. Not only were they to lose their political influence, but they also feared that they would be forced to accept the supremacy of the Presbyterian Church, favoured by Monck, or the Church of England, the faith of the King and the leading Royalists. John Maidstone, former steward of Oliver Cromwell's household, lamented the demise of Independency in a letter to John Winthrop: 'The interest of religion lies dreadfully in the dust, for the eminent professors of it, achieved formerly great victories in the war, and thereby great power in the army, made us of it to make variety of changes in the government, and every one of those changes hazardous and pernicious. . . . They were all charged upon the principles of the authors, who, being Congregational men, have not only made men of that persuasion cheap, but rendered them odious to the generality of the nation.'

With Monck triumphant, there remained the possibility that he might be tempted to seize supreme power himself. The French ambassador, Bordeaux, told Clarges that Cardinal Mazarin would do all he could to help if this was Monck's wish, but Clarges rebuffed the overture. Hesilrige and Scot, as a last resort, are supposed to have offered Monck the crown on 13 March. As Baker recounts in his *Chronicle of the Kings*, they tried to point out the danger of acting as kingmaker, quoting historical precedents, and dismissed with arrogant contempt the idea that 'the people are always bad judges of what is best for themselves'. Would it not be better, they urged, overturning their lifelong devotion to Republicanism, for Monck to seize the crown himself, to which the general gave the brusque reply, that he 'had rather be torn to pieces by wild horses, than be so treacherous to the country's freedom'.

Meanwhile, the general was inundated with gifts. A delegation of Irish officers presented him with a gold sword, a rich hatband and an embroidered belt, showing, as Ludlow, dismissed as commander-in-chief in Ireland, noted bitterly, 'their acknowledgement and acceptance of his good service in betraying the publick cause'. Monck appeared to be enjoying the trappings of power, parading through London, as Lady Willoughby commented, 'with four silver trumpets before him and twenty troopers in black velvet coats'. He was, however, intelligent enough to turn down parliament's offer of the royal residence of Hampton Court, realising that it would deeply offend all Royalists. But a gift of £20,000 from parliament more than made up for any feeling of deprivation.

The general was fêted by the great livery companies in the City. He celebrated at a dinner at the Grocers' Company on 28 February, which ended, in the words of Ludlow, in 'dissolute and unbecoming debauchery, for it was his custom not to depart from these publick meetings till he was drunk as a beast'. In the following weeks he was entertained by the

Clothworkers, the Drapers, the Skinners and the Vintners. By then even Monck's legendary capacity for food and drink was exhausted, and he was reduced to abstinence, claiming sound religious reasons for his forbearance, 'as not agreeable to the distemper of the times, and the season which the Church of England hath heretofore appropriated to abstinence and humility rather than to triumphs or entertainments'.

Monck's behaviour was typical of a growing disenchantment with the Puritan ethic, seen as ineffectual and hypocritical. A pamphlet, printed in 1659, entitled A *Character of England*, opposed to the increasing liberality of society, railed against taverns where 'fury and intemperance reign . . . ladies of the greatest quality suffer themselves to be treated in one of those taverns, where a curtezan in other cities would scarcely vouchsafe to be entertained; but you will be more astonish't when I shall assure you that they drink their crowned cups roundly, strain healths through their smocks, daunce after the fiddle, kiss freely, and tearm it an honourable treat'. Hyde, ever keen to moralise, had written of the young people 'educated in all the liberty of vice, without reprehension or restraint'. Doubtless the Chancellor would have disapproved of Pepys, who ended the month enjoying an outing to Cambridge, where he was reunited with his father and brother, 'playing the fool with the lass of the house at the door of chamber'.

On 15 March, the Long Parliament, perhaps the most influential in English history, sat for the last time. Whig historians, led by Lord Macaulay, have always stoutly defended the early achievements of 'that renowned Parliament which, in spite of many errors and disasters, is justly entitled to the reverence and gratitude of all who, in any part of the world, enjoy the blessings of constitutional government'. Contemporaries held a less exalted opinion at the time of its demise; one commented: 'The Long Parliament did great things for the first eight years. Then, I confess, it is best to sigh them out in sorrowful silence.' Londoners celebrated with bonfires the expiry with 'many sad pangs and groanes' of this universally despised institution.

The final acts of this famous parliament showed how out of touch it was with the mood of the country. A futile attempt was made to debar from the forthcoming election all who had fought for the Stuarts, and a vindictive attack was directed at the Church of England and all Roman Catholics. Mr Crewe, a zealous Presbyterian, urged his fellow members that 'before we dissolve ourselves, we should bear witness against the horrid murder of the King, and protest that we had neither hand nor heart in that affair'. Some MPs hastened to offer their support, but Thomas Scot remained implacably hostile. With foolhardy bravery he declared that he 'desired no greater honour in this world, than that the following inscription should be engraved on his tomb: "Here lieth one who had a hand and heart in the execution of Charles Stuart, late king of England."' These words were to sign Scot's death warrant when he was tried for the crime of regicide in the autumn.

There were fierce arguments among members over the writs to be issued for the forthcoming elections. No one but the King had power to summon parliament. Whether writs were to be issued by peers in the King's name, or by Monck, or even Richard Cromwell, they were still illegal. Under the Commonwealth, with the monarchy abolished, this had not mattered, but now, with the restoration a real possibility, it assumed great importance. The final compromise, that they should be issued in the name of the keepers of the liberties of England under the great seal of the realm, satisfied nobody.

Giavarina, susceptible to the mood of the populace, reported the King's restoration 'is absolutely necessary if this nation wishes to live at peace; otherwise it can only expect constant trouble and disaster'. The evening of parliament's dismissal, the painter Michael Darby was passing the Royal Exchange when he noted an empty niche where the statue of Charles I had once stood with the inscription 'Exit Tyrannus'. Darby set up his ladder and proceeded to replace the inscription with 'Vive le Roy', whereupon he threw his cap in the air and cried out, 'God save King Charles the Second.' The assembled crowd, full of admiration for Darby's daring, took up the cry.

Pepys, observing the growing swell of Royalist sentiment in London, listened to a sermon on a theme from the book of Ezra, 'Pray for the life of the King, and the King's son', before leaving the capital. On 23 March he embarked with Montagu in the *Swiftsure* at Greenhithe. The admiral, however, was still unsure of the loyalty of his fleet and had drawn up a list of the religious and political inclinations of his captains. Lawson had already submitted his suggestions for naval appointments to parliament on 22 February, many of them, including the Anabaptist George Dakins, well-known radicals, but Montagu had very different ideas. His list included men who were loyal to him personally and excluded the radicals. It was a tense moment when Lawson's squadron greeted its new commander with a broadside of such violence that it shattered all the windows in Pepys's cabin. A few days later the diarist heard a report of 'a great whispering of some of the Vice-Admiral's [Lawson's] captains that they were dissatisfied, and did intend to fight themselves to oppose the General [Montagu]. It was soon hushed, however, and the Vice-Admiral did wholly deny any such thing, and protested to stand by the General.' Lawson made no move while Montagu proceeded to weed out Anabaptists and other disaffected officers. Dakins of the *Worcester* and Algate of the *Oxford*, the two most dangerous captains, were to be left behind when the squadron sailed across to Holland to collect the King. All these events Montagu recorded in letters to Charles, who was kept closely informed 'what officers he was confident of, and of whom he was not assured'.

With the Royalists everywhere in the ascendancy, all eyes were directed towards Monck. This 'dull, heavy man', in Pepys's opinion, continued to send out confusing signals. Rumours abounded. He was reputed to be strongly influenced by his forceful, low-born wife, nicknamed 'Dirty Bess', known to have Royalist inclinations, and it was said that his son Kit had overheard his parents talking in bed of the King's restoration. Dr Barwick, one of the most intelligent and well-informed Royalist agents sending regular reports to Brussels, was unable to fathom his intentions. On 10 March he wrote: 'On Wednesday he declared himself to my friend that he would acquiesce in the judgement of the parliament both in relation to your Majesty and the House of Lords; and yet yesterday he told him, in great passion, he would spend the last drop of blood, rather than the Stuarts should ever come into England; though I hear from other hands he was in good temper again the same night.'

The fiery Republican Henry Marten, fearful for the future, came to take his leave of Monck on 16 March before departing England for Holland. When asked what form of government he meant to establish, the general replied: 'A Commonwealth'. The incredulous Marten retorted: 'I ought to believe your excellency, but will you give me leave to tell a story? It was this: a city tailor was met one evening in the country with instruments of husbandry, and was asked what he was going to do. "To make measure for a new suit," he answered. – "What! With a spade and pick-axe?" – "Yes, these are the measures now in fashion."'

There was one Royalist who held the key that would unlock this close-guarded man's mind but he had been denied the opportunity to employ it. Sir John Grenville, a fellow Devonian and a cousin of Monck's, carried messages from the King to the general. On several occasions he had waited in the reception chamber of St James's Palace, hoping to secure a private interview with the general, who greeted him cordially but would always excuse himself by claiming that he had urgent business to deal with or needed to retire to bed. When pressed, he urged Grenville to give his message to Monck's close confidant William Morice. This Grenville refused to do. Finally, on 16 March, on the dissolution of parliament, Morice informed him that the general would see him in his quarters the following evening.

On entering Monck's chambers, Grenville immediately notified the general of his royal commission, stating 'that he was infinitely obliged to his Excellency for giving him this opportunity of discharging himself of a trust of great importance both to himself and the whole Kingdom that had been long deposited in his hands: and that, whatsoever became of him, he thought himself very happy to have this good occasion of performing his duty, in obeying the commands of the King, his master'. Grenville then handed the general a letter from the King with the commission authorising him to deliver it.

Monck remained cautious, holding the letter in his hand and frowning. But, once he was reassured that Grenville had kept secret the fact that he had sent Nicholas Monck to meet his brother the previous summer with a message from the King, his frown was replaced by a smile. He complimented his cousin on the 'prudence, fidelity, care and constancy you have shown in this great affair, and I am much pleased also at your resolute secrecy in it'. At last the general read the King's letter, before uttering the momentous words: 'I hope the King will forgive what is past, both in my words and actions, according to the contents of his gracious letter, for my heart was ever faithful to him. But I was never in a condition to do him service till this present time. And you shall assure his Majesty that I am now ready to obey his commands, but to sacrifice my life and fortune in his service.' He then added: 'To witness this I call this honest man from the door.' Crossing the room, Monck summoned Morice, who had been waiting outside, to join the two men. Ever cautious, however, the general refused to put anything in writing, but asked Grenville to return two days later, when Monck would give him his reply to the King.

On 19 March, the expectant Royalist made his way once again to St James's. He was handed a letter which he memorised before the general threw the incriminating piece of paper on the fire. Grenville was to repeat the contents to the King alone, possibly because he had little confidence in Hyde, whom he suspected of plotting against him. Monck advised Charles to write to both himself and parliament, outlining his terms for a restoration. These included a general pardon and a land settlement favouring the present pattern of ownership, a highly contentious issue, since it meant that all those Parliamentarians who had acquired Royalist land during and after the Civil Wars would not be obliged to hand back their newly acquired estates.

In Brussels, Charles had no idea of the success of Grenville's mission. But, on receipt of a letter from Mordaunt assuring him of Monck's change of heart regarding a restoration, he decided to write again directly to the general. He began the letter in cautious fashion. 'If this be the first letter you have received from me,' Charles wrote, 'it is only because some of your friends have not found a convenience of delivering one to you, which they have had long in their hands. And you cannot but believe, that I know too well the power you have to do me good or harm, not to desire you should be my friend.' He then appealed to Monck's patriotism as 'a great lover of your country and that you desire to secure the peace and happiness and to advance the honour of it, and knowing very well that my heart is full of no other end, which I am sure you will know yourself as soon as you know me'.

This letter proved unnecessary, since Grenville was already en route for Brussels, taking care to avoid the floods that had inundated London. Four days after departing the capital, he arrived in Brussels. On his journey he had been accompanied by Mordaunt, who knew nothing of the vital message he was carrying. On his arrival, the King and senior Royalists gathered in Hyde's lodgings: Hyde himself, Grenville, Mordaunt, Ormonde and Nicholas. The King was anxious to know how he should reward Monck. Grenville offered sound advice: 'Wait till he sees Your Majesty in Whitehall.' Charles now felt less obligation to enter into negotiations with the Presbyterian leaders in England, who were confident that Monck, as a fellow Presbyterian, shared their views. He gave no more than a vaguely encouraging response to overtures from the Earl of Manchester and Sir Denzil Holles, both of whom Charles I had attempted to arrest in 1642. As the King noted to Grenville with considerable satisfaction: 'Little do they in England think that General Monk and I are upon such good terms.'

Charles was more concerned with acting upon Monck's advice. He and his advisers decided that they would let parliament decide the thorny question of the land settlement. Hyde, Ormonde and Nicholas now proceeded to draw up an Act of Indemnity with the major exception of the regicides, about whom the King was adamant. As Hyde recorded: 'No man was more disposed to a general act of indemnity and oblivion than his majesty was.' 'But', he continued, 'he thought it neither consistent with his honour, nor his conscience, that those who had sat as judges, and condemned his father to be murdered, should be comprehended in that act of pardon.'

Charles had been devoted to his father. They had been drawn together during the First Civil War. From 1642 to 1644 the Prince of Wales had barely left his father's side. He and his brother James had been present at the battle of Edgehill, when Charles had bravely attempted to charge a Parliamentarian dragoon, and later had accompanied the King on a triumphant campaign in the west, and celebrated his father's victories at Cropredy Bridge and Lostwithiel. Charles I had sent the Prince of Wales away from Oxford, the Royalist capital, in the spring of 1644, in order to prevent his possible capture, but had continued a regular correspondence with his son. The Prince had been powerless to prevent his father's capture in 1646, but had attempted to lead a fleet to his rescue on the Isle of Wight during the Second Civil War. He had been stunned on receiving news of Charles I's execution in 1649. The King would never forgive those who signed his father's death warrant.

Interestingly, all the key meetings of senior Royalists discussing the restoration were held without James, Duke of York. Charles's brother, four years his junior, had been his companion since the Duke's escape from England in 1648 and had earned his reputation as an able soldier, serving in the French army, while the exiled Court was based in Paris. However, his political judgement was faulty. There had been trouble in 1656 when he had initially refused to obey Charles's command to leave the French army and to join the King on his move to the Spanish Netherlands (France and the English Commonwealth being at war with Spain). The Duke of York had listened to his friend Sir John Berkeley, an inveterate intriguer, who had unwisely urged him to defy his brother. Like his father,

James had a rigid and dogmatic mind and was incapable of making compromises. Moreover, his choice of advisers was often poor, and this had led to clashes between the two brothers. These traits, which were to prove so disastrous when he eventually succeeded Charles, meant that the King preferred to rely on Hyde and Ormonde at this crucial juncture.

Hyde was busy working on the document known as the Declaration of Breda, but his work was interrupted constantly by the hordes of supplicants who inundated the Royalist Court. Both the King and his Chancellor could see how difficult it would be to satisfy all parties and to impose a lasting settlement. Some came looking for a pardon, 'others brought good presents in English gold to the king', as Hyde wryly noted, a far cry from the desperate poverty and crushing debts the exiles had been living in and under but a month before.

Charles was willing to accept any supporters, however recently they might have decided to join his cause. Sir Anthony Ashley Cooper, now a leading member of the Council of State, had started the First Civil War fighting for the Cavaliers, before changing sides and becoming a member of Cromwell's Council of State. Charles II had appealed for Ashley Cooper's support in 1655 but without eliciting a response. On 15 March 1660 he tried again: 'I value myself upon being a good Englishman, and do as much, if not more, than any man, desire the peace, happiness, and security of the nation, and why you, who have so fair a share in it, should not be willing to assist me in the right way of procuring it, I cannot imagine.' When the King received no reply, he authorised Ashley Cooper's brother-in-law Henry Coventry to go to London and win him over, if necessary with the offer of a title. Two months later, Ashley Cooper was a member of the delegation conveying the official invitation for the return of the King. He was to give a typically Machiavellian defence of his behaviour, that 'the less he was thought to be the King's friend, the more he had the power of being it'. Not surprisingly, Hyde regarded him as a man of a 'slippery humour'. More reassuring was an address from the noblemen and gentlemen of

Scotland, anxious to make known the zeal and loyalty of the King's subjects 'in this your antient kingdom'.

From the Hague, appeared two commissioners from the Netherlands. After the usual flowery compliments, the Dutchmen, in the words of Giavarina, 'begged him [Charles] not to take it ill that they had been in constant correspondence with his rebels, as the States were obliged to take their course in their own interests and to preserve trade'. Considering their previous complete indifference and hostility to his fate, the King must have smiled ruefully at the commissioners' emphasis on their 'ancient friendship'. He was to prove Holland's most acrimonious foe in the years ahead and led his country into two bitterly fought wars with the Dutch, in a determined effort to destroy their maritime supremacy.

12

MONCK TURNS ROYALIST

By the end of March 1660, Monck was ready to declare his Royalist allegiance publicly. The last hurdle to overcome was the resistance of die-hard Republicans in the Army, many of whom were likely to resist the idea of the Restoration. The general, with the advice of Clarges, preferred to entrust his person to the London Militia, who had shown sympathy for the Royalist cause. Six hundred of these men, under the command of Maj Gen Richard Browne, soon to lead the procession welcoming Charles back into this capital, kept guard outside Monck's quarters in Whitehall in addition to the general's own troops.

The leaders of the Rump, following the lead of Hesilrige, had submitted to Monck. Some of the secluded members, however, now that they had regained power after an absence of eleven years, still contemplated restoring the King with conditions, with Presbyterianism as the state religion. But they were fatally disunited. Some of their leaders, such as Sir William Waller, Sir Denzil Holles and Lord Willoughby, had been secret Royalists for years; others, such as Sir Harbottle Grimston, soon to be Speaker of the Commons, had only just renounced their Republican sympathies.

Royalists who had spent so long fretting over Monck's intentions were now reassured that he had returned to his former allegiance. Mordaunt reported to the King on 24 March: 'His frank and absolute refusal of the legislative power, preferred him, under what title soever he should choose, by the corrupt officers of the army and all eminent Rump-men, gives good evidence of his honesty and future resolutions.' Col Charles Howard, soon to be appointed Governor of Carlisle, was equally optimistic four days later, writing to his sovereign: 'Monk is now far from being your enemy, but he will go his own pace. . . . Meanwhile, do not entangle yourself in any foreign treaty, how specious soever, nor in any engagement to particular persons that are obnoxious to the power here; for nothing besides, in my poor opinion, can hinder the happy close of your affairs.'

Monck's own directives acknowledged the new dispensation. In a note sent to Robert Stent on 29 March he declared: 'I appoint you, by virtue of the power delegated in me by King Charles II, as firemaster of the garrison of Dunkirk.' This was the town whose capture by Cromwell was one of the most celebrated achievements of the Commonwealth. Its governor, Lockhart, soon to be replaced by Col Edward Harley, formerly a secluded member, had proved immune to Royalist overtures, happy to lock up anyone he felt threatened the Commonwealth. On the mainland, well-known Cavaliers such as Sir Horatio Townshend were rewarded for their loyalty with the appointment of Governor of King's Lynn.

Everywhere, emblems of the Commonwealth were hastily being taken down and replaced with the royal arms. There was a semi-hysterical reaction to anyone suspected of showing insufficient loyalty to the Stuart dynasty. Hyde was gratified to hear from a correspondent in London how the King's picture 'is hung up in many places in the streets, and all that goe by stop to look upon it; amongst whom there was one yesterday that said he had seen him lately and that he was not so handsome as that picture, at which the people were so angry they fell upon the man and beat him soundly, by which you may judge their inclinations'.

The European powers had been monitoring the extraordinary turn of events across the Channel. Cardinal Mazarin, fresh from his triumph at the Treaty of the Pyrenees, which had brought to a conclusion the long war with Spain, instructed his ambassador Bordeaux to strive to win the friendship of Monck, reminding him of Cromwell's friendship for France. The general, however, remained as taciturn as ever when Bordeaux went to see him, and seemed impervious to the ambassador's overtures, claiming that any alliance with France was dependent on the approval of parliament. Mazarin knew that he could expect few favours from Charles if he was restored. The King had never forgiven his removal from France in 1654 on the orders of Mazarin, as a central part of the treaty he had negotiated with Cromwell. The Cardinal had continued to ignore Charles subsequently, most recently at Fuenterrabía the previous autumn. The King's ministers were also suspicious of Mazarin's support of Henrietta Maria and her Catholic entourage based in Paris, who were hostile to the cause of the Church of England championed by Hyde and Ormonde.

The Dutch, who had also ignored the Royalists, were anxious to make amends. When Ormonde crossed the border to deliver a letter from Charles to his sister Mary at the Hague, he was immediately confronted by Jan de Witt, the Grand Pensioner of Holland. De Witt, a stalwart Republican and opponent of the House of Orange, had previously refused every overture from the Royalists, but the Dutchman 'assured him [Ormonde] of his utmost readiness to serve his master'. The Marquis of Ormonde and his fellow Royalists, remembering how they had been ignored by the Dutch government even when Holland had been at war with the English Commonwealth, treated these honeyed words with due caution. Hyde wrote on 27 March: 'I do assure you, that all that was ever yet proposed from foreign powers was so without foundation of reasonable hope that the King never gave further ear to it than by returning thanks for their good affections.' John Evelyn reported to the Chancellor his conversation six months previously with the Dutch ambassador who told him: 'His nation mind only their own profit, do nothing out of gratitude, but collaterally as it relates to their gain or security; and therefore the English were to look for nothing of assistance to the banish'd King.'

The Spanish ruler of the Netherlands, the Marquis of Caracena, and the Governor of Brussels, Don Alonso de Cardenas, who had witnessed the lowest point in Royalist fortunes while the exiled Court was based first at Bruges and then at Brussels, seemed unaware of the upturn in

Royalist fortunes. They continued to deprive Charles of funds, Cardenas showing no compunction in withholding 100,000 ducats sent from Spain for the King. Their masters in Spain were equally uninterested in the possibility of a restoration. When Hyde wrote to Sir Henry Bennet, Charles's minister in Madrid, to inform the Spanish government, Bennet replied that he did not dare report the matter, since it regarded Royalist hopes as 'without foundation of sense', and the King's condition as 'most deplorable, and absolutely desperate'. Nevertheless, Spain was still at war with the English Commonwealth. In the unlikely event that Charles was restored to the throne, the Spanish would suddenly be in possession of an extremely valuable hostage. The Portugese, engaged in a desperate struggle for independence from Spain, and anxious to make an alliance with the King, realised the danger Charles was in. Their ambassador in London warned Monck, who, in turn, informed Grenville.

When Grenville arrived in Brussels, he passed on Monck's warning. On 3 April the King asked permission from the Marquis of Caracena to visit his sister Mary in Breda. A strong-minded, proud character, acutely conscious of her Stuart blood, which did little to endear her to the republican Dutch government, Mary was the closest in age to the King and had proved his most loyal supporter. Although her husband, William II, had died very young in 1650, she remained unbowed and was an endless source of support for Charles and his brothers with her youthful high spirits.

There was nothing strange about the King's request to visit his sister. But the Spanish authorities, suddenly aware of the changing situation, were suspicious. The night that Charles requested permission to visit Breda, Hyde was woken by William Galloway, Irish page of Cardenas, who had come to tell him that the Spaniards had decided to put the King under guard. To prove his story he produced a note he had found on Don Alonso's bedside table. Hyde sent Galloway on to the King who read Cardenas's note in bed. Summoning Ormonde, Grenville and his equerry, Nicholas Armorer, he hastily dressed and saddled his horse.

By three o'clock in the morning the royal party was safely outside the walls of Brussels. Five hours later the Spanish guard arrived to find that the royal bird had flown.

As soon as Charles and his party had crossed into Dutch territory, he entrusted Grenville with a copy of the Declaration of Breda to take to England. This was Hyde's masterpiece, a document carefully designed to restore the King to his rightful position and to appeal to all parties. The three key issues: the offer of a general pardon, the desire for 'a liberty to tender consciences', and the ownership of land, were referred to the judgement of parliament. Hyde's caution was well judged. It was to take a generation of intense political struggle before the latter two contentious issues were finally resolved. Grenville had asked for no reward for himself for the crucial role he had played in negotiations with Monck but, as he departed, the King slipped a letter into his pocket. The faithful Cavalier was appointed Groom of the Stole and First Gentleman of the Bedchamber, important posts that gave the holder constant access to the sovereign. Charles offered to pay all of his and his father's debts and settled on Grenville land worth £3,000 p.a. Lastly, he was to be created Earl of Bath. Greatly encouraged by this largesse, Grenville headed for England.

Copies of the Declaration of Breda were presented to Monck and Montagu, the Council of State, the House of Commons and the Lord Mayor and aldermen of the City of London. To show his fundamental belief in the restoration of the old order, Charles authorised Grenville to deliver one to the House of Lords, a body that had been abolished at the same time as the monarchy in 1649. This letter expressed the hope that the Lords would once again have 'the authority and jurisdiction which hath always belonged to you by your birth and the fundamental laws of the land'. This clear attempt to reinstate the old order was the firmest indication of the growing confidence of Hyde and his master.

Royalists flocked to Breda to greet the King in such numbers that the town almost ran out of food. They were rewarded with the sight of the royal family enjoying their change in fortune. The staunch Catholic William Blundell, who had suffered much for the cause over the years, wrote: 'I saw the Dukes of York and Gloucester with their sister the Princess of Orange, play a long time at ninepins upon a Sunday, whilst the King their brother looked on.' Roger Palmer, who came with 'great expenses, and a slender fortune', hoping for Hyde's help, found that it was his 'gay wife' who caught the King's eye instead. Barbara Villiers, an auburn-haired, blue-eyed beauty, was a cousin of the Duke of Buckingham, Charles's childhood friend. The young Barbara had recently married Roger Palmer, but had already enjoyed a full love life, including a wild affair with the Earl of Chesterfield, a notorious rake who had arrived in January at the Royalist Court after killing a rival in a duel in England.

Charles's ministers were besieged by supplicants, anxious to gain office. Sir Edward Nicholas tried to refrain from any definite decisions on preferment. When he came across a petition from 'John Stone, recommended by Mrs Monck, he being now her son's dancing master', he noted curtly: 'I never heard of such a place. Respited [delayed].' Hyde had to bear the brunt of dealing with these supplicants and was realistic about the merits of the King's myriad new-found supporters. 'They were observed to be most importunate who had deserved least,' he observed caustically. However, few were turned down flat, since the Royalists did not want to make unnecessary enemies, but they sometimes received lesser posts than they had hoped for. Sir Abraham Shipman had petitioned for the office of chief armourer in the Tower, but was made keeper of the lighthouse at Dungeness instead. Senior Royalists were equally anxious to cash in on their unstinting years of service. Mordaunt, who had so nearly lost his life for the cause, and had been rewarded with a viscountcy, was hoping to be made a Gentleman of the Bedchamber and to have the lease of a lucrative coal farm in Newcastle.

The Chancellor continued to keep up an immense correspondence, directing Royalist candidates in the election at the end of the month, and encouraging friends and supporters. It was vital that the Cavaliers should not appear vindictive, however much they had suffered for the cause. In particular, there must be no fallout over religion, which had been such a divisive issue during the Civil Wars. In April Hyde sent across George Morley, shortly to become Bishop of Winchester, to meet Gilbert Sheldon, soon to be Bishop of London and future Archbishop of Canterbury, and to hold discussions between leading Anglicans and Presbyterians. The Chancellor hoped that, if episcopacy was restored, some Presbyterians might be persuaded to apply to be bishops, since he had a cynical view of many former opponents' sincere attachment to Presbyterianism. He dismissed Sir William Waller's attachment to the passion and rigour of the Presbyterians' with the remark: 'My Lord Mordaunt will easily discover what place will oblige him.'

Some of the leading Scottish Presbyterians were equally biddable. Hyde had never trusted the Covenanters and had strongly disapproved of the King's taking the Covenant in 1650. As James Sharp, a prominent Presbyterian and future primate of Scotland, noted: 'No notice is taken of Scotland in the treaty [of Breda]: We shall be left to the King, which is best for us.' Like the equally ambitious Earl of Lauderdale, recently released from the Tower, where he had been incarcerated for nine years, Sharp was willing to sacrifice his beliefs in order to secure the alliance of the Anglican circle at the Royalist Court in exile. These two men were to become the dominant figures in post-Restoration Scotland.

The tension of the past few months was taking its toll of Hyde, a man almost 60 years old and suffering from gout. He described to his close friend Lady Mordaunt his exhaustion, 'so short of sleep he could hardly hold his head up and did not know what he was writing'. One of the reasons that the Chancellor was so tired was that he knew full well that his close alliance with the King had earned him many enemies. Lady Mordaunt was sensitive to his predicament, and wrote affectionately that 'her own kindness for Hyde is such that half the town believes him her gallant'. More importantly, Charles remained Hyde's greatest ally. He wrote from Breda to the Cavalier general Sir Alan Apsley, brother-in-law to the regicide Col Hutchinson, citing his numerous opponents: ''Tis from some of those who are not so much my friends that the report comes that the Chancellor should have lost my favour. The truth of it is, I look upon the spreaders of that lie as more my enemies than his, for he will always be found an honest man, and I should deserve the name of a very unjust master if I should reward him so ill that hath served me so faithfully. Therefore I do conjure you to let so many as you can of my friends know the falsehood and malice of that report, and I shall take it as a service.'

On a lighter note, money ceased to be in such short supply, and Hyde and his fellow Royalists no longer suffered from acute hunger. The high-minded Chancellor, determined to benefit from the upturn in his fortune, immediately sent off to his friend John Cosin to scour the bookshops of Paris and purchase all the books printed at the Louvre. They were to be sumptuously bound and gilded. So excited was Hyde by the prospect of enlarging his library that he was even prepared to offer a top Parisian binder travelling expenses for himself and his family to come to England, a free house there and similar wages to those he enjoyed in the French capital.

Charles's sister Mary had wasted no time in informing the States of Holland, who had prevented her entertaining her brothers in her own home and had snubbed the House of Orange in favour of an alliance with the English Commonwealth, of her brother's change in fortune. She was gratified to note their rapid change of heart, beseeching the King to grace their capital at the Hague with his presence, where a magnificent reception 'would testify the great joy of their hearts for the Divine blessings which Providence was showering upon his head'.

Charles had a less cordial relationship with his mother, who resented her son's refusal to take her advice, particularly on religion. Henrietta Maria complained querulously that the Spanish had not paid her pension for eighteen months (hardly surprising since she was living in France). On a more personal note, she even chided her son with the expense of enter-taining him during his fortnight's stay at Colombes the previous winter.

171

Montagu, waiting for orders from parliament to sail across the North Sea to collect the King, had transferred from the *Swiftsure* to his flagship, the *Naseby*. He continued to cashier officers he suspected of disloyalty but it was work that needed careful handling. The admiral confided to Pepys on 11 April that he had little confidence in John Stokes, the senior captain of the fleet, and was even unsure of his own flag captain, Roger Cuttance. Christopher Hatton, assigned by Hyde to keep watch of developments at sea, was over-optimistic when he reported a week later: 'All the Fanatics in the Fleet have been turned out of command.' Of Lawson's twenty-one captains, just seven accompanied Montagu when he crossed the North Sea to Holland. The admiral kept the appointment of officers entirely in his own hands, and even ignored Monck's choices, a clear sign of the distance between the two men.

Montagu was in constant communication with the King, at first in great secrecy, but by the end of April, 'all the world', as Pepys recorded, knew where the stream of messengers visiting the admiral's flagship were heading. A month previously his fellow admiral, William Penn, one of the leading Commonwealth admirals in the wars with Holland and Spain, father of the eminent Quaker and founder of Pennsylvania, and now an Admiralty Commissioner, came to dine with his old colleague. Penn had played his hand astutely, using his friendship with Monck and his contact with Royalists to ensure that he obtained a pardon from the King. He was to return from Holland with a knighthood. Monck was anxious that nothing should mar the restoration. Even the Republican Robert Blackthorne, who had protested so bitterly at Lawson's apostasy in early March, was changing his position. A month later he was reconciled to the King, this 'sober man', and after a further month he was enthusing: 'Our great expectations and longings are for the safe return of his Majesty, whom the hearts of the whole nation (as one man) are towards.'

Pepys was a novice to life at sea and remained insatiably curious. Despite a bout of seasickness, he was soon enjoying 'a barrel of pickled oysters', playing at ninepins and making merry with Will Howe, so that his clothes were spoilt with the ale that had been spilt on them. Pepys was, however, kept busy by Montagu, who was issuing a stream of orders concerned with victualling ships (the cheapest place in England to do this was Bristol), paying the seamen and trying to secure the release of prisoners, either taken in the war with Spain or by Barbary pirates operating from the ports of North Africa. They posed a substantial threat; the Irish Royalist Lord Inchiquin and his son were captured by pirates from Algiers as they were entering the port of Lisbon, and enslaved. The Admiralty Commissioners, meanwhile, were trying to bring an end to hostilities with Spain by instigating an agreement between Monck, in his role as general-at-sea, and the Marquis of Caracena, whereby all prisoners, past and present, were to be released immediately.

It appeared that the Republican cause had been totally defeated. Certainly any threat that Richard Cromwell might return to power had long disappeared. On 18 April the former Lord Protector wrote despondently to Monck that for some time he had been forced 'to retire into hiding-places to avoid arrests for debts contracted upon the public account'. A few days earlier Marchamont Nedham, editor of *Mercurius Politicus*, a staunch supporter of the Rump Parliament, and a keen observer of the political scene, absconded. Okey, a regicide and known troublemaker, published his *Lamentation* on 26 March, still breathing defiance, but was swiftly confined to his home and his regiment 'remodelled'.

It was evident that the forthcoming elections would return a clear majority of Royalists. Many members of the New Model Army, however, had little time for democracy. They belonged to a sect of the Anabaptists, known as Fifth Monarchy Men. Having supported the decision to execute Charles I, they were aghast at the thought of the restoration of his son at the head of the Church of England. It was rumoured that Desborough was planning to 'secure' Charles Stuart, his brothers, 'that villain' Monck and parliament, filled with 'carnal, selfish men'. A rising in Wales would sweep all before it. In this tense atmosphere, rumours abounded. Maj Wood wrote to Hyde that Monck's wife was seen crying because her husband had been poisoned. On 11 April, Monck was given some reassurance by the presentation of a declaration of loyalty by the Army. Those officers who refused to sign it were, effectively, handing in their resignations.

There was one man, however, who could unite these disaffected troops under his banner. On 10 April, Lambert escaped from the Tower. Thomas Rugg gave a graphic account:

> about 8 of the clock att night hee made his escape, hee haveinge got a rope tied fast to his windo, by which he slided downe, and in eatch hand hercher upon his descent; and six men were ready to receive him, who had a barge ready to hasten away, which was effectually don, shee that made the bed beeing privey to his escape; and that eveninge, to blinde the warder when hee came to lock the chamber doore, shee went to bede and possessed Colonel Lambertts lock the chamber doore according to his useall maner hee found the curtains drawne, and the said warder conceived it to bee Coll. John Lambert. Hee said Good night, my lord, to which a seeming voice replyd and prevented further jelouses. And next morninge hee came to unlock the doore, and espinge her face cryed out, In the name of God, Joane, what makes you heare?

It was little wonder that the news was reputed to have put 'the general [Monck] and the Council of State into a great agony'. A proclamation was immediately published against Lambert or anyone sheltering him, with a £100 reward for his arrest. The Council also ordered chains to be put across the streets of the City and three regiments of the trained bands to be on guard. Rumours abounded and widespread panic gripped the populace, convinced that his escape would lead to a renewed civil war.

Monck was informed by one of his officers: 'I have very good ground to beleive yt ye Agitators and Lamberts Agents are all over England privately creepinge amongst us & temptinge our men from us & their affecons & I beleive a Generall risinge is intended & very great endeavours to cause all or most of ye Army to revolt.'

Lambert had decided, after lying low in London for a few days, to head for the Midlands, where he hoped to raise his old followers for the 'Good Old Cause' at Edgehill, scene of the opening battle of the First Civil War. It was rumoured that men from his native York 'were all Lambertonians and sectaries', and that he was assembling a force of '7,000 Quakers and Anabaptists'. Lambert's problem was that, in order to gather his supporters, he must publish the fact, thus alerting the Government. A few stalwart Republicans, such as Cols Okey, Cobbett and Axtel, joined him, but many more potential allies, such as Ludlow, who had left London some time before, hesitated before committing themselves.

Monck sent popular Col Ingoldsby post-haste to Northampton to deal with Lambert, and there he was joined by Col Streater on 21 April. Monck had also decided what to do if his plan misfired. He summoned Grenville and gave him the news: 'I know not yet what may become of this revolt. If Ingoldsby is beaten, and the army goes over to Lambert [as it had done the previous April and October] that he cannot be suppressed but by a war, I am resolved to put off all disguise, declare the King's commission, own it for the authority by which I act, and call the royal party to arms in all places through England, Scotland and Ireland.' He then instructed Grenville to ask his brother to convey a letter to the King.

Monck's fears were never realised, although risings of some sort were attempted in at least nine counties. The next day, Easter Sunday, the two forces met outside Daventry. Ingoldsby rode up and down in front of Lambert's troops, haranguing them on the dangers of renewed civil war. Gradually, they began to hold 'the noses of their pistols to the ground' and to break ranks. Lambert was seized as he attempted to flee, 'mounted on a Barb, which might have hastened his flight, providence had so ordered it, that he was on ploughed land, where his horse could prove of little advantage to him'. Ingoldsby rode him down and 'vow'd to pistol him if he did not immediately yield'. As he was led back to captivity in London, he reminded the colonel of Cromwell's remark as they set out for Scotland a decade earlier with the cheers of the crowd ringing in their ears: 'These very persons would shout as much if you and I were going to be hanged.' As he stood beneath the gallows at Tyburn, a warning to other potential rebels, before being recommitted to the Tower, Lambert must have pondered Cromwell's words. Ingoldsby, as a regicide, was also in great danger from vengeful Cavaliers, but his prompt capture of Lambert was to stand him in good stead when he was put on trial in the autumn.

Hyde was very relieved that Lambert's precipitate action had led to his downfall. He wrote: 'It may very reasonably be believed that if he had, after he found himself at liberty, lain concealed till he had digested the method he meant to proceed in, and procured some place to which the troops might resort to declare with him when he should appear . . . he would have gone near to have shaken and dissolved the model the general had made . . . he precipitated himself to make an attempt before he was ready for it or it for him.'

In order to avert any further threat of mutiny, Monck continued his purge of officers suspected of fanaticism. Col Moss's regiment was under suspicion and was ordered to march to Kennington Common on 21 April, where the troops received their arrears of pay and were disbanded. On Easter Tuesday a general muster of the militia was held in Hyde Park. Monck, fresh from interviewing Lambert, took the salute alongside the Lord Mayor. The six regiments numbered some 14,000 men and were commanded by prominent aldermen with openly Royalist sympathies. Many of the troops, including men of rank serving as volunteers, were wearing the King's colours and drinking his health openly.

13

BRING BACK KING CHARLES

The weeks leading up to the election of the new parliament were ones of intense political activity. With the Republican party now in total retreat, a deluge of tracts, pamphlets and letters poured from the press, attacking the leading figures of the Interregnum, civilian, military and religious, who were declared to be knaves, villains and hypocrites. Proclamations ordering Cavaliers to leave London were ignored with impunity. The main issue was whether the King was to be restored with or without conditions. Many Anglican Royalists, who had suffered greatly over the past twenty years, blamed the Presbyterians for the original break with Charles I. The King and Hyde signalled their approval of the use by the influential Onslow family in Surrey of the rallying cry: 'No Rumpers, no Presbyterians that will put bad conditions on the King.'

When the results came in, Royalists of all types were everywhere returned in triumph. There were incidents of double counting, and where disaffected soldiers tried to prevent candidates they disapproved of from standing, but this did little to affect the result, a whole-scale rejection of the Commonwealth rulers. Many successful candidates were men who had defied the Army in the late autumn, such as Col Howard for Cumberland, Col Rossiter for Lincolnshire, Ashley Cooper for Wiltshire and Fairfax for Yorkshire. Monck took his seat for his native Devon. Sir George Booth and Sir Thomas Middleton, who had led the revolt the previous August, were among the successful candidates, as was Sir Robert Pye, who had been sent to the Tower in January for championing the secluded members. In London, despite the large number of candidates who stood, Alderman Robinson and Maj Gen Browne, both known Royalists, were elected unopposed.

Supporters of Lambert's coup were rejected to a man. In contrast, Ingoldsby, whose popularity was high following his arrest of Lambert, was elected. Col Hutchinson, however, a fellow regicide, despite having just quelled an outbreak of violence between soldiers and townspeople in Nottingham, was elected but then expelled for having participated in the King's trial. Anyone perceived to be likely to oppose the restoration of peace and order was voted out. Not a single sectarian or Republican was returned for a county seat. Sixteen members of the Rump Parliament were elected but they did not include Hesilrige. Two hundred gentlemen in Leicester had declared that they would spend no more money in the town should he be elected, and the abrasive Rumper, recently one of the most powerful men in England, was defeated.

Even Monck was powerless when he proposed candidates seen as opponents of the restoration. Speaker Lenthall, who had been elected to the Long Parliament back in 1640 and had sat through all the constitutional changes since, had the personal recommendation of the general. But he was decisively rejected for the seat of Oxford University, despite his son's best efforts to ply voters with roast beef and ale. The general consensus was, in the words of Henry Stubbs of Christ Church, that 'William Lenthall was a rogue who had run away with a mace to join the army in 1647.' Elsewhere the officials of Bridgnorth, when recommended by Monck to put forward Thurloe, replied that they did not dare make use of the general's letter.

Interestingly, Lawson, who had been such a popular commander of the Navy, still exerted considerable influence. Although he appeared to have given up his anti-monarchist sympathies, and had even responded gratefully to a letter of goodwill from the King in early April, he gave his support to the Republican Luke Robinson in his native Scarborough. Lawson's support was largely instrumental in ensuring the old Rumper's triumph over moderate and crypto-Royalist candidates. This was, however, an aberration. Elsewhere, the results showed the general disillusion with the constitutional experiments of the previous decade. The people, finally allowed a free vote, expressed their detestation of their military and civilian rulers.

On 25 April 1660 the Convention Parliament met, so called because it had the unique privilege of not being summoned by the monarch. For the King, his decision to take Hyde's advice and wait on events had succeeded beyond his greatest expectations. The large number of Royalists elected to the Commons, despite the efforts of the Rump to debar them, and the unopposed return of the peers, was a clear indication of the restoration of the old order. But even now he did not press for his return and determined to wait for an official invitation from parliament. Its mood was overwhelmingly in favour of the King. A quorum of ten former Parliamentarian peers (five earls, one viscount and four barons) sat in the House of Lords. By 27 April their number had swelled to thirty-six, and with the introduction of Royalist peers, it grew to 145. With supreme confidence, they brushed aside any act parliament had passed since the House of Commons (or more accurately the Rump of the Commons) had voted for their abolition on 6 February 1649, a week after Charles I's execution. The Lords had not forgiven their junior partners' declaration that 'the House of Peers in Parliament is useless and dangerous, and ought to be abolished'.

The Presbyterians' intention was to restore Charles with conditions agreed at the Treaty of Newport in 1648. Although they were no longer a majority, as they had been in the Long Parliament, they remained a powerful and well-organised party and they counted on Monck's support. As soon as parliament met, three Presbyterian divines, Reynolds, Calamy and Baxter, were summoned to preach services of thanksgiving. Sir Harbottle Grimston, another Presbyterian, was elected Speaker despite the protests of Anglican Cavaliers that he had been elected by a minority of members. As Mordaunt reported to Hyde, it was 'an irregular beginning . . . for they [the Cavaliers] had been artificially drawn out into a room, out of which they were forced to pass through a narrow door in a great throng, which took up the time till the clerk was chosen. So many freaks appear already that I fear we shall find high opposition.'

From the outset, harsh words passed between the two factions. The ex-Parliamentarian Lord Wharton was castigated as one of the 'rotten crew of lords who wish to bring the king in on hard conditions', in the words of John Shaw. Anglican clergy, anxious to proclaim their devotion from the pulpit, retaliated. On 10 May Richard Baxter preached before the Lord Mayor a sermon entitled 'Right Rejoycing', in which he complained bitterly that many ministers 'have their persons assaulted, their windows battered, their ministrations openly reviled, and that go in danger of their lives, from the brutish rabble'. Baxter was incensed by the insults directed at his fellow ministers, who were referred to as 'Pres-biters, Drivines, Jack-Presbyters, Blackcoats, Pulpeteers etc.', which induced the King to ask George Morley and John Barwick to use their influence to urge restraint.

The Chancellor knew how hard it would be for the Church of England to regain its position of dominance. Its morale had been disastrously affected by the abolition of bishops, the banning of the Prayer Book and the dispossession of large numbers of Anglican clergy from their livings during the Interregnum. Brian Duppa, former dean of Christ Church and fellow of All Souls, who had been in charge of Charles's schooling in childhood, lamented the Church's inactivity to Sir Justinian Isham: 'But where are we all this while, that we have so much leisure to busy ourselves in David's Psalmes? Parliaments and Armies, changes and revolutions fill the heads of other men, and we like Archimides are drawing lines, while Syracuse is taken.'

Despite these divisions, all Members of Parliament were united in their desire to thank Monck for his part in securing the peaceful election. The Speaker gave effusive thanks for the Commons: 'Your Lordship has been our physician. . . . Statues have heretofore been set up to persons meriting much of their country, but your Lordship hath a statue set up higher, and in another place, in the hearts of all well-wishers to the good of this nation.' The Commons proceeded to pass a vote of thanks to Ingoldsby for his part in arresting Lambert, despite the fact that he was a regicide.

As the month ended, the Duke of Buckingham, who had forsaken his monarch and friend by returning to England in 1658, could be seen openly wearing his Garter, the highest chivalric order bestowed personally by the sovereign. Even the implacable Hesilrige was begging for mercy. A couple of months earlier, Monck, as a joke, had offered to save his life for tuppence. On 30 April Hesilrige sent a note to Monck proclaiming: 'I have always acted with the authority of Parliament, and never against it . . . and have hazarded my all to bring the military power under civil authority. I forgott to give you the two pence it is here enclosed, and being assured of your lordshipp's promise, I hope to end the remainder of my days in peace and quiet.' The two silver pennies enclosed with the note were enough to ensure Monck's intervention when he was later on trial for his life. The death penalty was rejected by 141 votes to 116.

On 27 April Grenville appeared before the Council of State with the King's letter and the Declaration of Breda. The members of the Council were unsure whether they should read such a momentous document and Annesley, the President, commanded Grenville to present it formally to parliament on 1 May. Accordingly, four days later, as soon as parliament assembled, he repeated the process, appearing first at the Lords, as the senior house, and then at the Commons. 'I am commanded by the King my master', Grenville declaimed, 'to deliver this letter to you, and to desire that you will communicate it to the House.' Grimston proceeded to read out Charles's appeal for the members' support: 'We look on you, as wise and dispassionate men and good patriots, who will raise up those banks and fences that have been cast down.'

Charles included the important proviso that 'the King's authority is necessary for the preservation of Parliaments'. He also upheld the Protestant religion, justice, and law and order, ending with a wry statement that 'we hope that our subjects will be better from our experience of other countries, and what we have seen and suffered'. Morice's motion that the constitution resided in King, Lords and Commons was passed without dissent, and, without hesitation, the Commons voted for the King's immediate restoration. Grenville was thanked by parliament for bearing the King's gracious message and given £500 to buy himself a jewel (the money borrowed from one of the members, as the public treasury was almost empty), whereas, as Hyde noted, but three months earlier he would have 'undergone a shameful death, if he had been known to have seen the king'.

Grenville then proceeded to the City, where he delivered a similar message to the Common Council, expressing the King's thanks for its support. The members, keen to pass over London's role as the centre of opposition to the Crown all through the Civil Wars, and to prove their loyalty, immediately guaranteed a loan of £100,000, half for the King and half to pay the Army. Two further messages from Charles were handed over to Monck and Montagu for the Army and Navy. Monck summoned all the senior officers based near London to come to St James's, where he personally read out the letter, stressing that a similar message had already been given to parliament, which had enthusiastically endorsed it. The officers received his words with expressions of support.

The ever-thorough Montagu, waiting impatiently at Gravesend for instructions to set sail, was leaving nothing to chance. Before summoning his senior captains to a Council of War on 3 May on board the *Naseby*, to read the contents of the Declaration of Breda and a letter of goodwill from the King, he dictated a record of their unanimous approval. Pepys, who was given the honour of reading the letter from the King to the fleet, noted the officers' equivocal attitude: 'Not one man seemed to say no to it, though I am confident many in their hearts were against it.' But once Montagu had fired the first gun and cried 'God bless His Majesty!' there was no denying the enthusiasm of the sailors.

Throughout the fleet, while the cannon boomed and flags were waved, Pepys heard the men 'crying out "God save King Charles!" with the greatest joy imaginable'. That evening, after the commanders and gentlemen had drunk two pipes of good canary, Montagu showed his kinsman private letters from the King and the Duke of York 'in such familiar style as to their common friend, with all kindness imaginable'. Charles invited the admiral to come to the Hague where his brother James 'offers to learn the seaman's trade of him, in such familiar words as if Jack Cole and I had writ them'. Pepys was impressed with the way that Montagu had concealed an extensive correspondence with the King over the previous months.

As if on cue, the day ended with the arrival of a personal letter for Montagu from Charles, thanking him for all his work on behalf of his sovereign. The admiral immediately penned his reply, describing the day's events. 'I do much rejoice', he wrote, 'to see that the King will require no assistance from foreign countries, as he has strength enough in the love and loyalty of his own subjects to support him. His Majesty has chosen the best place, Scheveling [Scheveningen], for embarking; and there is nothing in the world of which I am more ambitious than to have the honour of attending his Majesty, which, I hope, will speedily be the case.'

Throughout England, Mayday was celebrated with the reintroduction of the maypole, banned for almost two decades. The antiquarian John Aubrey recorded that 'at the Strand, near Drury Lane, was set up the most prodigious one [maypole] for height, that [perhaps] was ever seen; they were fain [I remember] to have the assistance of the seamen's art to elevate it'. In Oxford, Aubrey's friend Anthony Wood enjoyed the sight of 'a May-pole against the Beare in Allhallows parish, set up on purpose to vex the Presbyterians and Independents. Dr (John) Conant, then vice-chancellor, came with his beadles and servants to have it sawed downe, but before he entred an inch into it, he and his party were forced to leave that place.' The people of Oxford were obviously devoted to their traditional pleasures. At the end of the month they 'were soe violent in opposition to the Puritans that there was numbered 12 Maypoles besides 3 or 4 morrises'.

As if a hurricane had finally blown itself out, people universally yearned for peace and the restoration of old traditions. Two decades of political experiment had ended with a government controlled by a clique of self-seeking generals and politicians. The legacy of Cromwell's military dictatorship had been political anarchy as, in the words of Lord Macaulay, 'feeble copies of a great original' displaying 'the restlessness and irresolution of aspiring mediocrity'. There was only one alternative: to put the clock back and restore the monarchy. Former Parliamentarians were prepared to join with their Royalist foes and welcome back the King whom they had shunned for so long. A Frenchman writing home summed up foreign amazement at the political volte-face: 'Good God, do the same people inhabit England that were in it 10 or 20 years ago?' But, 'Anything was preferable', as Macaulay wrote, 'to the yoke of a succession of incapable and inglorious tyrants, raised to power like the Beys of Algiers by military revolutions recurring at short intervals.'

The Commons prepared to send a deputation of twelve members to Breda, under the leadership of Sir Denzil Holles, and including in their number Thomas, Lord Fairfax. The Lords chose six members, led by the Earl of Manchester, another prominent Parliamentarian. With an almost heroic disregard for political reality, Ludlow had refused to take part in the nomination of the commissioners going to Breda, noting how previously staunch opponents of the King strove to be included in the parliamentary delegation, hoping 'to procure favour and preferment for themselves'.

The Presbyterian party, whose leaders had been so hopeful that they could impose conditions on Charles's restoration, made one last attempt. Sir Matthew Hale, an eminent lawyer, raised the question in the House of Commons. But his proposal was rejected by Monck, who argued that there should be nothing that might hinder or 'delay the present settlement of the nation'. His views were 'echoed with such a shout over the house, that the motion was no more insisted on'. With Royalist feeling growing stronger every day, it was now inconceivable that the Presbyterians, or indeed anyone else, would be able to impose conditions. 'I can now say I am a king, and not a Doge,' a relieved Charles exclaimed.

Thomas Clarges left London on 5 May with a message from Monck for the King. As he passed through Kent, he was treated as a hero. Senior Royalists were more cautious, still not wholly convinced by Monck's conversion to Royalism. Grenville and Mordaunt wrote ahead to Hyde and Ormonde, warning them 'to treat him with all manner of civility and respect . . . but do not trust him or give credit to him'. Five days later, Grenville himself set out, with news of the parliamentary commissioners' imminent departure and bearing £4,500 in gold, and bills of exchange for a further £25,000.

On 8 May members of the Convention Parliament met in Westminster Hall and proceeded to Palace Yard, where they stood bareheaded while heralds proclaimed Charles King 'to the sound of drum and fife'. They then proceeded to Whitehall, with Monck following the Speaker of the Commons, where the process was repeated, and on to Temple Bar where the Lord Mayor, in his robe of scarlet velvet, and the aldermen and companies of the City received the heralds. Monck played a more prominent part in the proclamation to the Army and took the salute at the Guildhall standing beside the Lord Mayor. London celebrated the event in a tumult of bells and bonfires, accompanied by guns firing from the Tower and all the ships on the Thames.

All over England, towns and villages joined in the celebrations. Even stalwart Republicans joined in. The regicide George Fleetwood commanded his men to assist the Mayor of York in proclaiming the King. In Cambridge the celebrations lasted for two days. All the foreign ambassadors, with the exception of the Frenchman Bordeaux, aware of the exiled Royalists' hostility to him, rejoiced at the prospect of the restoration. Only the Anabaptists seemed cast down. There is a sense of near hysteria in contemporary descriptions of these celebrations. Recent converts to Royalism were particularly anxious to demonstrate their loyalty. There was more than a hint of guilt in the behaviour of some, now 'drinking of the King's health upon their knees in the streets', as Pepys observed, 'which methinks is a little too much'. Alderman Robinson, who had played a key role in supporting Monck's actions in London in February, warned the King of the danger of inebriated threats of vengeance. Charles agreed, stating that the offenders were better off in gaol than 'governing in taverns'.

Although there was no mention of Scotland in the Declaration of Breda, an indication of the country's neglect after the Restoration, the imminent return of the King was celebrated with equal enthusiasm in the land of his ancestors. There was near universal joy at the demise of the Covenant, whose supporters had reduced the nation to such an impoverished condition in the preceding two decades. For the moment, any disagreement over religion between the Covenanters and the more moderate Episcopalians was set aside. When Charles was proclaimed King at the Mercat Cross in Edinburgh, the diarist John Nicoll recorded, it was done with 'all solemnities requisite, by ringing of bells, setting out of bonfires, sounding of trumpets, roaring of cannons, beating of drums, dancing about the fires, and using all other tokens of joy for the advancement and preference of their native King to his crown and inheritance'. Johnston of Wariston, who had returned to the Scottish capital, was typically disapproving of the 'great riot, excess, extravagance, superfluity, naughtiness, profanity, drinking of healths; the Lord be merciful on us'. But for the majority of his countrymen, it was a welcome chance to become 'not only inebriat but really intoxicate, not only drunk but frantic'.

In Ireland, Charles was formally proclaimed King on 14 May, but the prospect of the restoration only registered with the Protestant ruling class. Following Cromwell's brutal invasion in 1650, large numbers of Catholic peasants had been transplanted to the wilder areas of Connaught and Munster in the west, and large tracts of the more prosperous land given to English soldiers and adventurers. Owing to a number of recent alleged murders of English Protestants, any Englishman occupying land was to retain possession of it. In other words, the Irish who had been dispossessed of their own land were to have no redress, a position that was to cause an enduring hatred of the occupying power lasting for centuries. Sir William Petty, serving with the occupying English Army, described the squalid conditions of the natives living 'in a brutish nasty Condition, as in Cabins, with neither Chimney, Door, Stairs nor Window; feed chiefly upon Milk and Potatoes'. Francis Howgill, a Quaker missionary, painted a much bleaker picture. Within 50 miles of Dublin he encountered 'more desolate places than ever did I think behold, without any inhabitant except a few Irish cabins here and there, who are robbers and murderers that live in holes and bogs where none can pass'. It seemed that the return of the King would do little to improve the lifestyle of these pathetic creatures.

On 9 May a bill of Pardon, Indemnity and Oblivion was presented to the House of Commons, and given a second reading three days later. But an exception was made for regicides, whose position grew increasingly dangerous. Most were only too anxious to beg for mercy. Ingoldsby hoped that his recent action in arresting Lambert would count in his favour, and made a tearful speech in the Commons, claiming that Cromwell had forced him to sign the death warrant. His recantation was successful and earned him a pardon.

Col Hutchinson's wife recorded how her husband attempted to justify his participation at the trial of Charles I, owing to 'the inexperience of my age, and the defect of my judgement, and not the malice of my heart', but stating his willingness to lay down his life for he had 'made a shipwreck of all things but a good conscience'. His fellow Republicans, however, were unimpressed by his letter to the Speaker recanting his past misdemeanours, and thought that he was acting purely to save his own skin. Edmund Ludlow and Algernon Sidney, both of whom were about to endure a prolonged exile to escape vengeful Royalists, accused Hutchinson of betraying the Republican cause (he had attended every day of Charles I's trial as well as signing the death warrant). Both men felt that he had agreed to sacrifice Vane, an intransigent Republican but no regicide, in exchange for a pardon from the King. Sidney wrote dismissively: 'If I could write and talk like Col. Hutchinson . . . I believe I might be quiet. Contempt might procure my safety, but I had rather be a vagabond all my life than buy my being in my own country at so dear a rate.' Hutchinson was to be spared the death sentence and spent the remainder of his life in prison.

Seven regicides were excepted from the general pardon on 14 May and a vote was passed three days later to seize their estates and to guard the ports to prevent their escape abroad. Two of them showed commendable bravery in facing their accusers. Maj Gen Thomas Harrison, a leading Fifth Monarchy Man, was captured and sent to the Tower. He was, however, unperturbed, believing firmly that he had been carrying out the work of God. Ludlow, who had been elected to the Convention Parliament as member for Hindon in Wiltshire, had the temerity to take his seat, hoping to face down his enemies even though a warrant had been issued for his arrest. When he realised the full extent of the hostility of his fellow MPs, he changed his mind and departed from the capital, taking to by-roads to avoid pursuit. Ludlow's estates in Ireland had already been seized by the acquisitive Sir Charles Coote, himself a turncoat.

Other Commonwealth leaders had taken precautions against Royalist vengeance. Downing, who had been such a thorn in the side of the exiled Court from his base at the Hague, offered to trade State secrets with Charles II in exchange for a pardon. He used as his intermediary the ex-Royalist Thomas Howard, brother of the Earl of Suffolk, whom he had persuaded to betray important Royalist secrets, well aware that Howard would be arguing for his life. Knowing Charles's hatred of regicides, Downing was at pains to stress 'that he never was in arms but since the King's death, nor had never taken oath or engagement of any kind'. Ormonde informed Howard that the King would overlook Downing's past 'deviations' and he was knighted at Breda just before Charles sailed for England. Anxious to demonstrate his new allegiance,

Downing was soon busy hunting down regicides who had fled abroad. He was so despised as a turncoat by the Republicans that it became a proverbial expression among New Englanders, where he had studied at Harvard in his youth, to say of a false man who betrayed his trust, that he was an arrant George Downing.

The spymaster Thurloe was a prime target for Cavalier vengeance. But he issued a defiant warning that he possessed 'a black book which should hang half of them that went for Cavaliers'. Thurloe remained an influential figure in the run-up to the parliamentary election. As late as 24 April, Broghill, now thought to be a wholehearted Royalist, was writing to the former Secretary: 'I do monstrously dread the Cavalier party, and if the parliament should be such, God only knows what will be the evills.'

Fairfax was one of the few openly to acknowledge the role that he had played in the Civil Wars. He proclaimed: 'If any man must be excepted, I know no man that deserves it more than myself, for I was general of the army at that time, and had power sufficient to prevent the proceedings against the King; but I did not think fit to make use of it to that end.' His attitude, however, was in marked contrast with the majority of Englishmen's overwhelming desire to prove their loyalty. Sir John Lenthall, son of the ex-Speaker of the House of Commons, expressed the opinion that all who had fought for parliament were equally guilty: 'He that first drew his sword against the King committed as high an offence as he that cut off the King's head.' Fierce objections were raised, however, to his divisive and 'unseemly motion', and he was 'called to the bar, where on his knees he received a severe reproof, and by vote was degraded of his knighthood, and very narrowly escaped being sent to the Tower'. Lenthall's father adopted a different tactic, sending Charles £3,000 as a gift, asking that he be allowed to continue as Master of the Rolls.

Some Royalists demonstrated their loyalty by attempting to retrieve all the royal possessions dispersed during the Commonwealth. Those, like Lord Lisle, who had profited from the dispersal of the royal art collection after Charles I's execution, offered to return some pictures and statues they had acquired from the sale. Every effort was to be made to ensure that when the King arrived in England, he would find the royal palaces refurnished with appropriate splendour. No detail was spared. Even Mrs Monck was prepared to join in, offering to supply the linen, as Hyde heard, 'because it was (as she saith frankly) her old trade'.

Throughout May, the most important month of Charles's life, there was a marked contrast between his emotional reticence and his subjects' wild celebrations. The overriding impression the King made on all he met was one of sobriety. He was wary of the sudden, overenthusiastic response of his subjects. He realised full well how superficial was the conversion of many, if not most, of his subjects, but had learnt to disguise his feelings behind a courteous and charming mask. Hyde, who had suffered with his master, was equally sceptical. 'A man could not but wonder', he mused, 'where those people dwelt who had done all the mischief.'

Anxious to take full advantage of his astonishing change in fortune, Charles listened attentively to the foreign powers now queuing up to seek an alliance. He chose to ignore the way that they had spurned him for the past decade. The King was particularly cordial towards Gamarra, the Spanish ambassador at the Hague, realising the necessity of bringing an end to the war with Spain. Charles hoped that he had not caused offence at the manner in which he had vacated Spanish territory. He politely rebuffed the Marquis of Caracena's attempt to entice him back to Brussels, thanking his former host with delicate irony for the hospitality that the Royalists had received over the previous four years. Caracena vented his fury on Don Alonso de Cardenas, who, despite his long period as ambassador in England, had failed to understand the situation and had allowed this valuable hostage to slip from his grasp.

Mazarin, realising that his ambassador Bordeaux was inimical to the leading Royalists, turned to Henrietta Maria, who was living outside Paris. She sent her favourite and opportunist major-domo, Henry Jermyn, recently created Earl of St Albans, to Breda. But the King was not convinced by the overtures of the 'juggling cardinal', as Mazarin was known to the Cavaliers in Brussels, and turned down Jermyn's invitation to pass through France on his way to England, stating that it was impossible since he must pass through Spanish territory to do so. Charles was also unconvinced by Mazarin's suggestion that he might consider a French princess as a prospective bride. The Cardinal's first choice, known as La Grande Mademoiselle, daughter of Louis XIII's brother, the duc d'Orléans, had rejected Charles when he was first exiled to France fourteen years previously. Other nations were also considering whether they might be able to make a marital alliance with the young English King. The Portuguese, desperate for help in their fight for independence with Spain, had already lined up Catherine of Braganza, daughter of the King of Portugal, as a prospective bride.

The Dutch were hopeful that they could gain from the King's residence at Breda. Although their government had failed to help the exiled Royalists, some individual merchants had been more sympathetic, offering an invaluable secret loan of £300,000. Now the grateful King gave as his password the word 'Amsterdam' as an acknowledgement of this. And he was very happy to accept a gift of 300,000 guilders from the States General, as the ruling body in Holland was known. In addition, the Dutch gave their new ally a state bed, and this was soon to be followed by a yacht, the first to be seen in England.

While Charles was deftly turning aside prospective alliances, Montagu was preparing to sail over to Holland to escort the King back to his native land. Evidence of the Commonwealth was repressed. On 7 May the Admiralty authorised that all 'standards, flags, and jacks, be forthwith prepared for the fleet as were in use before 1648'. The Committee had obviously not yet appreciated the irony that Montagu's flagship was named the *Naseby*, honouring the decisive Royalist defeat in the First Civil War, with the figure of Cromwell trampling on six nations on the prow (oddly enough this figurehead was to survive for a further three years). On Sunday 13 May Pepys saw the tailors and painters on the quarterdeck of the *Naseby* 'cutting out of some pieces of yellow cloth into fashion of a crown and C.R.' Montagu was taking no chances with the crews of his ships. There must be no danger of a renegade sailor attacking one of the royal party on their triumphant homecoming. Two officers had been arrested and sent to the Tower, charged with planning to blow up the ship carrying the King back to England. On 17 May the House of Lords heard how the master of the *Newbury* had sworn that 'if ever the king come into England, he would be the first that would take away his life'. He was arrested at once.

It was much more difficult to control ships out at sea; it took time to inform them of the change of regime and ensure the crew's acquiescence. For the past fifteen years the Royalists had freely attacked Commonwealth shipping, one of the few ways to strike back at their opponents. As late as 16 May Capt William Barker of the *Lichfield* sent in a long report to the Admiralty describing his pursuit of a number of Royalist privateers. Near Swansea he finally captured 'the *Henrietta Maria*, commanded by George Doudall, an Irishman, having the Duke of York's commission. She had taken 13 sail within a week, and much annoyed the trade in the Channel.' The same day Capt Richard Hodges reported capturing two Royalist vessels near Whitby: 'only one of the enemy was killed and 2 of our men wounded.' Capt Vessey of the *Constant Warwick* blamed the storm battering his ship on the wrath of God sent to condemn England for bringing back the King; but when a loose rope struck him on the head, it was thought to be divine retribution for his disloyal words.

Montagu was waiting impatiently for the word from Monck to cross the North Sea. The King determined to act as soon as he had been proclaimed with due ceremony. On 10 May he sent word for Montagu to leave immediately for Holland. The admiral sent a message to the King to prepare for his arrival, and set sail the following morning, too soon to pick up the parliamentary commissioners, who failed to make the rendezvous off Dover, to their great chagrin. Three days later Montagu anchored off Scheveningen beach.

14

THE RESTORATION

On 14 May 1660 Charles left Breda by boat, much encouraged by the welcome news that he had been proclaimed King in London and that Dunkirk had declared for the monarchy. He sailed gently downstream in a magnificent barge, accompanied by Mary and her 9-year-old son William, and an escort of thirty yachts. Mary had retired to her bed but the rest of the royal party was up on deck to enjoy the celebrations as they passed Dort. Every cannon in the town had been primed and, 'as long as they could discover the flag of the ship, which carried the person of the King, with all the royal family, they thundered'.

Just occasionally we catch a glimpse of Charles's reaction to his extraordinary change in fortune. The fleet of yachts had moored for the night near Dort, when Grenville arrived, bearing news that parliament had voted for his unconditional restoration, and that Montagu and his fleet were waiting off Scheveningen beach, near the Hague. Without a moment's hesitation, Charles weighed anchor and sailed on past Rotterdam. The royal party landed at Delft at 5 a.m. on 15 May, where the citizens had been up for several hours to prepare for his arrival. Charles and his family transferred into a cavalcade of seventy-two coaches, each drawn by six thoroughbreds. Charles and his siblings were crammed into the leading coach. Prince William was obliged to sit on his favourite uncle James's knee, little dreaming that he would supplant him on the British throne twenty-eight years later.

The royal party was led into the Hague, the Dutch capital, in a splendid procession headed by 'some trumpets of the Estate, clad in coats of crimson velvet, embroidered with gold and silver'. At the palace of the

Mauritshuis, Charles was welcomed by members of the House of Orange and his favourite aunt, Elizabeth of Bohemia, of whom he remarked that she 'useth me more like a Mother than an Aunt'. Elizabeth, sister of Charles I, had been living in exile since her husband, the Elector Palatine, who had been elected King of Bohemia in 1618, lost that throne the following year. The royal couple had fled Prague in such haste that they almost left behind their infant son Prince Rupert, destined to become the most famous Royalist general, and later an admiral, in the Civil Wars. The 'Winter Queen', as Elizabeth was known, was a great supporter of Charles and had high hopes that he would marry her daughter Sophia. Instead, Sophia married the Elector of Hanover and their youngest son was to become George I. She was gratified to note the reaction to Charles's arrival and how 'the very common people are as hot for the king as any of us'.

On 16 May the King received the parliamentary commissioners, the deputation of twelve MPs and six Lords, in the Mauritshuis. The members of the Commons included past enemies, such as Fairfax and Holles, Sir George Booth, recently released from prison, and Charles's future minister and later opponent Ashley Cooper, whose carriage overturned en route to the Hague, causing him a painful internal abscess. John Evelyn, much to his chagrin, was still recovering from illness and had been forced to turn down the offer to join the deputation. Holles made a lengthy speech in praise of the King and condemning the government of the Interregnum, while at the same time upholding the 'ancient rights and privileges' of all Englishmen. The King made a gracious reply, promising his eager listeners that he would henceforward devote himself to the peace and happiness of his subjects. He cordially thanked them for their munificence in presenting him with a gift of £50,000, with a further £10,000 for his brother James and £5,000 for the Duke of Gloucester. But the King's caution at this crucial time was eminently justified. There was an embarrassing moment when bills of exchange for these vast sums were presented to the merchants of Amsterdam, who refused to honour them, referring them to the City of London. At the end of the meeting, he invited Fairfax, the old general, who had pursued Charles into the West Country in the dark days of 1644–5, and his chaplain Dr Bowles to retire for a few minutes to his cabinet. As a gesture of reconciliation, the King was to ride Fairfax's horse at his coronation the following year.

The only honours Charles distributed were to commissioners from the City of London who presented the King with a gift of £12,000. Charles, who knew well how dependent he would be on the City's financial support, expressed his particular affection for London, the city of his birth, carefully omitting any mention of the leading role it had played in defying his father. The commissioners' joy at these kind words redoubled when they were told to kneel and the King knighted them on the spot, 'an honour no man in the city had received in near twenty years', as Hyde noted.

Other honours distributed in this period demonstrate the King's realisation of the need to placate the men in power. Thomas Clarges, Monck's confidant, was also knighted, an appreciation for everything that Monck had done for his sovereign. On 6 May Samuel Morland, chief commissioner to spymaster Thurloe, had met the King, throwing himself on his knees and imploring pardon for his past errors. Morland had carried on an extensive correspondence with Charles, revealing numerous Royalist traitors, including Sir Richard Willis, a founder member of the Sealed Knot. Now he repeated his accusations. The King thanked Morland for his frankness and knighted him.

Just occasionally, the King revealed the steel lying beneath the charming exterior. He absolutely refused to acknowledge a message from the judges who had presided at his father's trial. And a group of Presbyterian ministers who had come to Holland, though armed with a strong letter of recommendation from Sir Thomas Wharton to Ormonde, stressing their good intentions, were little more successful. The last thing the King, a steadfast Anglican since returning to France in 1651, wanted was a reminder that he had signed the Covenant in 1650 on his humiliating expedition to Scotland. When the Presbyterian ministers proceeded to ask him to disown the Book of Common Prayer and to prevent his chaplains from wearing surplices, they were swiftly dismissed.

Pepys met his monarch for the first time on 17 May. Like many others, his initial reaction was to note Charles's reserve. 'The King seems to be a very sober man,' he recorded, quite at odds with the debauched figure of Parliamentarian propaganda. All his visitors seemed shocked at Charles's and his courtiers' 'sad, poor condition', as one told Pepys, 'their clothes not being worth 40/- the best of them'. One of the few times Charles let his true feelings appear was when Sir John Grenville presented the King with a trunkload of gold sovereigns. Unlike grandiose promises of future munificence, here was the actuality. Charles was so excited by the sight of the gold that he called over James and Mary to admire the money lying in the portmanteau.

The young diarist had been exploring the Hague, enjoying the ride into town in a coach with 'two very pretty ladies, very fashionable and with black patches, who very merrily sang all the way and that very well'. Pepys was inspired to begin playing his flageolette, but, in the excitement, dropped his rapier stick. Although forced to share a press-bed with a judge, Pepys was sufficiently elated by his visit to return two days later. This time he managed to meet the royal family and kiss their hands. As well as the King, the diarist saw Hyde, 'who did lie bed-rid of the goute', and the Queen of Bohemia, 'a very debonaire, but plain lady'. On 18 May Pepys decided to visit Delft, where he went to a 'Dutch house where there was an exceeding pretty lass and right for the sport; but it being Saturday, we could not have much of her company'. The next day the diarist's lust was stronger than ever and, as he was due to embark from Scheveningen, he borrowed a room, 'where in another bed there was a pretty Dutch woman in bed alone; but though I had a month's-mind to her, I had not the boldness to go to her'.

The King, surrounded by a horde of importuning petitioners, found a welcome escape in the society of his own family. During these last hectic days of exile, although he was compelled to dine in public, he spent every meal with his relations, seated between his sister Mary and his aunt Elizabeth. Both were devoted to Charles, Mary once declaring that she could never love her son William as much as her brother while the King lived. At the ends of the table sat Charles's brothers James and Henry. Their conversation was accompanied by 'a set of violins, which diverted pleasantly the King, during the repast', when he was able to enjoy the music above the continuous noise of bells ringing and cannons booming.

Of all Charles's close family, only his mother and his sister Henrietta Anne were missing, the latter especially often in his thoughts. At the end of April he wrote to her: 'I have yours of the 23rd in which I find so many marks of friendship that I knew not how to find words with which to express my joy. In return I assure you that I love you as much as is possible and that neither absence nor any other thing can ever cause me to depart in the slightest manner from that friendship which I have promised you. And, believe me, the friendship I have for you cannot be shared.' Ever thoughtful, the King ended by telling Minette that he had ordered Charles Sorceau, the leading Parisian tailor, soon to come to England and play a major role in introducing the French taste, 'to bring you some ribbon so that you may choose the trimming and the feathers. I thank you for the song you sent me.' He ended his letter with the affectionate words: 'If you knew how often we talk of you and wish you here you would say we are longing to see you, and do me the justice to believe that I am entirely yours. For my dear dear Sister.'

The Dutch were striving to secure the goodwill of the restored King and therefore determined to honour him with a farewell banquet at the Hague. Charles, anxious that his sister Mary and her young son should be looked after properly after his departure, knowing Mary's antipathy for the republican government, accepted with pleasure. After the lavish meal, held on 22 May, his hosts, led by Jan de Witt, a strong opponent of the House of Orange but now eager to reconcile himself with the

Princess Mary and her brother, presented the King with the gold plate off which they had just dined.

On 22 May the Duke of York, appointed High Admiral of England, accompanied by the Duke of Gloucester, was cheered onto the *Naseby*. Montagu entertained them to a feast, the silver dishes laden with great pieces of roast beef of such girth that it seemed that the whole fleet could dine on the leftovers. There were many important present and future naval figures on board Montagu's flagship that day: James and Montagu, both admirals, William Coventry, Pepys and Sir George Downing, all three destined to become major figures in the naval administration, two honoured Dutch guests, Prince Maurice of Nassau and Adm Opdam. Pepys joined in the celebrations, firing a gun outside his cabin, but, in the general excitement, 'holding my head too much over the gun', gave himself a black eye.

The next day, 23 May, a crowd of 100,000 gathered on Scheveningen beach to watch the King's embarkation. The sea was almost as crowded as the land, with boats of every shape and size on the water. The air was so thick with smoke from the continuous firing and salutes that 'those great floating castles [English ships] disappeared in a moment to the eyes of those that were on the land'. About ten o'clock the crowd parted and the King dismounted from a coach at the water's edge. Charles and his family stepped into a barque, provided by the Dutch, adorned with garlands and crowns of flowers. They were conveyed to a barge, where Montagu, dressed in clothes 'very rich as gold and silver can make them', awaited his sovereign. As the two men met, the King embraced the admiral, kissing him on both cheeks, and the sailors 'made the whole neighbour shore to rebound with their shouts . . . cast their caps up into the air', others into the sea, and even 'their doublets and waistcoats'.

At eleven o'clock Charles climbed aboard the *Naseby*, adorned with the royal standard, and was saluted by the crew with a great cry: 'We have him! We have him! God bless King Charles.' Montagu proceeded to host a dinner for the whole royal family in the coach, as the apartment adjoining the admiral's cabin under the poop deck was named. The admiral had ensured that no expense was spared for the occasion. The cabin was wainscoted and gilded, the bed furnished with the finest linen, the coverlets fringed with gold and silver, and Turkish carpets laid on the floor. After the meal, Charles used his royal prerogative to rename the *Naseby* the *Royal Charles*, while the *Richard* became the *James* and the *Speaker* was renamed the *Mary*. It was now time for the King's departure. Mary could hardly bear to be parted from her brothers after all their mutual vicissitudes, and was led ashore in floods of tears with her aunt and son. At four o'clock the fleet, with pendants streaming and guns blazing, slowly set sail, accompanied by loud cheers from the throng on the shore.

With his homecoming just hours away, the King could barely contain himself. A man with a passion for physical activity, as well as a lover of the sea, he carried out a careful inspection of the ship as Pepys watched transfixed, 'walking here and there, up and down – (quite contrary to what I thought him to have been), very active and stirring'. Charles then sat down on the quarterdeck to recount the miraculous tale of his escape from the battle of Worcester, soon to become the King's favourite subject, a story that he was to repeat dozens of times in the years to come until his courtiers dreaded the mention of the word 'Worcester'. He had not allowed himself to relate it in public before, in case it led to the betrayal of his faithful supporters who had sheltered him. Pepys was very affected: 'Where it made me ready to weep to hear the stories that he told of the difficulties that he passed through.'

Charles chose to concentrate on episodes that reflected the loyalty of his followers and omitted any mention of his enemies who had so nearly captured him. Surprisingly, the story of the King hiding up the oak tree, which was to become one of the most famous stories in British history and was to appear in every conceivable art form, from ceramics and prints to inn signs and stump-work, was not recorded by Pepys. It was, however, to become a central part of Charles's subsequent account of his escape that the diarist later recorded at Newmarket in 1680. Perhaps, at this point, his experience in the Boscobel Oak, and the time spent cowering in priest-holes, were simply too terrifying or too undignified to relate to strangers.

The King's first recollection was of the perilous days immediately after the battle when the Penderel family, illiterate Catholic yeomen, living deep in the Staffordshire woods, saved his life. He told Pepys how Richard Penderel tried to lead him out of the vicinity of the battlefield, 'travelling four days and nights on foot, every step up to the knees in dirt, with nothing but a green coat and a pair of country breeches on and a pair of shoes, that made him so sore all over his feet that he could scarce stir'.

Charles continued by relating an episode that demonstrated the extraordinary sangfroid he displayed throughout six weeks on the run, when he never knew who might recognise him and turn him in to the Government, which had offered a huge reward for his capture. 'His sitting at table at one place,' Pepys recorded, 'where the master of the house [Abbot's Leigh, near Bristol], that had not seen him in eight years, did know him but kept it private; when at the same table there was one [even though he] had been of his Regiment at Worcester, could not know him but made him drink the King's health and said that the King was at least four fingers higher than he.'

Pepys finished this shortened account with a touching episode at Brighton, the night before Charles's embarkation for France: 'In another place, at his Inn, the master of the house, as the King was standing with his hands upon the back of the chair by the fireside, he kneeled down and kissed his hand privately, saying that he would not ask him who he was, but bid God bless whither that he was going.' In view of the scores of Royalists already importuning the King for honours, he refrained from mentioning the innkeeper's final remark, that 'I do not doubt, before I die, but to be a lord and my wife a lady'.

For Lady Fanshawe, who had suffered the privations of exile alongside her sovereign, this was a truly marvellous moment. The weather was so favourable that 'the ships' wherries went from ship to ship to visit their friends all night long. But who can sufficiently express the joy and gallantry of that voyage,' she continued, 'to see so many great ships, the best in the world [the finest of the New Model Navy], to hear the trumpets and all other music, to see near a hundred brave ships sail before the wind with the vast cloths and streamers, the neatness and cleanness of the ships, the strength and jollity of the mariners, the gallantry of the commanders, the vast plenty of all sorts of provisions. Above all, the glorious majesties of the King and his two brothers were so beyond man's expectation and expression. The sea was calm; the moon shone at full; and the sun suffered not a cloud to hinder his prospect of the best sight.'

On the morning of 25 May the royal brothers breakfasted on typical sailors' fare of pork, boiled beef and peas. In a light-hearted moment, Charles measured his height, 'standing under a beam in the cabin,' as William Blundell noted, 'upon which place he made a mark with his knife. Sundry tall persons went under it, but there were none that could reach it.' The light relief over, the King prepared to land at Dover, accompanied by a footman and his favourite spaniel. As a gesture of respect for Montagu's vital assistance in engineering the Restoration, the King chose to go ashore in the admiral's own barge.

As Petty Officer Edward Barlow described: 'The Parliament had fitted a "brigitine", rowing like a galley with twelve oars, with galley sails and three small guns of brass over the prow, galley fashion, and gilt most bravely with silk colours . . . yet His Majesty would not go ashore in her, for he went ashore in the General's barge, the same boat he came aboard in. And all the earls and lords accompanied him ashore in other boats, whilst all the ships rang him a peal with their ordnance, which made the very hills and Dover cliffs to sound the echo with like harmony, as though they were all glad to bear him up and have the happiness to welcome home the true sovereign, King Charles II, for whom the land had so long grieved.' The vessel in which Pepys went ashore conveyed another of the King's dogs, 'which shit in the boat, which made us laugh and me think that a king and all that belong to him are but just as others are'.

The King knelt on the beach for a moment before rising to be greeted by Monck. He was then presented with a handsome bible, embossed in gold, which Charles, diplomatic as ever, 'took and said that he loved above all things in the world', as Pepys noted. The three royal brothers, accompanied by the general, took a coach for Canterbury, attended by vast crowds. At Barham Down, 'distinguished troops under several noble men', commanded by the King's old friend Buckingham, were drawn up to receive him.

The exuberance of the welcome Charles received in every town and village was exhausting. 'My head is so prodigiously dazed', he wrote to Minette, 'by the acclamation of the people . . . that I know not whether I am writing sense or no.' But he still remembered to add that he had left instructions with his sister Mary 'to send you a little present from me which I hope you will soon receive'.

A sense of reality soon impinged on the dreamlike homecoming. At Canterbury, having received 'a tankard of massy gold' from the mayor, the King found himself accosted by a stream of petitioners, all looking for a reward for their loyalty and demanding vengeance on their enemies. A flood of proclamations arrived from all over England, declaring his subjects' loyalty. One came from John Ellesdon, mayor of Lyme Regis, whose brother had failed to provide a boat at a critical moment during Charles's escape after Worcester. The suspicion remained that Ellesdon had intended to betray the King, who had a price of £1,000 on his head. Former Parliamentarians sought to redress the error of their ways. Col Morley, who had resisted Evelyn's attempts to persuade him to deliver the Tower of London to the Royalists, realised his mistake too late. On 24 May he came to see the diarist, who directed him to Mordaunt. Instead of playing a role scarcely inferior to that of Monck in engineering the restoration, he was reduced to buying his pardon for £1,000.

Francesco Giavarina had set off post-haste from London as soon as he heard news of Charles's arrival at Dover. Reaching Canterbury, the Venetian was gratified to find that he was the first ambassador to greet the newly restored monarch and noted with some satisfaction that 'I was the only minister who had not recognised the parliament.' Giavarina was impressed that Charles spoke to him in Italian, and spent some time, after the audience ended, observing the patience of the King, who, 'at great personal inconvenience he remained standing many hours to receive the great numbers who came on purpose to kneel and kiss his hand, according to the custom of the country'. He then went to meet the Dukes of York and Gloucester, both of whom also greeted him in Italian. Giavarina's impression was rather different from that of Hyde, who had himself been inundated with supplicants, and declared the King to be 'extremely nauseated' by their behaviour.

Charles showed his political skill by avoiding firm commitments. When Monck entered the royal chamber and, without preamble, gave the King a list of his supporters whom he considered fittest to serve his country, Charles, by now well practised in dealing with such requests, slipped the note into his pocket without reading it. Later, he showed it to Hyde. Both men were astonished at the lack of Royalists among a list of some seventy potential appointments. It was quietly set aside after the King had explained that he could not award these honours to men of whom he had no knowledge. Perhaps the two men recalled Colepeper's advice that, once Monck had committed himself, 'he will want you as much as you want him, and you may mould him into whatever form you choose'.

The King was, however, very conscious of the debt he owed the general. Charles decided to hold a chapter of the Garter in the ruinous cathedral at Canterbury, where the general was appointed to the Order, and given the signal honour of having his badge put on by the royal princes James and Henry. Montagu, whose support had been so vital in the past few months, was also made a Garter knight. Alongside the two former Cromwellians, Charles also appointed two Cavalier grandees: the Marquis of Hertford and the Earl of Southampton.

The sad condition of Canterbury Cathedral was an indication of the plight of the Church of England; no member of the Anglican Church had been at Dover to greet the King. There were, however, a number of eminent clergymen who had striven to keep the cause of Anglicanism alive. The most able and energetic of these was Gilbert Sheldon, who had led the resistance in England all through the Interregnum. He hastened down to Canterbury to meet Charles and had a lengthy secret meeting with his sovereign on the night of the 26th. Sheldon was soon coordinating the highly successful revival of the Anglican faith that was to lead to it regaining its predominant position above Presbyterianism and Nonconformism.

The award of honours to the different parties sums up the difficulties facing the King as he strove to impose some degree of unity on his subjects. It was impossible to please all the supplicants. Hyde had always expressed caution about giving honours while in exile and, at this extremely sensitive moment, had the unenviable task of turning down unsuccessful suitors, often loyal Cavaliers who had suffered much for the cause. Sir Richard Fanshawe, whom he had knighted at Breda in April, had been in exile since he and his wife had fled to the Scilly Isles with the Prince of Wales in 1646. As his wife Ann recorded: 'The King promised my husband he should be one of the Secretaries of State [the other was Sir Edward Nicholas], and both the Duke of Ormonde and Lord Chancellor Clarendon [Hyde] were witnesses of it.' But the King and his ministers were realists, who knew that they must court the most powerful figures ruling in London. On 5 May, William Morice was writing to Charles, thanking him for the prized appointment that Monck had informed him was to be his. In his defence, Hyde was later to write that Morice 'did the business of his office without reproach'. Fanshawe could only lament that he should be passed over in favour of Morice, 'a fierce Presbyterian, and one that never saw the King's face'. He had to make do with the post of ambassador to Portugal and then to Spain.

For the moment, Monck could have any honour he wanted. As well as becoming a Knight of the Garter, he continued in his post as commander-in-chief, where he played a crucial role in reconciling the soldiers to the concept of monarchy that they had so long resisted. In addition, the general, created Duke of Albemarle, was to be awarded three of the great offices of state. His choice was Lord Lieutenant of Ireland, worth some £4,000 per annum, Master of the Horse, with its extensive patronage, and Lord of the Bedchamber, which guaranteed the general constant access to the King. The posts reflect Monck's two major concerns: power and money. The first meeting of the Privy Council was held in Canterbury, attended by the three senior Royalists returned from exile: Hyde, Ormonde and Nicholas. Ashley Cooper, who had been made a Privy Councillor at the request of Monck, was seen by Hyde as a man to be watched, although, as he noted, 'it was believed that his slippery humour would be easily restrained and fixed by his uncle [Southampton, now appointed Treasurer]'.

On 28 April the royal party left Canterbury and headed for Rochester, where the King was presented with a silver gilt basin and ewer by the mayor and corporation. He stayed at the home of Francis Clark, who would boast thereafter that he had given the royal brothers 'the first dish of meat they had from any private person' on their return. The next day, Tuesday the 29th, was Charles's thirtieth birthday. It was an auspicious day on which to celebrate the culmination of the recent astonishing events: the King's entrance into London.

Beneath a clear blue sky, Charles, mounted on horseback, rode through the lanes of Kent, waving and smiling to his ecstatic subjects. Almost none of them had seen their monarch before. The tall, graceful figure, 'black and very slender-faced', a natural horseman, cut a splendid figure, adorned with the blue ribbon of the Garter. He was dressed in a doublet of cloth of silver, a cloak adorned with gold lace, and a hat with a plume of red feathers, while, sitting beside him, the Duke of York wore a white suit and the Duke of Gloucester one of green. Rochester had welcomed its sovereign with Morris dancing, and Deptford saluted him with 100 virgins dressed in white, who strewed flowers beneath his horse's feet.

The most difficult moment in this triumphant day was at Blackheath, where 30,000 soldiers were drawn up to salute their sovereign. Monck read out a declaration of loyalty on behalf of the troops, so many of whom had fought the Royalists in the Civil Wars. Compared with the enthusiastic reception the King had encountered everywhere since his arrival, the greeting from the soldiers was muted. One of them, observing the brilliant clothes of the Cavalier entourage, is supposed to have whispered in Monck's ear: 'You had none of these at Coldstream; but grasshoppers and butterflies never come abroad in frosty weather.' In a highly symbolic gesture, the troops laid down their arms as servants of the Commonwealth, and picked them up as soldiers of the King.

The royal party then moved to St George's Fields in Southwark, where they were greeted by the Lord Mayor, Thomas Allen, who presented the City's sword on bended knee. He was duly knighted for his pains (the only honour to be granted that day), before he entertained Charles to a lavish lunch in a richly adorned pavilion. The procession then entered the City of London. The streets, crammed with expectant crowds, were garlanded with spring flowers and arches of white hawthorn. From wooden balconies projecting into the streets hung brilliantly coloured tapestries. Above them, flags bearing the royal coat of arms and inscribed with loyal mottoes fluttered from the roofs. Fountains ran with claret all day. The ceaseless cheering and the peeling of bells were overwhelming. John Ogilvy had devised a complex decorative scheme, with Charles portrayed as the God Jupiter, the Roman Emperor Augustus, the biblical hero King David and St George, patron saint of England, on a series of triumphal arches spanning the streets. Around these images were allegorical allusions to Truth, Peace, Plenty and Concord.

For seven hours the procession of some 20,000 passed before the exultant Londoners, who had seen nothing like it in living memory. Baker, in his *Chronicle*, described the full pageant:

The procession was led by major-general Brown, who had a troop of three hundred, all in cloth of silver doublets; then followed twelve hundred in velvet coats, with footmen and liveries attending them in purple: then another troop led by alderman Robinson, in buff coats with cloth of silver sleeves and very rich green scarfs: And after these a troop of above one hundred and fifty blue liveries, laced with silver lace, with six trumpeters and seven footmen in sea-green and silver: then a troop of two hundred and twenty, with thirty footmen in gray and silver liveries, and four trumpeters richly cloathed: then another troop of one hundred and five, with gray liveries, and six trumpets: and three troops more, two of three hundred, and one of one hundred, all richly habited, and bravely mounted. After these came two trumpets with his Majesty's arms: the sheriff's men in red cloaks, richly laced with silver lace, to the number of fourscore, with half-pikes in their hands: then followed six hundred of the several companies of London on horse-back, in black velvet coats with gold chains; each company having footmen in liveries attending. After these came a kettle-drum, five trumpets, and three streamers, and many rich and red liveries with silver lace: after these twelve ministers, and then another kettle-drum, and four trumpets, and his Majesty's Life-Guard commanded by lord Gerrard: then three trumpets in rich coats and satin doublets; and the city marshal, with eight footmen in french-green, trimmed with crimson and white: the city waits, and all the city officers in order: then the two sheriffs, and all the aldermen of London in scarlet gowns, and rich trappings; with footmen in liveries, red coats laced with silver, and cloth of gold and silver: the heralds and maces in red coats: Then the Lord Mayor carrying the sword bare; and next to him the Duke of Buckingham and the general [Monck]; then the King Majesty betwixt the Dukes of York and Gloucester: then followed a troop of horse with white colours; and after them the General's Life-Guard, led by Sir Philip Howard: the five regiments of the army-horse, led by colonel Knight: and after them, two troops of noblemen and gentlemen.

Charles greeted members of both Houses of Parliament at Whitehall Palace, seated beneath a canopy in the Banqueting House, the very room from which his father had stepped onto the scaffold eleven years earlier. So exhausted that he was barely able to comprehend their speeches of welcome, he replied: 'I am so disordered by my journey, and the noise still sounding in my ears, that I cannot express myself so full as I would wish.' A service of thanksgiving in Westminster Abbey was postponed, although there was no escaping a ceremonial dinner in public so that the adoring people could have one final look at their sovereign. The Earl of Leicester, one of many courtiers who queued up to pay their respects, noted the exhaustion of the King amid the chaotic tumult that surrounded him: 'There was so great a disorder and confusion', he recorded, 'that the King scarce knew or took notice of anybody.'

But there was no containing the unconfined joy of the crowd. No attention was paid to a proclamation 'against debauched and profane persons, who, on pretence of regard to the King, revile and threaten others, or spend their time in taverns and tippling houses, drinking his health'. But there was a darker side to the universal celebration. In order to show their devotion to the new regime, many people wanted to celebrate the demise of its predecessor. Effigies of Cromwell, along with the Commonwealth coat of arms, were burnt on top of bonfires three or four storeys high. The few intransigent republicans still in London could only lament the wholesale destruction of their cause. Edmund Ludlow and John Milton, hiding in Holborn and Bartholomew Close respectively, knew full well that they could expect little mercy from their foes. Ludlow was shortly to flee into exile abroad, while Milton remained to face his accusers. He was arrested briefly during the summer, but released on payment of a fine, and suffered the indignity of having some of his more radical tracts burnt by the common hangman.

For all true Royalists, however, the Restoration was nothing less than a miracle. John Evelyn summed up their feelings: 'I stood in the strand, & beheld it, & blessed God: And all this without a drop of blood, & by that very army, which rebell'd against him; but it was the Lord's doing, for such a restoration was never mentioned in any history, ancient or modern, since the return of the Jews from the Babylonish captivity.' Before he went to bed, the King looked round at the assembled courtiers, many of whom had yet to prove their loyalty, and said, 'I doubt it has been my own fault, that I have been absent so long – for I see nobody that does not protest he has ever wished for my return.' He finished with a rhetorical question: 'Where are all my enemies?' thus showing clearly to all present that he wished to establish a distance from his subjects, who were never to be privy to his innermost thoughts. His physical needs were another matter entirely, and legend has it that the King ended his triumphant day by retiring into the willing arms of his new mistress, the voluptuous Barbara Villiers, who gave birth to her son exactly nine months later.

CONCLUSION

The Restoration of Charles II is one of the great set pieces of British history. It appeared that Hyde's dictum that the Restoration would only occur when the English people came to their senses had been fully vindicated. Charles II was re-established at the apex of the age-old trinity of King, Lords and Commons, and the Chancellor's desire to wind the clock back seemed even more successful with the revival of the Church of England, which soon reasserted its position as the dominant religious body, led by a formidable bench of bishops. The major players in the months leading to the Restoration either became enthusiastic converts to Royalism or else were consigned to imprisonment, exile or death.

But the reality was very different. The titanic political and religious struggle that had convulsed Britain for twenty years had left ineradicable marks. The 1640s and '50s was a heroic age, one dominated by figures larger than life. Many of them died for the cause for which they were fighting. Charles I was the chief victim of the brutality of the Civil Wars, publicly executed outside his palace of Whitehall, but his two chief ministers, Strafford and Laud, suffered a similar fate. Countless others died on the field of battle. The Marquis of Montrose, the greatest Royalist general in Scotland, was prepared to endure defeat, betrayal and a noble death at the hands of his Covenanter enemies. The Marquis of Ormonde, a man of integrity and honour, devoted to his monarch and the Anglican faith, was willing to lose his fortune and all his possessions in Ireland. This heroic quality is equally apparent among the Royalists' leading opponents. Parliament had won the Civil Wars but the victors had also suffered grievously. John Lilburne, leader of the Levellers, had endured imprisonment, whippings and stints in the pillory for defying the tyranny of Charles I. Having fought in the First Civil War, he was prepared to endure further terms of imprisonment for his unstinting attacks on the tyranny of Cromwell and the Army, whom he perceived to be the oppressor of civil liberties. William Prynne, whose ears had been cut off for his criticism of Henrietta Maria in 1634, proved an equally powerful champion of civil liberties, initially against Charles I and then against Cromwell in the 1650s. The Civil Wars produced heroines as well as heroes. With so many men fighting far away, women were often left to defend their homes. Lady Derby defied Roundhead forces for months in the siege of Latham House in Lancashire; her counterpart Brilliana Harley defended Brampton Bryan in Herefordshire for parliament with equal gallantry.

The most successful figure to emerge from this heroic age was Oliver Cromwell, but the anarchy that followed his death ushered in a more pragmatic age, and it was this pragmatism that enabled the King to be restored without a drop of blood being shed. It was the anti-heroic figure of Hyde with his policy of passive resistance, waiting on events while encouraging his agents to play on the deep divisions between his enemies, that proved so effective. The Royalist dream of a successful Cavalier rising avenging their defeats in the Civil Wars never occurred. Their cause triumphed when supporters of the illegal regime realised that they had failed and that the restoration of the monarchy was the only alternative to anarchy. There were three men in particular who brought this about, all close former colleagues of Cromwell: Monck, who governed Scotland for the Protector, Montagu, who offered him the crown in 1657, and Fairfax, his predecessor as commander of the New Model Army.

The most important of these three men was George Monck, who, although willing to take bold decisions on the battlefield, had always followed a pragmatic line. His switch from the Royalist to the Parliamentary camp in 1646, his willingness to serve under Cromwell as general and then admiral, rested on the assumption that this was the only way for orderly government to continue. Monck's actions during 1659–60 were guided in the same way. An excellent administrator, with a well-provided army at his back, and using his excellent contacts throughout Britain, he was able to calculate his movements very carefully. Even his gamble in defying Lambert in October 1659 was a measured risk that was to pay off within two months, when the cohesion of the English Army collapsed. There was nothing heroic in his subsequent actions. His crossing into England was unopposed, his stand against the Rump was made after he was certain that he had the support of both his troops and the population of London. Despite the rising tide of Royalism, Monck would never have agreed to meet Grenville, thus ushering in the Restoration, if he had not been sure that he could carry the Army with him. Unlike Cromwell, who indulged in profound soul-searching before taking vital decisions, the pragmatic Monck, in the words of Macaulay, had 'very slender pretensions to saintship'.

The King himself was also an archetypal anti-hero. Unlike his father, who had embraced the martyr's crown so willingly, Charles II was a survivor, determined never to go on his travels again. From his experiences while on the run after Worcester, he knew how fickle was the loyalty of his subjects. During recent months he had observed carefully the moment when his enemies changed sides, and knew they might be willing to switch allegiance again. Charles had learnt through the long years of defeat and exile to keep his own counsel. Once he regained the throne, he was determined to reign alone, and would never fully trust any of his subjects. The King encouraged his ministers to vie with each other for his attention. This helps to account for the complexity of Restoration politics, where the issues of the day are inextricably confused with the ambitions of the leading individuals. The very word Cabal, composed of the initial letters of the surnames or titles of his chief ministers – Clifford, Ashley Cooper, Buckingham, Arlington and Lauderdale – epitomises this complex and shifting political scene.

Charles realised that he was unknown to the vast majority of his countrymen and that he needed to provide something to unite the nation. It was impossible to put the clock back and rely on the idea of the Divine Right of Kings. Nor could he, given his history of exile and defeat, pretend to full-blown heroic status. So, Charles decided to invent his own legend, to complement that of his father, the royal martyr.

The legend he aimed to establish was as the unifier of his people. The King must be seen to be open to all Englishmen. From the moment he appeared in London, Charles went on daily walks in St James's Park, where he was happy to be accosted by anyone, from the highest to the lowest of his subjects. He was keen to indulge in the same pastimes as his fellow Englishmen and was seen to be at the theatre laughing at the bawdy comedies, swimming in the Thames and riding racehorses at Newmarket. Most of his mistresses were high-born ladies, but Nell Gwynn, a lowly actress with a far from unblemished record, was a great favourite with Londoners, especially when she had the wit to describe herself as 'the Protestant whore', in contrast with the King's grander, Catholic mistresses.

Above all, Charles propagated the story of his escape from the battle of Worcester and the day spent in the Boscobel Oak. If not in itself anti-heroic, it epitomises the King as a man of the people, disguised as the woodcutter Will Jackson, outwitting his enemies. Such was Charles's confidence that he actually spent most of the day asleep in the lap of his companion Col Careless. Fortuitously, he had chosen as his refuge an oak tree, an ideal symbol of sturdy English liberty. Charles I had used the paintings of Sir Anthony Van Dyck to bolster an image of aloof majesty. By contrast the scene of the Boscobel Oak appears in any number of images: on Delft plates, on glass, on stump-work, in engravings, and on pub signs as the Royal Oak, still widely popular today. The King's birthday, 29 May, the day that he had entered London in triumph, was celebrated as Oakapple Day. The coronation medal, showing an oak tree bursting into leaf with the motto *Iam Florescit* (Now it flourishes), provided yet another potent connection between the royal

House of Stuart and the archetypal English tree, both rooted in the soil and part of the very fabric of England. This was contrasted with the transient and anarchic folly of the Interregnum.

The legend that the King created played a key part in enabling him to survive the political turmoil of his reign. Charles's alliance with Catholic France, ruled by his cousin Louis XIV, was a dangerous and deeply unpopular policy, and nearly brought about disaster. Fear of Catholicism, so deeply ingrained in Protestant Englishmen, led to the Popish Plot and the Exclusion Crisis of 1679–82, when the King's ex-minister Ashley Cooper, now Earl of Shaftesbury, tried to prevent Charles from nominating his Catholic brother James as his heir. But the King, playing on his subjects' fears of a revival of the Civil Wars and utilising the full powers of the restored monarchy and his own popularity, defeated Shaftesbury and the Whigs. Although there was no return to his father's personal rule, no taxation without parliament and the Court of Star Chamber was abolished, Charles died in 1685 after a reign of twenty-five years, one of the most powerful monarchs to have sat on the English throne. His arrogant and intransigent brother was less successful. Within four years, his attempt to transform England into an absolutist, Catholic state led to his abdication, and his replacement by his daughter Mary and her consort William of Orange, James's nephew.

The Glorious Revolution, like the Restoration three decades earlier, was a peaceful event. This time it was fear of absolutism, rather than Monck's fear of anarchy, that induced Englishmen to turn against James II, but the effect was the same: the arrival of a king from over the water and a major constitutional change executed without violence. The peaceful transfer of power at the Restoration set a precedent for the events of 1688–9. Their emulation of events a generation earlier was rewarded by the establishment of a constitutional monarchy and freedom of religion that is still with us today.

NOTES AND SOURCES

Introduction

There is an enormous bibliography on the life and career of Oliver Cromwell, who still excites almost as much controversy as he did in his life. Among the earlier historians, the magisterial works of S.R. Gardiner (*Oliver Cromwell*, London, Longmans Green, 1901; *Cromwell's Place in History*, London, Longmans Green, 1897; *History of the Commonwealth and Protectorate*, London, Longmans Green, 1897) and his pupil C.H. Firth (*Oliver Cromwell and the Rule of the Puritans*, New York and London, Putnam's Sons, 1900; *Last Years of the Protectorate*, 1909) set a benchmark for grand historical narrative. J. Buchan's *Oliver Cromwell*, London, Hodder & Stoughton, 1934 and C.V. Wedgwood's *Oliver Cromwell*, London, Duckworth, 1939 are also well worth reading; both are excellent writers.

Among modern historians Barry Coward's short book on the Protector (*Cromwell*, London, Longman, 1991) is a good starting point. Antonia Fraser's much longer biography (*Cromwell: Our Chief of Men*, London, Weidenfeld & Nicolson, 1973), with its wealth of anecdotal detail, makes a good foil to this. Almost everything by Blair Worden repays study. The work of A. Woolrych (*Last Quest for a Settlement, Commonwealth to Protectorate*, Oxford, Clarendon Press, 1982) is of a similar high standard. J. Morrill (*Revolution and Restoration, England in the 1650s*, London, Collins & Brown, 1992) is also interesting. Christopher Hill (*God's Englishman*, London, Weidenfeld & Nicolson, 1990) is full of stimulating insights. F.D. Gow's excellent work on Scotland (*Cromwellian Scotland*, Edinburgh, 1979), with a succinct introduction by Firth, and T.C. Barnard's on Ireland (*Cromwellian Ireland*, Oxford University Press, 1975) give good overviews of the other two kingdoms. For more information on the fascinating dilemma Cromwell faced on the issue of kingship, see C.H. Firth, 'Cromwell and the Crown', *English Historical Review* (henceforth *EHR*) 17 and 18, 1902 and 1903.

The works of Cromwell's contemporaries are interesting but suffer from a natural bias. Clarendon's *History of the Great Rebellion and the Civil Wars in England*, ed. Macray, Oxford, 1888, the most ambitious piece of historical writing of the entire seventeenth century, is a worthy tribute to a great statesman. In the title, Clarendon makes the key constitutional point that the momentous events of 1640–60 were a rebellion i.e. an attempt, ultimately unsuccessful, to overthrow the established order. Although the work is always of interest, many readers, the present author excepted, will disagree with Clarendon's verdict that Cromwell was 'a brave bad man'.

Richard Baxter (S.M. Baxter, *Richard Baxter's Narrative*, London, 1696), Col John Hutchinson (Lucy Hutchinson, *Memoirs of the Life of Colonel Hutchinson*, ed. C.H. Firth, London, 1908) and Edward Ludlow (*The Memoirs of Edmund Ludlow*, ed. C.H. Firth, Oxford, Clarendon Press, 1894), all of whom knew Cromwell well, ended up as fierce opponents of the great man, and their writings reflect this. Bulstrode Whitelocke (*Memorials of the English Affairs*, 4 vols, Oxford, 1853, and R. Spalding, *The Improbable Puritan – A Life of Bulstrode Whitelocke*, London, Faber, 1975), one of nature's trimmers, was not so outspoken and remained within the Protector's circle until his death. Cromwell himself does not serve his own cause very well. His speeches and letters, which have been recorded for posterity, tend to be long and complicated, with his long-winded appeals for divine guidance, and it is difficult to gain a proper appreciation of the man and his achievements. The most sympathetic version is probably still that originally edited by Thomas Carlyle, a great admirer of the Protector (*The Letters and Speeches of Oliver Cromwell*, ed. T. Carlyle, London, Methuen, 1845). The quote by the Leveller William Howard at the beginning of the chapter comes from Underdown's book on the Royalist under-ground movement during the Commonwealth (see chapter 2). The analysis of Cromwell by Lord Rosebery, the Liberal Prime Minister, typifies the revival of Cromwell's reputation following the publication of Carlyle's work on the Protector.

The chronology of this book starts out with the death of Cromwell. For those interested in a more speculative approach to history, H.F. McMains,

Cromwell's Death, Lexington, 2000, offers a fascinating thesis on the Protector's death by poisoning.

1. Cromwell's Heir, His Generals and His Protégés

Richard Cromwell is best treated in general books on the period. The most comprehensive of these is by Godfrey Davies, *The Restoration of Charles II 1658–60*, London, 1955, which follows a similar formula to that of Gardiner and Firth. Earl M. Hause, *Tumble-Down Dick*, New York, Exposition Press, 1972, provides a good supplement to this. A good older account is by F. Guizot, *History of Richard Cromwell and the Restoration of Charles II*, trans. A. Scobie, London, 1856. Those who wish to discover more about Richard himself will find more material, but not necessarily more enlightenment, in Robert W. Ramsey, *Richard Cromwell*, London, Longmans Green, 1935, and John A. Butler, *A Biography of Richard Cromwell*, New York, Lewiston, 1994.

The correspondence of William Hooke, who emigrated to New England in the 1630s before returning to serve as Oliver Cromwell's chaplain, and John Winthrop, first Governor of Massachusetts, shows the close links between leading Puritans on both sides of the Atlantic (Sir Harry Vane, a key player in the events covered by this book, had also been Governor of Massachusetts). This correspondence is recorded in *Collections of the Massachusetts Historical Society*, 4th series, vii, Boston, 1865.

There is a great deal of material on Cromwell's generals. Maurice Ashley provides a clear overview in his *Cromwell's Generals*, London, Jonathan Cape, 1954, which covers all the key figures. A biography of Lambert (William H. Dawson, *Cromwell's Understudy*, London, W. Hodge & Co., 1938) conveys the capabilities of this charismatic soldier and statesman. Lucy Hutchinson's *Memoirs* are very revealing on her husband's colleague and later opponent. See also G. Heath III, 'Cromwell and Lambert', in I. Roots (ed.), *Cromwell: A Profile*, London, Macmillan, 1973. A shorter synopsis of Lambert's career and importance was written by Firth in the DNB. Harrison is also well served by his biographers Firth (*The Life of Thomas Harrison*, Worcester, Mass, Hamilton, 1893) and Simpkinson (*Thomas Harrison: Regicide and Major-General*, London, J.M. Dent, 1905), who capture the essential nobility of this religious visionary. M.A. Gibb, *The Lord General: the Life of Thomas Fairfax*,

London, 1938 places the first commander of the New Model Army in context. Whether Lady Fairfax's bold intervention at the trial of Charles I reflected her husband's opinion has never been established, but the general played no subsequent part in public affairs.

Much has been written on the men that these generals commanded. The best source is still C.H. Firth, *Cromwell's Army*, London, Methuen, 1962, and there is also C.H. Firth and G. Davies, *The Regimental History of Cromwell's Army*, Oxford, Clarendon, 1940. Mark A. Kishlansky, *The Rise of the New Model Army*, Cambridge, Cambridge University Press, 1979, provides a good supplement, emphasising the immense importance these men played in the whole history of the Interregnum.

Monck repays closer study than any of the other generals if one is to understand fully the events leading up to the Restoration. There remains considerable disagreement over his motives and the moment when he decided to revert to his former Royalist allegiance. Recent writers to tackle the subject include Maurice Ashley, *General Monck*, London, Jonathan Cape, 1977, an excellent biography but his opinion on the key question of when Monck became a Royalist is by no means conclusive. J.D.G. Davies, *Honest George Monck*, 1936, provides a balanced view of the enigmatic soldier. A great deal of interesting material is contained in F. Guizot, *Memoirs of George Monck, Duke of Albemarle*, trans. J. Stuart Wortley, London, R. Bentley, 1838.

Monck is well served by his contemporaries, including his chaplains Thomas Gumble, *Life of General Monck*, London, 1670, and John Price, 'The Mystery and Method of His Majesties Happy Restauration', in F. Masseres (ed.), *Select Tracts relating to the Civil Wars in England*, London, 1815, with their different analyses of their commander's actions. The two men, both of whom knew their subject very well, show how careful one must be in handling source material, since Gumble's Parliamentary sympathies and Price's Royalism colour every observation they make of the general. *The Clarke Papers*, ed. C.H. Firth, Camden Society, 2nd series, Vol. 62, 1901, include much interesting material, accompanied by Firth's excellent notes. Hyde's judgement of Monck is of interest because he is, largely, not complimentary about the general and seems to have consistently misjudged him throughout this crucial period.

There are good biographies of Montagu (R. Ollard, *Cromwell's Earl: a life of Edward Mountagu, First Earl of Sandwich*, London, HarperCollins, 1994, and F.R. Harris, *Life of Edward Mountagu, First Earl of Sandwich*, London, John Murray, 1912). The career of Broghill is covered by Kathleen M. Lynch, *Roger Boyle, First Earl of Orrery*, Knoxville, University of Tennessee Press, 1965 and *A Collection of the State Letters of Roger Boyle, First Earl of Orrery*, ed. T. Morrice, Dublin, 1743. Thurloe (P. Aubrey, *Mr Secretary Thurloe, Cromwell's Secretary of State*, 1652–60, Athlone Press, 1990) provides a synopsis of a career covered in detail in J. Thurloe, *State Papers*, ed. Thomas Birch, 7 vols, London, 1742. It reveals the clandestine world so brilliantly controlled by the spymaster. See also Roy Sherwood, *The Court of Oliver Cromwell*, London, 1977. R.W. Ramsey, *Henry Cromwell*, London, Longmans Green, 1933, gives a useful description of Richard's able younger brother.

The careers of Fleetwood, Desborough, Fauconberg, Downing and Lockhart are covered admirably in the *Dictionary of National Biography*, ed. L. Stephen and S. Lee, 63 vols, London, Smith, Elder, 1885–1900 (subsequently referred to as *DNB*).

2. Presbyterians, Republicans, Royalists and Foreign Powers

A number of the leading secluded members have merited biographies. William M. Lamont, *Marginal Prynne*, London, Routledge & Kegan Paul, 1963, helps to unravel the complexities of this prolific pamphleteer.

There is considerable material on the leaders of the Rump, who played such a key role in the events of 1658–60. There are good biographies of Hesilrige (B. Denton, *Only in Heaven: the Life and Campaigns of Sir Arthur Hesilrige*, Sheffield, Sheffield Academic Press, 1977) and the mystic visionary Vane (J.H. Adamson and Folland, *Sir Harry Vane and his Times 1613–62*, London, Bodley Head, 1974, and Violet A. Rowe, *Sir Henry Vane the Younger*, Athlone Press, 1970). Ludlow remains a prime source, though not always a reliable one. Those wishing to learn more about the memoirs of this important regicide should read E. Ludlow, *A Voyce from the Watchtower*, ed. B. Worden, Camden Society, 1978.

Blair Worden, *The Rump Parliament*, Cambridge, Cambridge University Press, 1974, provides a lot more information on all these key figures.

The convoluted career of Anthony Ashley Cooper is well covered in K.H.D. Haley, *The First Earl of Shaftesbury*, Oxford, Clarendon Press, 1968, and W.D. Christie, *Life of Anthony Ashley Cooper*, 2 vols, London, Macmillan, 1871, which attempt to unravel this subtle politician's ability to keep all sides guessing as to his true loyalty in the run-up to the Restoration. More information on parliamentary activity can be found in the *Old Parliamentary History*.

Of all the books written about Charles II, Gilbert Burnet, *History of My Own Time*, 6 vols, Oxford, Oxford University Press, 1833, provides the best contemporary insight. To this can be added S. Tuke, *A Character of Charles II*, London, 1660, and a mass of information in Sir Richard Baker, *A Chronicle of the Kings of England*, London, G. Sawbridge and T. William, 1670, though this is not always accurate. Hester Chapman, *The Tragedy of Charles II*, London, Jonathan Cape, 1964, provides the most perceptive analysis of his character and conveys the destructive influence exerted by the long years of exile. There is much interesting material in Eva Scott, *Travels of the King*, London, Constable, 1907. The best recent critical analysis of Charles's character is Richard Ollard, *Image of the King*, London, Hodder & Stoughton, 1979. The complex politics of the period is well covered by Godfrey Davies and Ronald Hutton, *Restoration, 1658–67*, Oxford, Clarendon Press, 1985. Antonia Fraser, *King Charles II*, London, Weidenfeld & Nicolson, 1979, offers a sympathetic and lively portrayal of the King. S. Coote, *Royal Survivor*, London, Hodder & Stoughton, 1999, describes his subject with few illusions. For information on Charles II's youthful love life, John Evelyn, *A Panegyric to Charles II*, 1661, lists seventeen mistresses he is supposed to have acquired in exile. Mme de Motteville, in her *Memoirs of Madame de Motteville on Anne of Austria and her Court*, trans. K. Wormsley, 1902, is a keen observer of Charles during his early period of exile.

Hyde has been well served by Richard Ollard, *Clarendon*, London, Hamish Hamilton, 1987, which acknowledges his crucial role in bringing about the Restoration. Hyde himself was indefatigable, both in his *History of the Great Rebellion*, ed. Roger Lockyer, London, Oxford University Press, 1967, and his correspondence (*The Clarendon State Papers*, ed. F.J. Routledge, Oxford, Clarendon, 1932). To avoid confusion, any mention of Hyde or his correspondence refers to *The Clarendon State Papers* (Hyde was not created Earl of Clarendon until 1661).

Ormonde's life had been fully covered by Carte (Thomas Carte, *Life of James, Duke of Ormonde*, 1735–6, London, J.J. and P. Knapton, 1851) but there may be room for a modern assessment of the noblest of Charles II's servants. Hyde's close colleague Sir Edward Nicholas, Secretary of State to Charles II throughout the 1650s, enjoyed a correspondence almost as copious as Hyde himself (*The Nicholas Papers: Correspondence of Sir Edward Nicholas, Secretary of State*, ed. Sir G. Warner, 4 vols, Camden Society, 1886–1920). A biography of Henry Bennet (Violet Barbour, *Henry Bennet, Earl of Arlington*, Washington, American Historical Association, 1914) is of particular interest in showing Bennet's ability to manage the King.

Much the best account of Royalist activity during the Commonwealth is David Underdown, *Royalist Conspiracy in England 1649–60*, New Haven, Yale University Press, 1960, which uncovers a great deal of new material. The role of Anglican divines such as Gilbert Sheldon, future Archbishop of Canterbury (Victor D. Sutch, *Gilbert Sheldon*, The Hague, 1973), and John Barwick (Peter Barwick, *Life of Dr John Barwick*, London, J. Bettenham, 1724), the key man in converting Monck's officers to the Royalist cause, is of particular interest. A new biography by Charles Spencer may well complement existing biographies on Prince Rupert, a leader of the Action party (see P. Morrah, *Prince Rupert of the Rhine*, London, Constable, 1976).

For a general assessment of the major European powers during the 1650s, see chapter 1. Col Holles's quote on the Cavaliers appears in J.G. Muddiman, *The King's Journalist*, London, John Lane, 1923. Edward Phillips, a prime source for Baker's *Chronicle*, was a cousin of Milton and shared his republican views. Lambert's quote on the Cavaliers reflects the inherent insecurity of the regime.

3. Trouble in the Army

Godfrey Davies's *Restoration* covers all the key events in some detail. The *Cambridge Modern History*, vol. iv, is also excellent on the political developments covered by this book. Thurloe's correspondence with Henry Cromwell and Viscount Fauconberg (see chapter 1) provides an insight into the close circle surrounding the Protector. Thurloe is interesting on the question of the succession and the growing concern in the Government at the role of the Army. Ludlow's *Memoirs* offer further analysis of the problems that beset the new Protector.

Mercurius Politicus, edited by the talented Republican journalist Marchamont Nedham, and a major purveyor of news, contains the numerous addresses sent in by Richard's loyal subjects to their new ruler. *The Clarke Papers, the Public Intelligencer*, Baker's *Chronicle* and Baxter's *Narrative* all describe contemporary reactions to his accession. Hyde and Nicholas provide a Royalist and therefore hostile commentary. W. Orme, *Memoirs of John Owen*, London, 1820, brings one of Cromwell's closest religious associates to life.

D. Massarella, 'Politics of the Army 1647–60', Ph.D. thesis, University of York, 1977, gives a good analysis of why the soldiers were so discontented. There is a considerable literature on the extremist sects which played such a vital role in Army politics. The most stimulating account is Christopher Hill, *The World Turned Upside Down*, London, Temple Smith, 1972. Other interesting works are B. Capp, *Fifth Monarchy Men*, London, Faber, 1972, and Louise Fargo Brown, *The Political Activities of the Baptists and 5th Monarchy Men*, Washington and London, American Historical Association, 1912. To avoid an overdose of Quakerism, on which subject there is any amount of material, you can restrict yourself to B. Reay, 'The Quakers, 1659 and the Restoration of the Monarchy', *History*, lxiii, 1978. Lockhart's worries over a potential mutiny are recorded in the *Thurloe State Papers*. A succinct analysis of Fleetwood's career can be found in Ashley's *Cromwell's Generals*.

Lord Colepeper's astute analysis of Monck, the most prescient of any Royalist, can be found in *The Clarendon State Papers*. Sir John Grenville, son of the Royalist hero Sir Beville Grenville, was related to George Monck, a crucial advantage in the months ahead. Sir Richard Willis, who also appeared to have impeccable Royalist credentials, was, in fact, a double agent in the pay of Thurloe. His betrayal of the cause caused confusion in the Cavalier ranks, and is well covered in Underdown's *Royalist Conspiracy*. Cromwell's cryptic remark on Monck's loyalty is quoted by Thurloe and Price's *Mystery and Method*.

There is an interesting short account on Viscount Mordaunt, the most active Royalist in England, and appointed King's Plenipotentiary, in

M. Coate, 'The Letter-book of John, Viscount Mordaunt', Camden Society 3rd series, lxix, 1945. Mordaunt attempted to form an alliance with former Parliamentarians, especially the Presbyterians, and this appears in G.H. Abernathy, 'The English Presbyterians and the Stuart Restoration', American Philosophical Society, 1965. Godfrey Davies has a great deal of material on the disputes among the factions surrounding Richard Cromwell and the arguments in the Privy Council.

The most interesting development in foreign policy occurred in the Baltic, where Sweden and Denmark, as so often, were at loggerheads. The best analyses of Cromwell's foreign policy are by R. Crabtree, 'The Idea of a Protestant Foreign Policy' in Roots's *Cromwell*, and Charles P. Korr, *Cromwell and the New Model Foreign Policy*, Berkeley, University of California Press, 1975.

Two good accounts of Oliver's funeral can be found in John Evelyn's *Diary*, ed. Guy de la Bedoyere, Bangor, Headstart History, 1995, and Richard Baxter's *Narrative*. Other sources are Francesco Giavarina's perceptive reports, sent weekly to the Venetian Senate, in the *Calendar Venetian* (ed. Rawdon Brown, London, Longmans Green) and, for the French ambassador Bordeaux's correspondence, see Guizot's *Richard Cromwell*. Abraham Cowley's account appears in *The Collected Works of Abraham Cowley*, ed. T. Calhoun, London and Newark, University of Delaware Press, 1989. *The Clarke Papers* record that the soldiers of the New Model Army intended to seize Cromwell's body for pay. The quotes by Fauconberg appear in Thurloe.

4. The Fall of the Protectorate

Mercurius Politicus covers the election to parliament. Thurloe, as the orchestrator of the government party, offers a more personal opinion of the voting. Further analysis is provided in Guizot's *Richard Cromwell*. G. Davies, 'The Election of Richard Cromwell's Parliament', *EHR*, lxiii, 1948, contains a great deal of useful detail. Hyde and Nicholas, in their copious correspondence, offer the Royalist perspective on the composition of the House of Commons.

Quotes by Hesilrige, Chaloner Chute, Speaker of the House of Commons, and Okey appear in the *Diary of Thomas Burton*, ed. J.T. Rutt, London,

H. Colburn, 1828. Burton also covers the release of Overton, whose plot to overthrow Oliver Cromwell appears in Gardiner's *Commonwealth and Protectorate*. Interestingly, Overton was arrested by Monck, and the relationship between the two men was to remain fraught in the months to come, with Overton holding a key position as Governor of Hull, which contained the main arsenal in the north of England. Burton also covers the description of the sufferings of the Cavaliers sold as slaves to the West Indies.

The actual debates in the new parliament are covered in G. Nourse, 'Richard Cromwell's House of Commons', *Bulletin of John Rylands Library*, lx, 1977–8. Ludlow in his *Memoirs* offers further commentary, particularly on the question that vexed the members, still relevant today, on whether the Scots and Irish should have representation. He was also much concerned with the composition of the Other House, which he saw as a threat to the supremacy of the House of Commons. For more information on the debates in parliament, the reader should consult Slingsby Bethel's *The Most Material Debates in that Pretended Parliament called by Richard Cromwell*, 1659 and 1680.

Mordaunt offers more insight into Royalist activity in his *Letter-book*. The copious correspondence of his rival Brodrick, secretary to the Sealed Knot, appears in *The Clarendon State Papers*. The charismatic but maverick figure of Buckingham, who exerted a fascination on Charles II throughout his life, often with disastrous results, comes to life in David Hanrahan, *Charles II and the Duke of Buckingham*, Stroud, Sutton, 2006.

The quote by Nehemiah Bourne appears in Firth's excellent introduction to *The Clarke Papers*. Thurloe and Ludlow describe the hostile relations between Ashfield and Whalley. Ashfield had served under Monck in Scotland, and the general had dismissed him, together with Gough, another known troublemaker, in a note to Thurloe in March: 'If they were here they would signify as little as any two officers in Scotland.' The story of the Protector's support for Ingoldsby is told at length in *A Second Narrative of the Late Parliament*, 1658, as recorded in Frith's notes on *Ludlow's Memoirs*. The quote by Col Parker appears in Burton.

The propaganda offensive instigated by the Rump, with its frequent references to the 'Good Old Cause', is noted by Austin Woolrych, 'The Good Old Cause and the Fall of the Protectorate', *Cambridge Historical Journal*, xiii,

1957. The petitions and addresses made by the soldiers to Richard are recorded in *Mercurius Politicus, The Clarendon State Papers*, Thurloe, Guizot and Clarke, with comments on their mixture of loyalty and discontent. The splits in the Army between supporters and opponents of Richard Cromwell are covered in Thurloe, Clarke and Ludlow. The attack on Maj Gen Boteler is recorded in Thurloe and the *Commons Journal*. For information on the activities of the radical group led by Sir Richard Tichborne, see *The Nicholas Papers* and Clarendon.

The *Calendar of State Papers, Domestic* and Guizot offer opinions as to the cause of Richard's fall. The picture they paint shows the Protector in a better light than history has allowed, but also demonstrate that, in the last resort, he was in an impossible predicament. Giavarina, in the *Calendar Venetian*, records the soldiers' loss of confidence in the Protector. Ludlow and Baker's *Chronicle* must be treated with caution, since their compression of events leads to possible confusion. *The Clarke Papers* offer a reliable perspective from north of the Scottish border. Royalists, such as Hyde and Nicholas, are naturally less sympathetic and their conclusions have been generally accepted.

The anguished correspondence between Richard Cromwell and his brother Henry reveals his bitterness at the betrayal of his relations Fleetwood and Desborough. The *Heath Chronicle* (*James Heath, A Brief Chronicle*, London, 1663) is interesting on Royalist attempts to persuade Richard Cromwell to declare for Charles II. Butler's *Richard Cromwell* cites the offers by Cromwellian loyalists to get rid of Fleetwood, Lambert, Vane and Desborough.

5. The Rump and the Army

The best analysis of the propaganda offensive waged by the Rump can be found in Woolrych's *The Good Old Cause*. The original material is all available in *Collection of the Pamphlets* collected by George Thomason, 1908 (known as the *Thomason Tracts*, BM, Dept of Printed Books, 1908). Sir Archibald Johnston (*The Diary of Sir Archibald Johnston of Wariston*, Scottish Historical Society, 1940), a fierce Covenanter and once the foremost enemy of Montrose, and Ludlow are both interesting on the negotiations between the leaders of the Rump and the Army. The restoration of the Rump is noted in the *Calendar, Domestic*. Analysis of its leaders, Hesilrige and Vane, is provided in the *Public Intelligencer* and Ludlow's *Memoirs*. The high-handed behaviour of the soldiers is well described by Giavarina in the *Calendar Venetian* when he recounts with horror how they broke into the house of his fellow ambassador from Denmark.

There are numerous publications by critics of the regime, notably the *Clarendon Calendar. England's Confusion*, London, 1659, by Annesley, a leader of the secluded members, appears in *Somers Tracts* (John, Baron Somers, *A Collection of Scarce and Valuable Tracts*, London, T. Cadell and W. Davies, 1809–15). Mordaunt's *Letter-book* records the Royalist viewpoint. Thurloe, and *The Clarke Papers*, showing the Committee of Safety's instructions to Monck, and Guizot all provide commentary on the gradual breakdown of the relationship of the two dominant parties. Even Sir Archibald Johnston, who served as President of the Council of State, was highly critical of the regime. Lucy Hutchinson's *Memoirs* and Ralph Josselin, *Diary of Ralph Josselin 1616–83*, ed. A. Macfarlane, London, Oxford University Press, 1976, provide further comments from the sidelines. G.E. Aylmer, *The State's Servants*, London, Routledge & Kegan Paul, 1973, portrays the role of the judges and other officials.

The Rump's cashiering of officers, so crucial to its hold on power, is noted in Baker's *Chronicle*, *The Clarke Papers*, and Firth and Davies's *Regimental History*. The *Calendar Venetian* gives the surprising account of the defeat of the senior officers' vote to restore the King by just six votes. Richard Cromwell's biographers describe the former Protector's fall from grace. Even Hyde is sympathetic to his predicament. The regicide Thomas Scot's boast about his part in Charles I's execution is recorded in Burton's *Diary*, the Thurloe *State Papers* and Barwick in his correspondence with Hyde. When the regicides were tried in the autumn of 1660, this remark was to cost Scot his life.

Suspicions of the loyalty of Ashley Cooper are well covered by his biographer, Haley. Morland's tendency to over-exaggerate his role as a Cavalier spy is given full scope in his *Autobiography* (*A Brief Account of the Life, Writings and Inventions of Sir S. Morland*, Cambridge, 1838).

The complex situation in Ireland is related in Lynch's biography of Broghill. Henry Cromwell's biographer Ramsey describes his resignation.

According to Ludlow, Henry contemplated armed intervention on behalf of his brother. *The Clarendon State Papers* show how Hyde tried to cash in on this.

The various sources on Monck relate his acceptance of the Rump's accession to power, while the *Calendar Venetian* notes the ambiguity of his letter of submission. Both Ollard and Harris record the complex situation in the Baltic, where Montagu's friendship with the Swedish king put him at odds with the Rump's wish for England to remain neutral. They also record Montagu's change of allegiance, and his decision to enter into a clandestine correspondence with Charles II. Information on the new Admiralty Commissioners Walton and Morley, and on Downing and Lockhart's activities, can be found in the *DNB*. Ludlow, as a leading member of the new regime, is interesting on his marked preference for Lawson over Montagu in the naval high command.

Lambert's record as a political theorist (he had drafted the *Instrument of Government* in 1653) is recorded by his biographer Farr and by Gardiner in his *History of the Commonwealth*. A measure of the importance of Harrington's role in attempting to change the whole political outlook of England can be gained in G.A. Pocock, *The Political Works of James Harrington*, Cambridge, Cambridge University Press, 1977. Johnston's *Diary, the Calendar Venetian* and *The Nicholas Papers* record the difficulty of passing the Act of Oblivion. Ludlow records the confrontation between Hesilrige and Lambert.

The Clarendon State Papers, and particularly Hyde's correspondence with Barwick, express the Royalists' hope to benefit from Lambert's dissatisfaction. Johnston, on the other hand, is sunk in gloom at the lack of success of the regime. Wood (*Life and Times of Anthony Wood*, ed. A. Clark, Oxford Historical Society, 1891), Conway (*The Conway Letters*, ed. M.H. Nicolson, Oxford, Clarendon Press, 1992), and Reay on the Quakers, all comment on the widespread fears of religious extremists; Reay includes Col William Parker's remark.

6. Booth's Rebellion

The background to the Royalist intrigues that dominated the summer can be found in *The Nicholas Papers* and *The Clarendon State Papers*, especially Hyde's correspondence with Brodrick, secretary to the Sealed Knot. Mordaunt's

Letter-book is vociferous in the viscount's dissatisfaction with the activities of the Sealed Knot, and his rivalry with Brodrick gravely harmed the Royalist cause. Hyde, in particular, reveals the general lack of preparation of the Cavaliers.

Underdown's *Royalist Conspiracy* provides a clear overview of the disastrous Royalist rising, and describes all the main characters. He notes the number of new Cavaliers, such as Willoughby, Browne, Massey and Booth himself, Presbyterians who had fought for Parliament in the 1640s. Many were secluded members; Popham, a Rumper convert, was still a rare breed. One of the most interesting characters is Sir Richard Willis, the Royalist double agent. Underdown shows how the Sealed Knot, of which Willis was a leading member, continued to defend him despite evidence mounting of his treachery. However, the appearance of his name three times in the *Council Register* amounts to proof of his treachery.

More detail can be found in R. Petty, 'The Rebellion of Sir George Booth', *Journal of the Chester and North Wales Architectural, Archaeological and History Society*, xxxiii, 1939, and J. Jones, 'Booth's Rising of 1659', *Trans. Lancashire and Cheshire Antiquarian Society*, lxix, 1959.

Among original sources, Hyde, Nicholas and Mordaunt in his *Letter-book* give extensive contemporary coverage of the events of the rebellion from the Royalist perspective. Whitelocke's *Memorials*, *Mercurius Politicus* and the *Calendar Domestic* present the Government's viewpoint and its activities to thwart the Cavaliers. The *Calendar Venetian* notes the mutinies of Lambert's men when setting off to confront Booth.

For an account of the Royalist 'army' in Flanders, see J. Childs, *The Army of Charles II*, London, Routledge & Kegan Paul, 1976, and *The Memoirs of James II: His Campaigns as Duke of York 1652–60*, trans. A. Lytton Sells from the Bouillon manuscript, 1962. James, as its commander, had proved himself a talented soldier, serving under Marshal Turenne in the French army. He had been very reluctant to give up his commission following Cromwell's decision to ally with France in 1654, which had compelled Charles to leave France. As allies of Spain, James and his brother Henry, Duke of Gloucester led the Royalist contingent against the Anglo-French force at the battle of the Dunes in 1658, shortly before Cromwell's death.

The commander of the Cromwellian troops was Maj Gen Thomas Morgan (see *DNB*), who was shortly to serve under Monck in Scotland.

The potentially crucial role of Montagu as a supporter of Booth is covered by both Harris and Ollard in their biographies. Jones's *Booth's Rising* and D. Ogg, *England in the Reign of Charles II*, Oxford, Oxford University Press, 1955, take Montagu's Royalist sympathies very seriously. There is a paucity of evidence, perhaps an indication of the admiral's success as a conspirator. Few letters survive between Hyde and Montagu, and there is no mention in Pepys of his cousin's dangerous correspondence with the King.

Monck's even more enigmatic role appears in Davies's biography. *The Clarke Papers*, although of great interest, do not reveal anything of the general's thinking. The mission of Nicholas Monck to his brother is fully covered in Price's *Mystery and Method*. The chaplain is also very good on Monck's almost incredible sangfroid on being given the news of Booth's defeat, if indeed the general was about to declare for the rebels.

7. A Split in the Army

The *Calendar Domestic* and Guizot's *Richard Cromwell* record the Rump's reaction to Lambert's victory. Hyde is much more astute on Lambert's relationship with Fleetwood than he is on Monck. Monck himself is very perceptive on Lambert's relations with the Rump. Lucy Hutchinson's *Memoirs* notes Lambert's vanity. Hutton's *The Restoration* is interesting on Lambert's promotion of religious extremists and Monck's reactions to it. This issue, of great importance in the break between the two men, has been underplayed by most previous historians.

The *Calendar Domestic* notes Hesilrige's rejection of Lambert's promotion and his ham-fisted attempt to make up for this by increasing the grant to the general following his victory. The Derby petition appears in *A Declaration of the General Council of Officers*. Thomas Rugg's *Diurnal*, London, Royal Historical Society, 1961, a compilation of newspapers and some personal entries, lists the petitions issued in London under the charge of Desborough. *The Clarke Papers* lists Monck's objections, his refusal to sign the petitions and his support for the Rump.

Ludlow's *Memoirs* and the *Calendar Venetian* describe how Fleetwood showed the petition to Hesilrige, and his incandescent response. See also J. Redmayne, *A True Narrative of the Proceedings in Parliament, the Council of State, the General Councell of the Army and the Committee of Safety*, London, 1659 and the Thurloe *State Papers*. R.R. Sharpe, *London and the Kingdom*, London, Longmans Green, 1894–5, describes how the Rump backed down over its involvement in the choice of the Lord Mayor of the City.

There are a number of graphic accounts of the events leading to the dismissal of the Rump (*Calendar Venetian, Weekly Intelligencer,* Johnston's *Diary,* Hyde and Ludlow). One suspects that Whitelocke was no hero, as he records how he and his family hid behind locked doors. Although Hutton defends Bradshaw as a champion of parliament against the military, it is worth remembering that the trial of Charles I, over which he presided, only took place after Col Pride had purged the majority of MPs who refused to be associated with this radical and, in their view, totally unconstitutional measure.

8. *Lambert versus Monck*

The copious sources on Monck and his activities north of the border are listed in Chapter 1, Cromwell's Heir. Guizot's *Memoirs of George Monk* and the *Weekly Intelligencer* describe Monck's purging of his regiments. Firth and Davies's *Regimental History* provides a list of those officers cashiered.

There is some interesting material on the religious extremists supported by Lambert, Lilburne and Overton in Capp's *5th Monarchy Men* and Reay's *Quakers*. James Nayler's entry into Bristol, based on Christ's entry into Jerusalem, was seen by most Englishmen as both scandalous and sacrilegious. Although some were horrified at the savage punishment meted out to him, it is, nevertheless, interesting that Lambert should have defended him (Nayler had formerly been a member of the New Model Army).

Monck's letters in the *Old Parliamentary History,* xxii show his mastery of propaganda. These can be compared with his opponents (*The Army's Plea for the Present Practice* and *A Declaration of the General Council of Officers*). James Welwood, *Memoirs of the most Material Transactions in England for the last Hundred Years, etc*, London, 1749, provides interesting detail on Monck's attempts to prevent agents from London infiltrating his troops. The Army's cashiering of Okey and Alured, staunch Republicans, is indicative of the fatal split among Charles II's opponents. These two men were to remain hostile to the idea of the Restoration to the bitter end (see Chapter 11). Godfrey Davies's *Restoration* describes the effect that these divisions had on local government.

The Clarendon State Papers and *The Nicholas Papers* offer a Royalist commentary on the changing situation, with hope gradually reviving. John Evelyn, *An Apology for the Royal Party*, published on 27 October 1659, gives a good idea of this new-found confidence. Mordaunt's *Letter-book*, Hyde and Barwick all note approaches made by Cavaliers to Lambert, Fleetwood, Lawson and other senior figures. Many were unsuccessful but the decision of Broghill, Charles Howard, Ingoldsby (see *DNB*) and others to switch allegiance encouraged Royalists to persevere. Interestingly, these former Parliamentarians, together with Montagu, now also a Royalist, had all been strongly in favour of Oliver Cromwell accepting the crown.

The Clarke Papers are particularly interesting in their detailed commentary on Monck's dealings with the Army grandees in England, and his determined efforts to control and educate his men so that they were united before he even contemplated marching into England. The *Publick Intelligencer* lists negotiations between Monck and the Army commissioners. Giavarina, writing in the *Calendar Venetian*, notes astutely how Monck used these negotiations to play for time.

Gumble's *General Monk* and Price's *Mystery and Method*, although they are both full of excellent anecdotal material, need to be treated with caution, since they view the actions of their commander with hindsight. Baker's *Chronicle*, based on the evidence of Monck's brother-in-law Thomas Clarges, is also questionable in some of its conclusions.

Lambert has been served less well. What evidence we have of the state of his troops stationed on the Scottish border during November and December 1659 appears in Dawson's biography, Clarke and Baker's *Chronicle*. Lucy Hutchinson's comments on the arbitrary nature of the English Army's government are representative of the widespread disillusion among former supporters of the New Model Army.

The crucial importance of London in the Army's loss of control of England is well laid out in V. Pearl, 'London's Counter-Revolution' in Aylmer (ed.),

The Interregnum, London, Oxford University Press, 1961 and S.R. Smith, 'Almost Revolutionaries: the London Apprentices during the Civil Wars', *Huntingdon Quarterly*, xxxxii, 1978–9. The best account of Monck's inspired choice of journalist to defend his cause is J.G. Muddiman, *The King's Journalist*, London, John Lane, 1923.

For the activities of Broghill in Ireland, busy planning a rising against Ludlow, see Lynch's *Roger Boyle* and Barnard's *Cromwellian Ireland*. Gumble and Price give graphic accounts of the primitive nature of Monck's quarters. Dow's *Cromwellian Scotland* comments on the general's agreement with the Scottish Royalists to remain quiet. J.G. Davies is good on the role of Fairfax and the intrigue between him and Monck. Fairfax took a very firm stand over some of his troopers' wish to sign a declaration of support for the Rump. He had no wish to see them becoming involved in politics, which had caused such problems in the New Model Army in the aftermath of the First Civil War.

For the role of Portsmouth in the fall of the Army, see C.D. and W.C.D. Whetham, *The Life of Colonel Nathaniel Whetham*, London, Longmans Green, 1907, and *A Letter from Sir Arthur Haselrigge in Portsmouth*, 1659. Orme's *Owen* describes how this champion of the Independent sects, so close to Cromwell in his religious beliefs, tried to stem the tide.

The *Publick Intelligencer* relates the actions of the Committee of Safety to prevent the publication of petitions in London. The *Unhappy Marksman* shows the Committee's failure. The *Calendar Venetian* notes the release at the beginning of November of many of the leading Royalists arrested after Booth's defeat.

Pepys, about to commence his *Diary*, already shows the full range of his descriptive skills in his account of the apprentices' riot on 5 December (*Letters and the 2nd Diary of Samuel Pepys*, ed. R.G. Howarth, London, J.M. Dent, 1932). Haley's *Shaftesbury* provides evidence for Ashley Cooper's growing influence. Ludlow in his *Memoirs* attempts to portray himself as acting as the mediator between the two sides. Soon, he is struggling to retain control of his command in Ireland. His angry comments on events in Dublin need to be read in conjunction with Firth's measured footnotes.

The role of Lawson in forcing the Army's hand is well described in M.H., *A Narrative of the Proceedings of the Fleet*, London, Streeter, 1659, and the *Publick Intelligencer*. Hyde, although no friend of Lawson, saw clearly the enormous advantage to be gained from this move. Vane's biographers Adamson and Folland describe the failure of Vane to persuade Lawson that only the Army could prevent the restoration. Vane provides a clear indication of the fractured nature of the Republican cause in his decision, despite his championship of parliament against the Army in 1648, 1653 and the spring of 1659, to have changed sides and thrown in his lot with Lambert and Fleetwood.

The Remonstrance & Protestation . . ., signed by all the major Commonwealth figures, apart from the English generals, demonstrates the ever-narrowing power base of the Army. Samuel Tuke's advice to Charles II is symptomatic of the majority of Royalists' desire to wait on events. The description in *Mercurius Politicus* of a proposed Royalist rising bears this out. Charles enjoyed a fraught relationship with his mother, owing to her militant Catholicism, which he feared would damage his chance of a restoration (E. Hamilton, *Henrietta Maria*, London, Hamish Hamilton, 1976). For further information on the King's burgeoning relationship with his favourite sister, Minette, which reveals the most charming side of Charles's nature, see C.H. Hartman, *Charles II and Madame*, London, Heinemann, 1934.

The *Publick Intelligencer* and the *Weekly Journal* both describe the restoration of the Rump. Whitelocke's *Memorials* is very interesting on the last days of Army rule and the collapse of Fleetwood. As Keeper of the Great Seal, one of the main offices, representing some continuity with the past, he should have been in an important position, but so discredited was the Government that he fled for his life, leaving his wife to hand over the seal to Speaker Lenthall. Hyde records Fleetwood's memorable comment on leaving office.

9. Monck's March on London

Patrick Morrah, *1660 The Year of Restoration*, London, Chatto & Windus, 1960, provides a very readable alternative to Godfrey Davies's more complex and detailed *The Restoration of Charles II*. For original sources, Gumble and Price both provide vivid descriptions of Monck's momentous march south.

J.G. Davies's *Fairfax* describes the veteran general's capture of York, his meetings with Monck after his arrival in the city and his subsequent decision to retire from the fray. See also, *Memorials of Thomas Fairfax*, ed. Brian Fairfax, 1699.

Samuel Pepys commenced his famous *Diary* (*The Diary of Samuel Pepys*, ed. R.C. Latham and W. Matthews, 9 vols, London, Bell, 1970–6) on the very day that Monck began his epic march. As with so many of the best diarists, Pepys contrives to be in the right place at the right time, and provides an invaluable commentary on the exciting events leading up to the Restoration. The *Diary* is worth reading in its entirety.

Giavarina, in the *Calendar Venetian*, also makes very interesting reading. The importance of the Turk's Head coffee shop marks the beginning of the role of the coffee shop, or café, in society. Monck reveals his much under-estimated political skill in his choice of subordinates: Muddiman as his propagandist, Gumble as his negotiator with the Republicans, Sharpe with the Presbyterians, Clarges with the Army grandees and Morice with the Royalists. Gumble records his determined resistance to the Council of State's attempt to force him to reveal Monck's intentions; furthermore, he offers his commander very sage advice on the Council's intentions.

Pepys records the outburst of propaganda as people felt increasingly confident in flouting the Rump's authority. One can sense the relish with which Brodrick, in his correspondence with Hyde, details Salwey's grovelling apology for his misdeeds. Mordaunt provides an acerbic commentary on Ashley Cooper in his *Letter-book*, but his superiors realised that they needed the little man's support and continued to make overtures. Howard and Ingoldsby, though rewarded by the Rump for their supposed loyalty, had already pledged their true allegiance to the King. Whitelocke gives a vivid description of the sudden change in fortune whereby one of the most influential men in England was now in hiding from his enemies.

Aldermen Wale and Robinson were to play an important role following the arrival of Monck in London (see A.B. Beavan, *The Aldermen of the City of London*, London, 1908). Like the Rump and the Army, Monck was to court the City, whose financial muscle gave its rulers great power. Evelyn's *Diary* relates his attempt to recruit his old schoolfriend Morley to the Royalist cause. It demonstrates clearly the crucial importance of timing. As Governor of the Tower of London, he held a key post and could have played a role almost as important as Monck or Montagu. Instead, he was to beg for mercy at the Restoration. Ludlow's *Memoirs* take on a bitter twist as he finds himself isolated in Ireland and realises belatedly that all his former colleagues have deserted the cause.

Hyde and Mordaunt's correspondence reveal the anguish of the Royalists as they tried to keep abreast of the rapidly changing situation. It is clear that they were no longer able to influence events. Nevertheless, the *Calendar Domestic*, in comments on the Royalist Dr Richard Allestree and his opponent Col Dixon, shows that the Government remained paranoid about security. Gibb's *Fairfax* records his meetings with Monck, although no one knows for certain what the two generals said.

Scot and Robinson, sent to monitor Monck's movements, were both fiercely republican in their views. Price offers a fascinating but hostile commentary on the commissioners, describing the way that they spied on the general like true commissars.

The detailed research that Clarges carried out on the disposition of the troops around London shows how careful Monck was in his dealings with the New Model Army, which had so often participated in the dismissal of parliament, most recently in October 1659. The petitions made to him are listed in Davies's *Restoration*, the *Thomason Tracts* and the *Calendar Domestic*.

The stoical Hyde's lamentation on the poverty and hunger endemic at the exiled Court shows how low Royalist morale remained despite the supposed upsurge in their fortunes. Pepys, in contrast, rejoices in his ostentatious dinner at Montagu's lodgings (two dozen larks, etc.). Never overburdened by his conscience, he nevertheless ends his entry for the month with a moment's reflection on his witnessing the execution of Charles I eleven years earlier. For the rest of his life, Pepys was always nervous of anyone who knew that he had seen the event, in case they remembered his remark to his friends, on returning to school, that if he had to preach a sermon on the King, the text would be: 'The memory of the wicked shall rot.'

10. The Fall of the Rump

Hugh Peters was not a regicide but was accused by Royalists after the Restoration of plotting Charles I's death with Cromwell and Ireton (*DNB*). Although Peters was a famous preacher (he preached at Cromwell's funeral), Price was disgusted at the sermon he preached to Monck at St Albans. Pepys and *Mercurius Politicus* give accounts of the Army in London's mutiny. In addition, five companies mutinied when ordered to Gravesend for passage to Dunkirk. An idea of the unpopularity of the Rump and the Royalist revival can be gauged in *Rats Rhymed to Death*, 1660 and *Rump: or an Exact Collection of the Choicest Poems and Songs relating to the Late Times*, 1662.

The sources on Monck and the *Old Parliamentary History* describe his attendance in parliament, and his dismantling of the City gates, although there is no consensus on why he obeyed the Rump's order. Guizot records Hesilrige's cry of triumph.

Baker's *Chronicle* and many others give accounts of Monck's momentous decision to readmit the secluded members into parliament. Price, anxious to promote his general's Royalist credentials, needs to be treated with some scepticism. The general, 'a dull, heavy man', in the words of Pepys, was a master at disguising his intentions. The Royalists were left constantly in the dark (see Hyde and Mordaunt), but even Monck's colleagues were seldom in agreement. Bishop Seth Ward, in his funeral sermon, summed up the general very well: 'He was a man great of pleasure, little of Speech, no lover of wast words or fine composed orations, but a great affector of what was short and plain, easie and inaffected.'

Pepys's account of the impact made by Monck's decision is one of the best pieces of reportage in the English language. For a different interpretation, see Denton's *Hesilrige*. Haley's *Shaftesbury* records Ashley Cooper's quickness of mind to avert a potentially calamitous situation.

Hyde is again good on the tension afflicting the Royalists in Brussels. Carte's *Ormonde* notes the approaches to the Marquis, with news of the fall of the Rump in London. The role of the King at this period has been underestimated, due to its essentially passive nature. Nevertheless, critics of Charles's character, such as Ollard in his *The Image of the King*, fail to give Charles due credit for his masterly ability to wait on events while maintaining the morale of his followers. He still had all to lose. Newcastle, Charles's governor in childhood, has been well covered in Margaret Cavendish, *The Life of William Cavendish, Duke of Newcastle*, ed. C.H. Firth, London, 1886.

There is something wonderfully gallant about Hesilrige's pigheaded refusal to face the facts. Pepys, Clarke and the *Mercurius Politicus* note the meeting of Monck, the Rumpers and the leading secluded members. Baker, Gumble and Ludlow, in addition, depict the crucial meeting of Monck and his close associates, when the decision was taken to admit the secluded members. Pepys is again excellent on the next day's events. Prynne had proved one of the most aggressive of the secluded members, determined that those responsible for his expulsion from parliament in 1648 should be held to account. John Aubrey, *Brief Lives*, ed. Richard Barber, London, Folio Society, 1975, describes his tripping up the former Parliamentarian Gen Waller.

11. Monck's Great Decision

Pepys's unlikely mention of Richard Cromwell's name alongside those of Monck and the King shows the generally chaotic political situation where even the perceptive diarist was totally in the dark over how events would turn out. Bordeaux (*Calendar Venetian*) was more accurate, certainly compared with the Royalists Barwick and Hyde.

The *Calendar Domestic* lists the complaints of the armed forces, both military and naval. Guizot is interesting on the City's refusal to loan Monck money until he had reorganised the militia. The argument over control of the militia had played a key role in the build-up to the First Civil War. Contemporary accounts differ over Monck's successful handling of the Republicans in the New Model Army, always likely to prove his most dangerous opponents, as their previous interventions in politics had proved. Hutton in his *Restoration* picks his way carefully between the discrepancies in Pepys, Baker, Price, Hyde, Guizot, Gumble and Rugg's *Diurnal*, and his conclusion seems entirely accurate.

Pepys records the swelling tide of Royalism, but his ignorance of his cousin Montagu's correspondence with the King is a good example of the great care the leading figures took in guarding their true loyalty as they calculated when to change sides. In Woolrych's excellent analysis in his introduction to Milton's *Complete Prose Works*, he argues that in the *Readie and Easy way to establish a free Commonwealth*, Milton was not fighting a hopeless cause. Marchamont Nedham, *True and Good News from Brussels: Containing a Sovereigne Antidote agst the Poysons and Calumnies of the present time*, 2 April 1660 (using the old calendar, not changed till the eighteenth century), was the most successful of a number of slanders printed against the King; it is listed in the *Calendar Venetian*. Evelyn's rebuttal of Nedham, *The Late News or Message from Bruxels Unmasked*, appears in G. de la Bedoyere, *The Writings of John Evelyn*, Woodbridge, Boydell and Brewer, 1995.

The best account of the role of the Presbyterians, former opponents but now Royalists, and the dominant group among the secluded members, can be found in G.H. Abernathy, 'The English Presbyterians and the Stuart Restoration', American Philosophical Society, new series part 2, 1965. Hyde's correspondence gives an excellent view of the increasing confidence of the Royalist Court during the spring of 1660. Price's report of Monck's view of the restoration of bishops must be treated with caution, owing to his desire to portray the general as a closet Anglican.

For an analysis of the House of Lords, see *The Clarendon State Papers* and C.H. Firth, *The House of Lords during the Civil Wars*, London, Longmans Green, 1910. Davies's *Restoration* gives a good synopsis of the various accounts (Baker, Clarendon, Bordeaux, *Calendar Venetian* and *Mercurius Politicus*) in his description of Monck's meeting with the officers of the New Model Army at St James's.

Guizot describes Bordeaux's offer to Monck. The French ambassador remained an opponent of the Stuart Restoration long after all his fellow ambassadors had seen the light. Consequently, Charles II refused to have anything to do with him, and there was considerable friction between the two governments when Bordeaux was sent back to France by the newly restored monarch. Baker's account of Hesilrige's offer of the crown to Monck is questionable. Critics of the general liked to concentrate on his vices, citing his acquisitiveness (his delight in receiving £20,000) and his general boorishness (Ludlow on his drunken behaviour).

Lord Macaulay, as the high priest of the Whig cause, is a brilliant and persuasive champion of the Parliamentarian cause in his *History of England*, Folio Society, 1985. Davies notes Crewe's denial of the Rump's part in the execution of Charles I. Ludlow, on the other hand, as a fellow regicide, fully acknowledges Scot's pride in his participation. This was not the first time Scot had made such a boast (see 'The Rump and the Army'). Pepys and several other sources note the painter Darby's action at the Royal Exchange.

Pepys is also interesting in Montagu's continued efforts to weed out disaffected officers in the Navy. Davies comments on the role of Lawson, still an influential figure and a known republican. Barwick, writing to Hyde, attempts unsuccessfully to fathom the conflicting signals that Monck continued to send out. This was probably a deliberate tactic of the general, who was still acutely aware of the gap that remained between the strongly republican Army and the increasingly Royalist desires of the civilian population.

There are differing accounts of the key meeting between Monck and Grenville. In general, I have followed the chronology set out in Hutton's *Restoration*. Hyde cites Monck's defence that he could not have revealed his Royalist sympathies earlier, although this remains very much open to doubt. For the part played by William Morice, see Mary Coate, 'W. Morice and the Restoration of Charles II', *EHR*, xxiii, 1918. Interestingly, Mordaunt, who accompanied Grenville to Brussels, had no idea of the nature of his visit, so careful was Grenville to keep his momentous news for the King's ears only.

As the Declaration of Breda was to be Hyde's finest hour, everything he writes about this key period is worth reading. In view of James's subsequent disastrous political career and his religious bigotry, it was surely right that he should be excluded from the delicate negotiations with Monck, and the inclusion of the concept of religious toleration in the Declaration of Breda. *The Clarendon State Papers* list the growing number of supplicants inundating the exiled Court, asking for jobs following the Restoration. Christie is good on the role of Ashley Cooper, whose importance was accepted by Hyde despite his suspicion of his newly acquired Royalist sympathies.

12. Monck Turns Royalist

Abernathy's *English Presbyterians* gives a good account of this important faction. The *Calendar Domestic* notes the dismantling of the Commonwealth. Hyde and Mordaunt give more colour in their writings as they note, with some relish, the universal desire of Englishmen and women to present their Royalist credentials.

The Harleys had been staunch supporters of parliament during the First Civil War and Lady Brilliana's epic defence of her home at Brampton Bryan had earned her a legendary status. There could be no clearer sign of change than the replacement of Lockhart as Governor of Dunkirk by Col Edward Harley, now a committed Royalist.

To what extent Charles resented the Dutch government's neglect of his sister Mary is difficult to calculate, but there is no doubt of his personal antipathy to the Dutch, evident in the two bloody wars that he was to wage on them in the years to come (John Miller, *Charles II's Foreign Policy*, Huntingdon, Royal Stuart Society, 1991). Although Charles had little love for Mazarin or his ambassador Bordeaux (see Chapter 11), he felt much more affinity for France, and Louis XIV was to prove his closest ally. The Spanish rulers of the Netherlands had treated the Royalists with mild disdain while Charles had been based in Bruges and Brussels. The way that Caracena and Cardenas allowed the King to escape to Breda typifies this disdain.

Grenville's absolute discretion had earned him his place at the Royalist high table. The copies of the Declaration of Breda were to be presented to the key players: parliament and the Council of State, representing the government, Monck and Montagu, as heads of the armed forces, and the City, representing financial power. William Blundell (*Cavalier: Letters of W. Blundell to Friends*, ed. Margaret Blundell, London, Longmans Green, 1933) was a recusant Royalist who had suffered much for the cause, but was to receive little restitution at the Restoration.

Barbara Villiers was to become the King's chief mistress immediately after the Restoration. It is still open to dispute who was the father of her daughter Anne, born exactly nine months after Charles's entry into London on 29 May. She was the only one of six children whom her hapless husband claimed as his own. For more information on her tempestuous love life, see Elizabeth

Hamilton, *The Illustrious Lady: a Biography of Barbara Villiers, Countess of Castlemaine and Duchess of Cleveland*, London, Hamish Hamilton, 1980.

The correspondence of Hyde and Nicholas continues to list hundreds of Royalist supplications, most of whose expectations far exceeded the reality. Underdown's *Royalist Conspiracy* and R.S. Bosher, *The Making of the Restoration Settlement*, Oxford, Oxford University Press, 1951, note the important mission of Morley to Sheldon, so crucial to the re-establishment of the Church of England. Sir William Waller (*DNB*) has already appeared, flat on his face, after being tripped by Prynne in the House of Commons on 21 February.

Sharp and Lauderdale (*DNB*) were the two men responsible for the reintroduction of Episcopalianism (i.e. bishops) at the expense of Presbyterianism. Both men, having thrown their hands in with the restored King, were regarded as turncoats by their former religious allies. In 1679 Sharp was murdered by the Covenanters, whom he had systematically persecuted since the Restoration.

Sir Alan Apsley (*DNB*) was commander of the Royalist infantry at the battle of Naseby. Hyde's friend Brian Cosin was a staunch defender of the Anglican faith and unwilling to make concessions to the Presbyterians. For Charles II's fraught relationship with his mother, see Hamilton's *Henrietta Maria*.

Guizot comments on the coolness between Montagu and Monck, joint commanders of the Navy. William Penn (*DNB*) was another who made the successful transition from Cromwellian to Royalist. His son, a prominent Quaker, became a good friend of the King, who granted him the land in America which was to be named Pennsylvania in his honour. The *Calendar Domestic* records the conversion of the formerly diehard Republican Robert Blackthorne. The problem of hostile Arab corsairs patrolling the western Mediterranean was a perennial one. In this context, the acquisition of Tangier in 1661, as part of Catherine of Braganza's dowry, assumed great importance.

Capp records the activities of the Anabaptists. Rugg's *Diurnal* and *Mercurius Aulicus* give a sensational account of Lambert's escape. Further, more accurate, if less entertaining, information appears in the *Clarendon Calendar*, *Mercurius Politicus* and the *Calendar Venetian*.

Monck's words to Grenville on the Cavaliers show the essentially passive nature of the Royalist participation in the Restoration. Of course this gravely weakened their position when they demanded lucrative posts, and diminished their chances of exacting retribution on their enemies. Of all the regicides, Ingoldsby tried hardest to make amends; his role in defeating Lambert was crucial to his success in escaping execution. Baker is good on Lambert's capture. Underdown cites the marked Royalist sympathies of the muster of the militia in Hyde Park.

13. Bring Back King Charles

Davies's *Restoration* is very good on the propaganda preceding the election of the Convention Parliament, and the details of the election itself. Wood's *Life* gives a vivid idea of the passions aroused by the election in Oxford in his description of the rejection of Speaker Lenthall's son. *The Parliamentary Diary of Sir Edward Dering* (New Haven, Yale University Press, 1940) gives further information on the activities of the Convention Parliament.

Bosher's *Restoration Settlement* describes the split between the Anglicans and the Presbyterians. This is supplemented by L.F. Brown, 'The Religious Factors in the Convention Parliament', *EHR*, xxii, 1907, in which she disputes the fact that the Presbyterians formed a majority in the new parliament. Hyde, Barwick and Baxter provide further evidence of this split, from their differing viewpoints. The new Speaker of the House of Commons, Sir Harbottle Grimston (*DNB*), was one of a number of leading Presbyterians who felt confident in their position and were to be totally surprised by the speed and efficiency of the revival of the Church of England, spearheaded by Sheldon and Morley.

Buckingham's wearing the Garter was a definite sign that the Restoration was a foregone conclusion. Guizot records Hesilrige's abject submission to Monck. Hyde records the various letters that Grenville delivered to parliament, the Council of State, the City and the armed forces. Sharp's *London and the Kingdom* comments on the enormous loan of £100,000 (never to be realised) voted by the City.

Pepys notes the equivocal reception given by the senior naval officers to Charles's letter, compared with the enthusiasm of the common sailors. He is very impressed with Montagu's skill as a conspirator on inspecting the correspondence he has been carrying on with the King and the Duke of York. Wood gives an amusing insight into the restoration of May Day, banned during the Commonwealth.

Lord Macaulay is a great champion of the Parliamentarians, whose cause ended so ignominiously. The majority of the deputation sent by parliament, as represented by Holles and Fairfax, were secluded members, i.e. former opponents of the King who had played little part in politics since Charles I's execution. Burnet's *History* comments on Sir Matthew Hale's last-ditch attempt to impose a conditional restoration.

Bordeaux played his hand very badly. Not only had he tried, unsuccessfully, to offer Monck the crown, but he had also, as the *Calendar Domestic* recorded, attempted to seize Charles I's tapestries, which he was about to send to France. J. Nicoll, *Diary of occurrences chiefly in Scotland, Jan 1650 to June 1667*, Bannatyne Club, 1836, records the reaction to events in Scotland. Davies provides more information, both in Scotland and Ireland.

Ludlow gives the most vivid picture of the net closing in on the regicides. For a less heroic view of Col Hutchinson, see Derek Hirst, 'Remembering a Hero: Lucy Hutchinson's Memoirs', *EHR*, cxix, no. 482, June 2004. For Thurloe, Broghill and Fairfax's biographers, see Chapter 2. *Calendar Domestic* has details of the return of the royal collection.

Although a great deal has been written about Charles II in the run-up to the Restoration, it is very difficult to gain an impression of his thoughts during the most dramatic month of his life. Sir William Lower, *A Relation In Form of Journal, Of The Voyage and Residence Which the most Excellent and most Mighty Prince Charles the II King of Great Britain etc, hath made in Holland, from the 25th May to the 2nd of June, 1660* [old calendar], The Hague, 1660, gives a wealth of information. For Mazarin's intervention, see Guizot's *Richard Cromwell*; Giavarina in the *Calendar Venetian* records that there was no love lost between Charles and the French cardinal. The *Calendar Domestic* provides information on the difficulty of contacting all the ships at sea to inform their captains of the fall of the Commonwealth.

14. The Restoration

Lower continues his account with a detailed description of Charles's journey through Holland, and his reception at the Hague. The King's female relatives, with the exception of his mother, doted on him, particularly his youngest sister, Minette (see Hauptman). It is fascinating to speculate on the possible relationship between Charles and Elizabeth's daughter Sophia, who was less smitten with her cousin. Turning down any chance of becoming Queen of England in favour of marrying the Elector of Hanover, she was nevertheless to found a dynasty that lasted long after the Stuarts had died out.

Charles's natural cynicism, honed through years of exile, can only have been increased by the lavish gifts of the parliamentary commissioners. There are numerous accounts of their meeting with the King. Of all these men, it is interesting that Charles should have wished to speak alone with Fairfax. The King granted no honour to the Parliamentarian general, but when he rode to his coronation the following year, Charles was seated on a horse given by Fairfax, whose mare the general had ridden at the battle of Naseby.

In view of the difficulty of disentangling the truth from Morland's reports, it is rather strange that the King should have chosen to knight him, but his knowledge of agents and double agents was potentially very dangerous. There can be little surprise at the King's coolness to the Presbyterian ministers from even the most peripheral reading of Charles's dealings with the Scottish Covenanters in 1650–1 (see Chapman and Fraser's books on Charles II).

Pepys provides an interesting portrait of the King at the Hague. His description of Charles's excitement on seeing a trunk of gold sovereigns, so aptly contrasted with the poor quality of his clothes, rings very true. Charles's devotion to his family is well recorded.

Among other gifts given by the Dutch government were yachts for Charles and his brother James. Their passionate adoption of the new sport of yacht racing was to set a fashion that continues to this day. The dinner given by Montagu included men who were to feature prominently in the maritime history of England and Holland (for William Coventry and Downing, see *DNB*).

Charles retained an affection for Montagu much deeper than he ever held for Monck. Pepys's description of the King on the quarterdeck of the *Royal Charles* is yet another example of his almost miraculous ability to be in the right place at the right time. For the first time, the King could relate in public a tale that must have consumed so many of his waking hours through the long years of exile since his escape from Worcester. Pepys conveys the freshness of the dramatic story, highlighting the events brought to life in the King's description.

There is a bitter sweetness to Lady Fanshawe's account of the King's return (*The Memoirs of Ann, Lady Fanshawe*, ed. E.J. Fanshawe, London, 1907). Alhough she, as someone who had accompanied Charles on his flight from England to the Scilly Isles and on to Jersey in 1646, felt great delight in his triumphant return, her husband was shortly to receive the unwelcome news that the position of Secretary of State, offered to him by the King, was to go to Monck's accomplice Morice (see M. Coate's 'W. Morice').

Montagu's biographers Harris and Ollard give thorough coverage of Charles's landing at Dover. *The Flemings in Oxford*, ed. J.R. Magrath, Oxford, Oxford Historical Society, 1904, comments on the King's reception of the bible on the beach. Giavarina in the *Calendar Venetian* records his visit to greet Charles at Canterbury; with typical astuteness, he was the first foreign ambassador to welcome the King, and was impressed with the fluency with which Charles and his brothers spoke Italian.

The King's secret meeting with Sheldon was of great importance. As his biographer Sutch relates, Sheldon, as chaplain to Charles I during his captivity, had been entrusted with many 'secret and last counsels, especially commands to be delivered to his son'. This was Sheldon's chance to deliver Charles I's charge. The revival of the Church of England probably owes as much to this meeting as any of the more public activities of Hyde and other Anglican Royalists. The King's attempts at religious toleration were to founder on the rock of Sheldon's steadfast and immovable Anglican beliefs.

Hyde's comments reflect his indignation at the audacity with which Monck presented his list of supporters to Charles. The award of the Order of the Garter, the greatest honour the King could bequeath, and carefully divided between old Anglican Royalists and Monck and Montagu, both such recent converts, indicates Charles's desire to placate all sides. The meeting of the Privy Council appears in E.R. Turner, *The Privy Council in England*, Baltimore, Johns Hopkins University Press, 1927.

There are numerous contemporary accounts of Charles's entry into London. Baker's *Chronicle* is interesting on the King's meeting with the New Model Army on Blackheath, the most awkward moment in his day of triumph. Baker gives a full description of the iconography designed by John Ogilvy. The poignancy of the King's final public appearance in Inigo Jones's Banqueting House cannot have been lost on anyone present.

An easy way to show enthusiasm for the new regime was to join in the destruction of its predecessor. The burning of effigies of Cromwell at the Restoration was a prelude to more drastic measures. Within a few days the bodies of Cromwell, his son-in-law Henry Ireton, perceived to be the strongest advocate of the decision to put Charles I on trial in December 1648, and John Bradshaw, chief judge at the trial, were dug up. After a symbolic hanging at the foot of the gallows at Tyburn, the bodies were decapitated and the heads put on spikes at Westminster. The headless bodies were thrown into a common pit, from where they were later rescued by their families.

Ludlow and Milton both survived and, unlike so many of their fellow Republicans, never recanted their beliefs. As has been often remarked, many of the best lines in Milton's masterpiece *Paradise Lost*, London, Longman, 1998, are given to Satan, who strives to overthrow the established order. To what extent they relate to Milton's fierce opposition to the Restoration, the reader must judge for himself. Ludlow lived on into old age, and his *Memoirs* is a determined attempt to set the record straight, and a chance to take a swipe at all those he perceives to have sold out. They represent a tiny minority willing to take a stand on principle. John Evelyn's remark in his *Diary* sums up the opposite view of all those Royalists who had longed for this day and could scarcely believe, after all they had endured, that it had come to pass without a drop of bloodshed.

The end of the most momentous day of Charles's life sums up different facets of his character. His farewell remark to his courtiers, quoted by Antonia Fraser in her biography of Charles II, is a masterly dismissal, to which there was no answer. Even if he did not retire to bed with Barbara Villiers, the very fact that so many people believed that he did sums up the legend that was already being created of the 'Merry Monarch'.

INDEX

Index